MW00749030

# RECLAIMING WRITING

"Teaching writing in an era of scripted curricula and standardized testing can be lonely and discouraging. *Reclaiming Writing* brings together a community of support, providing us research, experience, and strategies for (once again) engaging in the joyful and passionate work of being writers and teachers of writing. It is an inspiring read for those already teaching and for those learning to teach."

**Donna Kalmbach Phillips, Pacific University, USA**

"… reclaims power for students and teachers, which has been stripped off in today's standards-driven environment. This book sheds light and hope in our education with vivid examples of teaching writing in the crack of the dark age or in open opposition to dehumanized standardization."

**Danling Fu, University of Florida, USA**

With passion, clarity, and rich examples, *Reclaiming Writing* demonstrates possibilities for reclaiming spaces for writing in classrooms in this era of high-stakes testing and mandated curricula. Classrooms and out-of-school settings are described and analyzed in exciting and groundbreaking narratives that provide insights into the many possibilities for writing that support writers' searches for voice, identity, and agency. Offering pedagogical strategies and the knowledge base in which they are grounded, the book looks at writing within various areas of the curriculum and across modes of writing from traditional text-based forums to digital formats. Thematically based sections present the pillars of the volume's critical transactive theory: learning, teaching, curriculum, language, and sociocultural contexts. Each chapter is complemented by an extension that offers application possibilities for teachers in various settings. *Reclaiming Reading* emphasizes literacy as a vehicle for exploring, interrogating, challenging, finding self, talking back to power, creating a space in the world, reflecting upon the past, and thinking forward to a more joyful and democratic future.

**Richard J. Meyer** is Regents' Professor, University of New Mexico, College of Education, Department of Language, Literacy, and Sociocultural Studies, USA.

**Kathryn F. Whitmore** is the Ashland Inc./Nystrand Chair in Early Childhood Education, College of Education and Human Development, University of Louisville, USA.

# RECLAIMING WRITING

## Composing Spaces for Identities, Relationships, and Action

*Edited by Richard J. Meyer and Kathryn F. Whitmore*

Routledge
Taylor & Francis Group

NEW YORK AND LONDON

First published 2014
by Routledge
711 Third Avenue, New York, NY 10017

and by Routledge
2 Park Square, Milton Park, Abingdon, Oxon OX14 4RN

*Routledge is an imprint of the Taylor & Francis Group, an informa business*

© 2014 Taylor & Francis

The right of the editors to be identified as the authors of the editorial material, and of the authors for their individual chapters, has been asserted in accordance with sections 77 and 78 of the Copyright, Designs and Patents Act 1988.

All rights reserved. No part of this book may be reprinted or reproduced or utilised in any form or by any electronic, mechanical, or other means, now known or hereafter invented, including photocopying and recording, or in any information storage or retrieval system, without permission in writing from the publishers.

*Trademark notice*: Product or corporate names may be trademarks or registered trademarks, and are used only for identification and explanation without intent to infringe.

*Library of Congress Cataloging in Publication Data*
Reclaiming writing : composing spaces for identities, relationships, and actions / edited by Richard J. Meyer and Kathryn F. Whitmore.
     pages cm
   Includes bibliographical references and index.
   1.  English language–Composition and exercises–Study and teaching. 2.  Composition (Language arts)–Study and teaching. 3.  Language arts–Correlation with content subjects. 4.  Reflective teaching–United States.  I. Meyer, Richard J., 1949– II. Whitmore, Kathryn F., 1959–
LB1576.R428 2013
372.62'3044–dc23                                                    2013017161

ISBN: 978-0-415-82704-1 (hbk)
ISBN: 978-0-415-82705-8 (pbk)
ISBN: 978-0-203-49460-8 (ebk)

Typeset in Bembo & ITC Stone Sans
by Cenveo Publisher Services

We dedicate this book to the next generation of writers who will compose across many modalities, for a variety of reasons, and with heartfelt purposes and intents as ways of contributing their thinking and actions to create a more just world.

# CONTENTS

*Preface*                                                                xi
*Acknowledgments*                                                        xv

1   Introduction: Reclaiming Writing                                      1
    *Richard J. Meyer and Kathryn F. Whitmore*

**PILLAR I**
**Learning**                                                            **11**

2   Shoshana Learns to Write: A Longitudinal Study                       12
    *Yetta M. Goodman and Kenneth S. Goodman*

    Chapter 2 Extension: Reclaiming Identities and
    Learning to Write                                                    24
    *Bobbie Kabuto*

3   Artful Bookmaking: Learning by Design                                28
    *Kathryn F. Whitmore and Marie Gernes*

    Chapter 3 Extension: The Circus of Design                            38
    *S. Rebecca Leigh*

4   Learning to Respond in Writers' Workshop                             42
    *Allen Koshewa*

Chapter 4 Extension: Learning Authentic Genres in
a Community of Writers                                                    53
*Michael L. Shaw*


**PILLAR II**
# Teaching                                                               **57**

5   When the Water Goes Bad and Other Essential Reasons to
Argue and Write About Science in Elementary Classrooms       58
*Lori Norton-Meier and Brian Hand*

Chapter 5 Extension: Young Mathematicians
Writing for Real Reasons                                                 70
*Elisa Waingort*

6   Teaching the Joy of Writing Through Wikis                    73
*Shannon Blady and Roxanne Henkin*

Chapter 6 Extension: After-School Technology Possibilities   83
*Lindsay Laurich and Kathryn F. Whitmore*

7   Supporting Writers as They Learn to Spell:
A Holistic Approach                                                      87
*Maryann Manning and Marilee Ransom*

Chapter 7 Extension: Constructivist Spelling, Yes!
Constructivist Grammar, Too!                                            98
*Sandra Wilde*


**PILLAR III**
# Curriculum                                                            **103**

8   Reworking Writing Workshop                                    104
*Kathryn Mitchell Pierce*

Chapter 8 Extension: Creating Gems of Writing                114
*Dick Koblitz*

9   Writing Pictures, Drawing Stories: Reclaiming Multimodal
Composing in First Grade                                                119
*Prisca Martens, Ray Martens, Michelle Hassay Doyle,
and Jenna Loomis*

Chapter 9 Extension: Reclaiming Multimodal Responses in
Fifth Grade    131
*Renita Schmidt*

10 Sing Me a Song of Writing: Transforming the Writing
Curriculum With the Help of One Child's Determination    135
*Jane Baskwill*

Chapter 10 Extension: Trusting Students' Visions for a
Participatory Video Project    146
*Lenny Sanchez*

**PILLAR IV**
# Language    **151**

11 Using Multiple Languages to Write With Passion and Purpose    152
*Katie Van Sluys*

Chapter 11 Extension: Translanguaging: A Language Space
for Multilinguals    164
*Susana Ibarra Johnson and Richard J. Meyer*

12 Intentional Moves to Build Community in Writers' Workshop    168
*Amy Seely Flint and Sanjuana Rodriguez*

Chapter 12 Extension: Uncovering Children's Expository
Writing Within Home and Community Lives    178
*Charlene Klassen Endrizzi*

13 "Learning How to Mean:" Writing and Gardening
in Two Urban Schools    182
*Patricia Paugh, Mary Moran, and Geoff Rose*

Chapter 13 Extension: "So My Grandpa Knows What Way to
Drive the Tractor:" Children Engage Rural Ways of Knowing    193
*Lori Norton-Meier*

**PILLAR V**
# Sociocultural Contexts    **197**

14 Producing Cultural Imaginaries in the Playshop    198
*Karen Wohlwend and Carmen Liliana Medina*

Chapter 14 Extension: The Girls Go to the '70s and the '80s:
Self-Produced Videos and Play                                                          210
*Chuck Jurich and Richard J. Meyer*

15  Digital Media, Critical Literacy, and the Everyday:
Exploring Writing in the Twenty-First Century                          214
*Vivian Maria Vasquez, Peggy Albers, and Jerome C. Harste*

Chapter 15 Extension: Writing as Designing: Reclaiming
the Social and Multimodal Aspects of Writing                          224
*Candace R. Kuby*

16  Democratic Writing in Video Production:
Reclaiming the Social Nature of Writing Practices                    228
*Chuck Jurich and Richard J. Meyer*

Chapter 16 Extension: Democratic Writing and
Multiliteracies Work in Schools and Community Centers          240
*Linda Skidmore Coggin and Carmen Liliana Medina*

17  Listening to Compose Spaces for Identities, Relationships,
and Actions                                                                                  244
*Richard J. Meyer and Kathryn F. Whitmore*

*Contributors*                                                                             254
*Index*                                                                                        257

# PREFACE

During the summer of 2008 we were fortunate to meet with some colleagues following the *Literacies for All Summer Institute* in San Diego. We asked this small group of highly respected literacy scholars, thinkers, and teachers to help us consider the state of literacy education in the country. The meeting was being held during the decade-plus-long dark ages of education, referring to the intensely scripted, policy-influenced, and legislatively induced era when many educators forfeited outstanding literacy practices. Those educators were acting out of fear, coercion, or not knowing how to respond to imposed curriculum (for many, because they were so new to the profession). Often the fear, coercion and not knowing dissolved into one another as teachers were intimidated and isolated. Teachers were required to attend so-called professional development sessions at which they were told what they would be doing (with no questions allowed), and professional learning communities were bastardized into guilt-ridden data exposés during which children's and teachers' lives were reduced to studying and responding to often ridiculous tests (Goodman, 2006). Story after story was told as participants recounted the horrors of what we were witnessing, which was essentially the appropriation of our imaginings about what could happen in schools. Reading curriculum was reduced to one-size-fits-all and publishers were getting rich in the process (see Altwerger, 2005). There was no room or time for child-centered or culturally responsive teaching because curriculum for reading was "canned," delivered as canned foods are delivered to supermarkets. And among the casualties of the clampdown was writing: the joys of writing disappeared because writing wasn't tested and therefore did not matter.

The intensity of our discussions led to considerations of actions that we might take. We, the editors of this book, agreed that one action would be the initiation of the reclaiming of the literacy possibilities that were emerging prior to the onset of the dark ages of education. This book is the second in a series that we are composing with the goals of reclaiming reading (see Meyer & Whitmore, 2011), reclaiming writing (in this volume), and reclaiming assessment (which is in the planning stages). *Our goal across all these books is to reclaim the imaginative literacy work that is important to teachers, students, families, researchers, communities, and other supporters of public education, and reflects the productive and process traditions of progressive literacy research.*

Throughout this book, which focuses attention on writing, readers will peer into exciting classrooms and communities where teachers, students, and families engage in productive and fulfilling composition in many forms. In these spaces, developing composers explore who they are and what they think, inquire into the world around them, and grow a sense of their own agency within that world. The work in this volume is evidence that the progressive tradition of writing workshops has grown in these spaces, but mostly "in the cracks" – the quiet places between the mandates that dominate schools and place test scores ahead of students. Some teachers, students and researchers write "under the radar," sometimes with the support of administrators; we know that many more teachers in public schools suffer the angst, stress, depression, and oftentimes deep sadness that accompanies leaving their progressive writing practices behind. Yielding to the pressures of policies and laws is not something we condemn because we appreciate the realities of educators' lives: We understand that teachers need to keep their jobs and support their families and that they continue to love working with children while they search for shreds of hope that these dark ages will end soon.

This book is saturated with inspiring stories of hope. The progressive tradition of writing has not disappeared, but is realized in spaces like those described throughout these chapters. Authentic, intentional writing that we know well from decades of classroom-based inquiry and writing workshops now includes multimodal composing that marks that essence of writing in the new century. It is also critical as children assume agency, question power structures, talk back to power, challenge each other, interrogate ideas, and compose themselves as authors.

This is the imaginative work that we are reclaiming; it is work that must develop from the local contexts in which educators and students live as it concomitantly addresses our deepening understanding of the expectations that a democratic nation holds for writers who can not only write with accuracy, but with voice. The children and educators that we present in these pages inspire us to continue to learn about writing and the teaching of writing so these actions can be realized in others.

In *Reclaiming Reading*, a basic premise of each chapter was that reclaiming joy is essential to reclaiming reading activities within our classrooms. We explained that our deepening understanding of joy involved the feelings that are experienced when readers engage in hard, challenging work, when they invest hours reading, thinking, arguing, and making meaning, and when they appreciate the broad spectrum of interpretations that may arise from one text across different readers. We are committed to the same premise throughout this book. Readers of this volume will vicariously experience the complexity of joy inherent in the challenges, arguments, tones, tenors, excitement, urgency, demands, needs, languages, cultures, and contexts of writers engaging in work that is important to them. The chapters provide insights into the joys of watching: a grandchild growing as a writer over many years, children designing books as objects of art, children composing wikis, writers conferring with each other and teachers, writing to make the case for healthier water, designing spaces in which writers can compose using different modalities and different languages, and more. We invite you to engage in the joyful, intense, exhausting, contentious, and exciting work of reclaiming spaces for composing – by understanding and nurturing identities, building relationships, and taking actions to compose a more just and truly democratic world.

## Center for the Expansion of Language and Thinking: Authors of this book

The participants at the meeting we described at the opening of this preface included many members of the Center for Expansion of Language and Thinking (CELT). The authors of the chapters in this book are members or affiliated with members of CELT, which was founded in 1972 as:

> a nonprofit educational corporation, international in scope, whose members believe in the principles of education for democracy with a focus on natural language learning and inquiry. These principles are supported by beliefs in learners and learning, teachers and teaching, and language and curriculum. The members of CELT are dedicated to the improvement of education through a greater understanding of the relationship between language, thought, and learning. CELT includes a rich diversity of people who share similar beliefs about language and learning but have widely varied background experiences (visit www.celtlink.org).

The Center for the Expansion of Language and Thinking remained committed to progressive literacy practices during the dark ages of education and, further, remained strong voices of dissent and discontentment during that time. As we complete this book we sit on the eve of the massive imposition of the Common Core State Standards in the United States and similar challenges around the globe and, more importantly, the ensuing high-stakes tests that accompany such impositions on literate children. As you read, know that you are in the company of the valiant voices of continued contention to any policy, law, or mandate that imposes upon the practices of informed, intelligent, reflective educators. We are – and we implore you to be part of – the rising tide of voices opposing mandated and legislated malpractice.

## References

Altwerger, B. (Ed.). (2005). *Reading for profit: How the bottom line leaves kids behind*. Portsmouth, NH: Heinemann.

Center for Expansion of Language and Thinking (2013). Home. Retrieved from www.celtlink.org.

Goodman, K. S. (2006). *The truth about DIBELS: What it is, what it does*. Portsmouth, NH: Heinemann.

Meyer, R. J., & Whitmore, K. F. (2011). *Reclaiming reading*. New York: Routledge.

# ACKNOWLEDGMENTS

This book has been a massive undertaking as we embarked upon a journey to have many voices heard. We gratefully acknowledge the members of the Center for Expansion of Language and Thinking (CELT) for helping us think about this volume and for their contributions as authors and as part of the remarkable thought collective that sustains our professional lives. We also thank the many children, their families, and teachers that were part of this work. They are part of a cadre of thinkers and composers that provided us with creations, reflections, and ideas that reclaimed and staked out new territory in writing. Their work reminds us of the infinite possibilities that exist when children and adults wonder together about what is important to them and how they might act upon our world.

Our families continue to be extremely supportive of our work, our passions, our commitment, and the many hours that our thinking and writing consume. It is essential that we name them in print. Thank you Tom Barten and Patricia Meyer for being patient with the hours you spent watching us work and hearing us Skype, and reminding us to come up for air to go to a volleyball game, cook a meal, watch the sunset, or walk the dog.

Naomi Silverman continues to be our supporter and advocate, finding importance and relevance in our work and making the case for it to be published. Others at Routledge have consistently provided outlets for our work and we look forward to working with them in the future. We gratefully acknowledge the wonderful contribution of Ray Martens as part of our cover design.

Little did we know when Kathy moved that deep in the heart of Kentucky we would find a superwoman who could work with efficiency, grace, and understanding. Thanks to Emily Boyle for working with us to bring this book to fruition.

# 1

# INTRODUCTION

## Reclaiming Writing

*Richard J. Meyer and Kathryn F. Whitmore*

A letter has been received, read and discussed by several members of the family. It is then laid on the table. Harold (a three year old) takes it up. He looks it over and walks around thoughtfully with it under his arm. Presently, turning up the blank side of the sheet, he says, "I want to write." He is supplied with paper and pencil, seated in his little chair, and is much occupied for five minutes. He then takes the scrawled-over sheet to his grandmother, with the request that she read it. Does she hesitate? Not at all. She promptly reads from it such sentences as he might have given expression to, greatly to his joy and satisfaction. He is learning to write. (Iredell, 1898, p. 235)

Well over one hundred years ago Harold observed the significance of writing and understood how it positioned the writer in a place of importance in a family. His wanting to write is an indication of his understanding that there are multiple ways to compose and relate meaning; he might have painted, spoken orally, danced, or gestured. His intuitive sense about and approximation of written language was supported when his writing was received as genuine and authentic meaning making. He learned that writing enriches relationships, presents voice, and births joy, drawing the writer and reader into an intimate space in which ideas, passions, questions, challenges, and feelings are acknowledged, shared, and confirmed. Harold joined the group of literate souls who form the literacy club (Smith, 1988) in which members understand that writing matters; it gets messages across, is steeped in relationships, and can be used to initiate and forge bonds while delivering meaning.

The nature of the literacy club has changed considerably since Harold was a young child. Today, many of us are familiar with the image of a young child leaning over a magazine and touching photographs in anticipation of them opening files, games, or movies. Or, perhaps we have been witness to young children reaching for a family member's phone and opening virtual spaces in which to play, compose, and read. These youngsters were engaged in contemporary literacy activity. In our highly technical world, writing has become hybridized in that there are many tools with which to compose and many ways in which to respond. Authentic writing remains an intensely social act because it is invented within, across, among, by ignoring, or in tension with others. As much as being a source of joy, it may be a vehicle for contention and interrogation.

Yet, for many writers in schools across our country, something went dreadfully wrong during the more-than-decade long dark ages of education when the Elementary and Secondary Education Act was known as *No Child Left Behind (NCLB)*. Authentic writing got left behind because the impact upon schools of reading and math tests were so intensely punitive that many teachers had little choice but to comply with mandated, often scripted, programs that left little time for authentic writing. As we will demonstrate, prior to NCLB, we were on an exciting trajectory of supporting students as authors, inquirers, thinkers, and more, but were interrupted by legislation, policies, and mandates that closed writing down for many teachers and the children in their care. This book is a journey through classrooms and other venues in which teachers, researchers, and students reclaim writing by using the lessons of the past and the tools and thinking of the present to open (and reopen) spaces for an exciting future for many different ways with writing.

## Reclaiming Writing: Joyful and Political Work

Writers compose for a veritable infinite spectrum of reasons. We write to: discover self, uncover ideas, express emotions, make sense of and explore content, be passionate, lie, talk back to power, tell secrets, tell truths, explain scientific findings, politicize, mollify, comply, complain, untangle our thoughts and relationships, tangle up our thoughts and relationships, compose who we are or want to be, set ourselves free, oppress others, step into the world, emancipate, and so much more. Writers' voices are organic and change over time, contexts, and relationships, moving from joy to interrogating to tension and more. We assert our presence as we write. Most of our work as writers is joyful, but:

> that joy is not a simple feeling of euphoria or pleasure; it is also found in moments of intensity when dealing with something powerful and important. Such moments of joy may be responses to negative ideas or occur during disheartening events, when there is a growing awareness, understanding, consciousness, and conscientization of the participants in the event (Meyer & Whitmore, 2011, p. 280).

Reclaiming writing is something that will take much joyful work as we engage in the pedagogical and political struggles necessary to bring back into our classrooms the diverse writing voices of our students.

Our focus in this book is on reclaiming the complexity and intensity of children engaged seriously as composers. When Harold picked up that pencil, he was playing at what more mature writers do. He was doing what kids do best when they are at play: taking risks, pretending as a way of becoming, pretending as a way of extending and expanding, and experimenting in a safe environment as a way of seeing what happens when he writes. Vygotsky (1962) explains that "a child at play is a head taller" (p. 102), and Harold is a head taller as he writes. Through his play, he enacts the *stuff* of what writers do, presenting his understanding of that at a given point in time. Children at play are more willing to try again and again (revising), and even willing to be tentative about their final products, often abandoning them because the process was more important than the product. Central to reclaiming writing is the very political notion that opening spaces in which writers can play is essential to their processes as writers. Inquiring about writing is political because critical inquiry demands interrogation and contention, voice and joy. In this book, contributors help us *question* how tools are used, how to work alone or in groups, the reasons to write, audiences, the tone and tenor of different pieces of writing, voice, and much more because asking questions is at the heart of reclaiming writing. In the final chapter of this volume, we shall return to this idea of questioning by considering the ways in which we *listen* for answers.

In *Reclaiming Writing*, we seek to re-ignite (or ignite for the first time) educators' and students' dedication to, love of, and passion for composing. In a fashion parallel to our work in reclaiming authentic reading (Meyer & Whitmore, 2011), we intend to reclaim the joys of the writing pedagogies of writing workshops and the potential those spaces hold. Reclaiming in this sense involves relocating the inertia of an earlier time and using it to move forward to support and enhance our students' lives, delightfully complicated by multiple interpretations of composing, including: remixes (Lankshear & Knobel, 2006), art, movie making, script writing, book designing, social networks, public service announcements, dance, gardening, and play. Our goal is to reclaim (or claim for the first time) writing for critical work in classrooms in which children compose pieces that serve to address issues of immediate importance, joy, curiosity, and social justice (Lewison, Leland, & Harste, 2008). They may do so in very traditional ways of writing or as "bedizens" (Luke, 1999), born into a citizenship of the Internet and actively contributing to and participating in the critical composing, relationships, and conversations that technology affords (Vasquez & Felderman, 2013).

Our orientation is that "children's experiences, desires, and hopes play a crucial role in learning and in working toward developing a strong sense of agency [as] writers" (Salvio & Boldt, 2010, p. 197). In a critique of marketed writing programs, Salvio and Boldt found the programs "hold much in common with behaviorist approaches to teaching and learning. They assume that learning can be controlled and urged on through the rational actions of a reasonable teacher who regulates conversations and the production of final products …" (2010, p. 198). Such regulation reigns in the playful nature of composing, disrupts the safety of the context, eliminates voice and joy, and reifies writing into providing what the teacher wants. Our work with reclaiming writing involves bringing classrooms of writers back to the most essential reasons for writing and doing so in ways that are rooted in the ways that contemporary writers write and the reasons that writers do their work. This certainly includes a traditional sense of writing that occurs with paper and pencil as well as the many creative and hybridized formats and forums (web pages, social media, blogs, podcasts, wikis, movie making, etc.).

## The Roots of Reclaiming Writing

The reclaiming we call for in this volume has a rich and articulated past that was inspiring new directions, experimentation, and invention prior to being interrupted. A brief tour of the roots of our work serves to connect teachers to a taste of the progressive traditions in which this book is rooted. As early as 1939, Hildreth found that children are quite interested in writing, often engaging for hours at a time. She reported that "children increasingly practice writing through preschool years and that as they mature they demand more help from their elders in achieving skill in writing" (p. 302). The dialectic between invention and convention (Goodman, 1988) was evident to Hildreth as she saw children eager to learn conventions of print and almost simultaneously involve themselves in inventing writing, pretending that they could write conventionally in order to explore authentic functions of print.

Burrows (1951) understood that writing is not simply putting to paper that which we already know. The very act of writing ignites joy and creativity that often surprise (Murray, 1985) the writer and, Burrows suggested, it is these surprises that are essential to a democracy. "For it is through honest revelation that real satisfaction is achieved, that genuine needs are met, that learning is promoted, that the creative urge is strengthened. And creativeness is essentially valuable in a democracy where uniqueness, not uniformity, is a source of strength" (Burrows, 1951, p. 207). She understands children's need for

> [b]eing in the role of authority over one's characters [as] a vicarious and constructive way of balancing the scores. That children use such media spontaneously, often violently, with no hint of self-consciousness is all the more evidence of their essential need [to write] (Burrows, 1951, p. 137).

Parke (1959), in a thorough history of writing instruction in the 1940s–1950s, discussed the "vitalization of the curriculum ... [and] [i]ncreased communication among children in primary grade classrooms in a more permissive atmosphere" (p. 107) as having an effect on what and how they choose to compose. Parke presented many studies that support the tenet that "the mechanics of writing should be subordinated to the substance of ideas" (p. 110). In other words, voice and joy trump mechanics.

We use these somewhat distant historical references as evidence of the consist-ent finding – across decades and centuries – that children *want* to engage in acts of composing. This is as true today as it has been throughout history. Moving momentarily from a rich progressive past to the present, Jurich and Meyer (2011) find that fourth through sixth grade children whose classroom writing lives con-sisted of twentieth-century writing tasks that left those children bored and dis-connected become quite engaged and rejuvenated writers when they work with twenty-first-century literacies by collaboratively writing scripts for movies, revis-ing, recording, often revising again, and presenting their movies to colleagues and families. Sadly, as Ives (2012) points out, in contemporary classrooms, many teach-ers and students continue to engage in "showdowns" (p. 55) during which teach-ers and students struggle over permissible writing topics, imposed standards, and the uses and definitions of conventions in writing. Ives concludes that, "Authoritative discourses of accountability, achievement, equity, and excellence shaped by hegemonic centripetal forces working to sort, order, standardize, and rank are ubiquitous in current educational policy and practice" (p. 61). Yet the goals of excellence and achievement need not be reified into discrete measures that neither accurately portray nor represent the writers we wish to cultivate. Greene (2013) suggests that "By allowing students to be partners in their own educational experiences, teachers and students can begin to loosen the chains of testing that can potentially bind us" (p. 13).

The progressive roots of reclaiming writing certainly emanate from Freire's (1970) explanation of praxis, which places teaching at the nexus of research, theory, practice, contexts, and relationships. This is a huge responsibility because it means that teachers need to understand how writers write, their development possibilities over time, the contexts of their lives, and the times when specific instructional strategies are to be used. There's a wonderful tension here, one that we believe was intended to be part of writers' workshops since their inception by Graves (1973). It's a tension that makes one day in the classroom appear smooth and well planned, and the next day, in the very same classroom, seem chaotic and unpredictable. Graves (1981) writes that

> The complexity of the writing process and the interrelationships of its components have been underestimated by researchers, teachers, and other educators, because writing is an organic process that frustrates approaches to explain its operation (p. 227).

An *organic process* suggests a gardening metaphor (Santa Ana, 2002), which is appropriate in our reclaiming work. Classroom activities are the soil, water, and sun, but the seeds are the writers in our classrooms. It is up to us to cultivate with care and respect in order to understand what has been planted and what will grow. Yet there is a concomitant mystery in authentic written language activity, almost as though one does not know what seeds were planted or what fruit or flowers will grow. First grade teacher Mary Ellen Giacobbe (1986), one early explorer of Graves' ideas about the teaching and learning of writing, understands that

> Learners need time, choice, and response. I do not think teachers need to choose between learning to write or writing to learn. A productive class-room in any subject should provide opportunities for the student to wonder, to pose questions, to pursue possible answers, to discuss with others, to come to some conclusions – all in writing and all in an attempt to come to a greater understanding of what they are trying to learn. … writing can be the vehicle for learning – for learning about writing and for learning about particular topics in content areas (p.147).

If children are challenging (even interrogating) us, then we know we're doing things in a way that supports their exploration of written language and the power it has (Elbow, 1981). If they are complying, looking for our approval, meandering around the room being truly lost (not the contemplative meandering of writers at work), then we know they bracketed (or were forced to bracket) their voices and the joy that writing can provide.

Reclaiming writing is an investment by teachers in helping our students to read the world (Freire & Mercado, 1977) in which they live and see the multiple layers of texts, textures, and textualities that inhabit those worlds in order to support our students in writing and rewriting their worlds. Reclaiming writing for our students involves living the life of a writer–teacher–researcher in classrooms that honor fair-ness, kindness, responsibility, and human decency as the cornerstones of critical literacy (Bomer & Bomer, 2001). Reclaiming involves understanding that our work is advocacy (Smith & Whitmore, 2006), involves positions and relationships (Janks, 2010; Jones, 2006), and teaching with intention (Van Sluys, 2011). Reclaiming writing relies on the past, honors the rich cultural, linguistic, social, political – and even spiritual – present, and serves as the origin for meaningful futures.

## Organization of This Book

As in *Reclaiming Reading* (Meyer & Whitmore, 2011), we organized the chapters of *Reclaiming Writing* based upon five pillars that Goodman (1991) developed: learning, teaching, curriculum, language, and sociocultural contexts. The pillars are all related and each chapter has elements of all of the pillars, yet authors high-light one of the pillars in their individual chapters. The chapters are comple-mented by *extensions*, which are short pieces that elaborate upon the meaning and expand the audience of the chapter. Some readers may find they enjoy reading these brief complementary pieces prior to reading the full chapter; others may find the opposite to be true.

Reclaiming is political because it involves teachers being cognizant of and responding to what is happening in the lives of our students and relying upon those realities as the substance for what happens with writing in our classrooms. Reclaiming demands being professionally informed about the many facets of teaching and learning writing, understanding curriculum, valuing languages, and reading sociocultural contexts.

The *Reclaiming Learning Pillar* offers descriptions of writing development and learning that grow from students' identities, lives, relationships, concerns, loves, hates, feelings, and interests. It begins with Goodman and Goodman's longitudinal study of a biliterate writer, Shoshana, and the premise that within a single developing writer exists a theory for all writing learning. Kabuto's extension considers this idea with examples from Emma, a child simultaneously learning to write in alphabetic and non-alphabetic systems. Whitmore and Gernes emphasize the role of design as children learn to write, describing how second graders with whom they worked activated understanding of voice as they designed books as objects of art. The second graders cause Leigh to think back to a time when she was not allowed to design a book as a child, and how she came to understand the relationship between art and writing in a teenager's learning. Koshewa narrates how children learned to respond to each other's composing in his classroom by creating a classroom of trust that allows for productive critique. His chapter is extended by Shaw, who describes how letter, persuasive essay, and magazine writing were genres that encouraged his students' authentic writing.

The chapters in the *Reclaiming Teaching Pillar* offer insights into the pedagogical acts in which teachers engage. It begins with Norton-Meier and Hand's description of the teaching actions that supported elementary students' science writing through a lens of "argument-based inquiry." Waingort extends these ideas with examples from her bilingual classroom when she taught students to write as mathematicians. Blady and Henkin move the discussion to digital writing contexts and tell how Blady increased the authentic nature of writing for her fourth graders by introducing wikis. A "technology think tank," which Laurich and Whitmore describe, offered fourth graders digital literacy invitations in an after-school setting and shifted power dynamics for children perceived to "struggle." Manning and Ransom complete the pillar by offering a developmental description of spelling growth and a constructivist view of teaching spelling. Wilde offers examples of three lessons that teach grammar within the same constructivist frame.

The *Reclaiming Curriculum Pillar* focuses on characteristics of how writing is organized in classrooms, the nature of the writing process and the products that writers compose. Pierce presents a realistic account of the challenges and joys of creating writing curriculum in contemporary times and Koblitz shares his experiences to illustrate how writing "gems" were composed within his classroom's writing workshop. Martens, Martens, Doyle, and Loomis explain the relationship between art and writing, arguing that composing multimodally challenges children to think, create, and problem solve in multidimensional ways that they cannot do with written language alone. Schmidt shares examples from fifth graders for whom access to drawing and thinking multimodally supported their critical responses to literature. The multimodal discussion turns to music as Baskwill tells a story of how the writing curriculum was revitalized when a first grade teacher listened intently to one child's need to write songs. The story reminds Sanchez of his work with third graders and their teacher when the children's insistence on creating videos to present their community-based learning led to writing that mattered.

The *Reclaiming Language Pillar* focuses on the ways in which language, including relationships between oral and written language, bilingualism and biliteracy, theories of language development, and the study of languages, enhances the writing lives of students. The pillar begins with Van Sluys' argument that continuous and consistent inclusion of the many languages children bring to school supports multilingual writers in engaging with intensity and purpose. Ibarra Johnson and Meyer further her argument with a rich example of "translanguaging" in a fifth grade classroom as a way of honoring the linguistic richness of the students. Flint and Rodriguez continue the conversation as they recount ways that Rodriguez supported her young students' writing development by encouraging their oral stories from home. Endrizzi offers examples of similar intention in an after-school family literacy context where families and teachers grew to appreciate the functional everyday writing they did at home with their children. Paugh, Moran, and Rose describe academic writing practices that occurred within an urban gardening theme and were consistent with a theory of language as it functions in context. In a contrasting setting, Norton-Meier found that a teacher's learning to value rural "ways of knowing" was pivotal to curriculum that integrated writing with investigative science.

The *Reclaiming Sociocultural Contexts Pillar* demonstrates how teachers' knowledge of individual learners' multiple identities and the funds of knowledge (González, Moll, & Amanti, 2005) they bring to school transacts with how written language grows in the twenty-first-century, multimodal world. Wohlwend and Medina demonstrate how children took up more than character identities as they played with global and cultural texts, power relations and familiar media roles in separate kindergarten and drama "cultural imaginaries." Jurich and Meyer look to an after-school elementary video club to further explore play and composing in movie making. Vasquez, Albers, and Harste illustrate the possibilities of twenty-first-century writing in the intersection of digital and critical literacies. An example of second graders who created 3D puppets and scenery on a Smart Board, shared by Kuby, shows how children effortlessly move between various modes and materials to communicate. Finally, Jurich and Meyer analyze the interactions and activities of multiple authors and the tools and objects elementary students use while democratically composing and producing videos. Coggin and Medina's description of digital composition in the contexts of a research project in a rural primary classroom and a community literacy program for immigrant Latino families round out the section. In the closing chapter, we elaborate on the significance and power of listening to compose spaces where identities, relationships, and action enable writing to thrive.

## Reclaiming Potential and Possibilities

The standards and test driven environment of the Common Core State Standards and the writing-void environment of NCLB silence(d) and repress(ed) the possibilities and potentials that we were only beginning to uncover prior to those harmful initiatives. It is our hope that this book will support and enhance the reclaiming of writing activities and writers' lives as we write our way towards a more democratic and just world.

## References

Bomer, R., & Bomer, K. (2001). *For a better world: Reading and writing for social action.* Portsmouth, NH: Heinemann.

Burrows, A. (1951). Children's writing and children's growth. *Elementary English, 28,* 205–207.

Elbow, P. (1981). *Writing with power: Techniques for mastering the writing process.* New York: Oxford University Press.

Freire, P. (1970). *Cultural action for freedom.* Cambridge: Harvard Educational Review and Center for the Study of Development and Social Change.

Freire, P., & Macedo, D. (1987). *Literacy: Reading the word and the world.* South Hadley, MA: Bergen & Garvey.

Giacobbe, M. E. (1986). Learning to write and writing to learn in the elementary school. In A. Petrosky & D. Bartholomae (Eds.), *The teaching of writing: Eighty-fifty yearbook of the national society for the study of education* (pp. 131–147). Chicago: University of Chicago Press.

González, N., Moll, L. C., & Amanti, C. (Eds.). (2005). *Funds of knowledge: Theorizing practices in households, communities, and classrooms.* New York: Routledge.

Goodman, K. (1988, July). *Language and learning: Toward a social-personal view.* Presented at Brisbane conference on language and learning, Brisbane.

Goodman, K. (1991). In the mail. In K. Goodman, L. Bird, & Y. Goodman (Eds.), *The whole language catalog* (Inside Cover). Santa Rosa, CA: American School Publishers.

Graves, D. (1973). *Children's writing: Research hypotheses based upon an examination of the writing processes of seven year old children.* Unpublished doctoral dissertation, State University of New York at Buffalo, Buffalo.

Graves, D. (1981). An examination of the writing processes of seven year old children. *Research in the Teaching of English, 9,* 227–241.

Greene, K. (2013). Breaking free. *English Journal, 102* (4), 13–14.

Hildreth, G. (1939). Developmental sequences in name writing. *Child Development, 7,* 291–303.

Iredell, H. (1898). Eleanor learns to read. *Education,* 233–238.

Ives, D. (2012). Kristina's ghetto family: Tensions and possibilities at the intersection of teacher and student literacy agendas. *Research in the Teaching of English, 41*(1), 39–63.

Janks, H. (2010). *Literacy and power.* New York: Routledge.

Jones, S. (2006). *Girls, social class, and literacy: What teachers can do to make a difference.* Portsmouth, NH: Heinemann.

Jurich, C., & Meyer, R. (2011). The reading–writing connection in video production. In R. Meyer & K. Whitmore (Eds.), *Reclaiming reading: Teachers, students, and researchers regaining spaces for thinking and action* (pp. 273–276). New York: Routledge/Taylor & Francis Group.

Lankshear, C., & Knobel, M. (2006). *New literacies: Everyday practices and classroom learning*. New York: Open University Press.

Lewison, M., Leland, C., & Harste, J. (2008). *Creating critical classrooms: K-8 reading and writing with an edge*. New York: Routledge.

Luke, A. (1999). What next? Toddler netizns, playstation thumb, techno-literacies. *Contemporary Issues in Early Childhood*, *1*(1), 95–100.

Meyer, R. J., & Whitmore, K. F. (2011). *Reclaiming reading: Teachers, students, and researchers regaining spaces for thinking and action*. New York: Routledge/Taylor & Francis Group.

Murray, D. (1985). Writing and teaching for surprise. *Highway One*, *8*(1–2), 174–181.

Parke, M. (1959). Composition in primary grades. *Elementary English*, 107–120.

Salvio, P., & Boldt, G. (2010). Who let the dogs out? Unleashing an uncanny sense of audience in the writing workshop. In M. O'Loughlin & R. Johnson (Eds.), *Imagining children otherwise: Theoretical and critical perspectives on childhood subjectivity*. (pp. 179–206). New York: Peter Lang.

Santa Ana, O. (2002). *Brown tide rising: Metaphors of Latinos in contemporary American public discourse*. Austin, TX: University of Texas Press.

Smith, D., & Whitmore, K. F. (2006). *Literacy and advocacy in adolescent family, gang, school, and juvenile court communities: CRIP4LIFE*. Mahwah, NJ: Erlbaum.

Smith, F. (1988). *Joining the literacy club: Further essays into education*. Portsmouth, NH: Heinemann.

Van Sluys, K. (2011). *Becoming writers in the elementary classroom*. Urbana, IL: National Council of Teachers of English.

Vasquez, V., & Felderman, C. (2013). *Technology and critical literacy in early childhood*. New York: Routledge.

Vygotsky, L. (1962). *Thought and language* (E. Hanfmann & G. Vakar, Eds. and Trans.). Cambridge, MA: MIT Press.

# PILLAR I
# Learning

# 2

# SHOSHANA LEARNS TO WRITE

## A Longitudinal Study

*Yetta M. Goodman and Kenneth S. Goodman*

In this chapter, we tell the writing history of our granddaughter, Shoshana, learning to write from preschool to secondary school, which leads to a theory to test against other developing writers. Much of what is known about language and literacy development comes from case studies of researchers' children such as those conducted by Bissex (1985) and Halliday (1975). Our purpose is to show how Shoshana learned to write in order to reclaim the importance of understanding how all children learn to write.

## An Informal Longitudinal Case Study

Shoshana is our daughter Karen's daughter. When she was little, Shoshana loved to make up stories to tell the family. At age three and a half she ended one of her elaborate stories with, "And none of it was nonsense." Yetta included her ending in a presentation in London that year and Betty Rosen decided to use it as the title of her book about children's storytelling (Rosen, 1988). Yetta has been studying Shoshana's writing for years. She interviewed Shoshana and Karen after they read a final draft of this chapter to verify and extend our insights. We used Yetta's concept of kidwatching (Goodman, 1985) and considered the social context of her writing for our analysis. The evolution of Shoshana's writing shows how she, like all children, dynamically built concepts about writing while using it for authentic purposes.

## The Learner is in Charge

Young children are surrounded by visible literacy, in print and digital modes. As a result, they come to know writing and its role in society. A main thesis of this chapter is that the learner is in charge of learning and that "the most *basic* writing skill of all – the capacity for social participation and effective communication – ... means the capacity [for learners] to read a social situation and to adapt one's symbolic and cultural resources so as to have one's say" (Genishi & Dyson, 2009, p. 109).

Duckworth's (1987) concept, *the having of wonderful ideas*, highlights the importance of allowing "children to accept their own ideas and to work them through" (pp. 12–13). It is the "person's own repertoire of thoughts, actions, connections, predictions and feelings ... the individual has done the work of putting them together ... And they give rise to news ways to put them together" (Duckworth, 1987, pp. 12–13). We make no claims that Shoshana's writing is typical of all learners. What she demonstrates, however, supports Halliday's (2004b) conclusions that, whenever humans use language, they are "learning language, learning through language and learning about language" (p. 308).

## Shoshana's Sociocultural History

Shoshana grew up in Tucson, Los Angeles, and Houston, and graduated from college with a degree in Fine Arts. She is bilingual and biliterate; Spanish is used by her native-speaking father and by her bilingual mother, but English is her dominant language. Shoshana visited family in Mexico regularly and lived in Colombia, South America, for six months when she was nine. Shoshana was also influenced by our Jewish family, especially during holidays.

Shoshana loved to read to her brother Noah before he was reading independently. Her writing and art projects were done at a small desk in the playroom with access to many materials. Sometimes Karen suggested that Shoshana write to family members or send an invitation. Although she answered Shoshana's questions and responded when she asked for homework help, Karen did no direct teaching of writing conventions.

## Shoshana's Early Schooling

Shoshana attended preschool with children from diverse backgrounds in a Los Angeles public school and then a science magnet school. The curricula in these schools were based in a transmission model. Yetta visited Shoshana's kindergarten where the five-year-olds sat with their hands folded on their desks waiting quietly for the teacher's instructions then moved to centers to independently complete worksheets while groups worked with the teacher. When Shoshana was in first grade she called us and said eagerly, "It's 'C' week." Another time she told us that her teacher encouraged her to spell any way while writing, "Just like you do Grandma!" In second grade, Karen remembers Shoshana saying, "My teacher thinks I'm a dummy." After six weeks, she brought home a report card that showed *S* (satisfactory) marks in achievement for handwriting, oral language and the subject matter areas and Ns (needs to improve) in *reading, written composition, spelling,* and *mathematics.* In Work Habits she had six Ss and three Gs (good) for *is courteous, obeys school rules* and *listens to and follows directions.* And in a box next to *May be retained,* there was an X.

Karen asked the teacher to explain the alarming report card. "Where do you think your daughter stands academically?" the teacher replied pointing to Shoshana's low first grade test scores. After the teacher enumerated problems in Shoshana's reading, writing, and arithmetic, Karen asked, "Can you tell me something that Shoshana does well?" The teacher replied, "She's a good listener, good in stories and social studies, but those are things I can't grade."

Karen wrote a letter to the school staff that she titled, *A Parent's Assessment of Shoshana's Abilities.* Here are some of her comments:

> Shoshana writes letters, stories, poems, signs and journal entries that are well structured, meaningful and reflect appropriate literary style. A year ago, her invented spelling was barely decipherable. Now anything she writes is easily understandable and she is rapidly moving toward convention. She was not reading on her own before first grade and now reads independently … beginner books. She has had excessive phonics instruction since kindergarten and is convinced that reading is "sounding out" word by word despite her mother's efforts to the contrary. Her reading instruction involves the whole class reading aloud from a second grade reader, which is beyond her; this year she has begun to feel that she is not a good reader … She is polite and defers to adult authority. … She becomes overwhelmed if she understands that she is expected to strive toward what she sees as perfect models of writing and reading.

Karen decided to enroll Shoshana in University Elementary School where Shoshana enjoyed theme projects, teachers were sensitive to children's individual interests, and there were no traditional grade levels; however, there was a lot of social and academic competition among the children, who included children of Hollywood celebrities. Shoshana remembers conversations about who lived in the best neighborhood, and she often felt she was an outsider to the wealth and status.

There were other positive influences in Shoshana's writing history. Now, as an adult, she remembers in some detail the teachers who encouraged her. Although she still lacks confidence as a writer and a speller, she was convinced by supportive teachers that she expresses herself well. One middle school teacher held regular writing conferences and pointed to her writing as evidence of her creativity and engaging language use. She was in a secondary English class in which the teacher involved the students in developing an online journal. In her middle and secondary classes, she wrote poetry and essays, and learned to organize for writing a paper, which she continued to use successfully to write *A* papers in college.

## The Context of Situation

By carefully examining specific features of Shoshana's writing over time, we provide evidence of her coming to know written language. Each literacy event was unique, took place in a specific context, and posed problems that contributed to her learning to write. She showed evidence of the social conventions that she already knew. In each piece, she showed invented new forms she needed to make sense to her audience. Her decisions were based on her purpose and the functions the writing served.

Halliday (2004a) conceptualizes the *context of situation* that frames all language use in order for meaning making as "the *social system*.... The context for an *act of meaning* is the *situation*... which ... consists of a *field* of social process ..., a *tenor* of social relationships and a *mode*" (pp. 121–122, emphasis in the original). Shoshana's composing, as for all writers, was unique within each context or situation. We present Shoshana's examples chronologically and compare similar genres to provide evidence of her developing language knowledge in relation to her genre choices, literary style, sensitivity to audience, and linguistic features, including orthography, phonology, spelling, and grammar. Shoshana's writing in this chapter is represented in italics and retains spelling, spacing, and other features exactly as in her originals.

## Shoshana's Letters Over Time

> *Dere gamoe i*
> *hoqe you are feelg*
> *Badre i hoqe you*
> *wiae llik my*
> *ladre say i Love*
> *you to gaqoe*
> *ffr me*
> *i Love you to*
> *Love Shoshana*

Shoshana's letters and greeting cards that we received prior to this *Dere* (Dear) *gamoe* (grandma) letter, which she wrote when she was 7 years 2 months, were addressed to both of her grandparents. Shoshana wrote this letter only to Yetta who was recuperating from an operation. It illuminates Shoshana's social sensitivity, which is evident in all her writing. She wanted to make sure that Grandpa wasn't forgotten, so she wrote: *say i Love you to gaqoe* (grandpa) *frr* (for) *me*. Shoshana used appropriate conventions for someone being ill. She was aware of her audience and her writing was comprehensible.

Shoshana used conventional spelling for most pronouns and the function words and a few content words that she used frequently (you, are, my, say, love). She invented the spelling of less familiar words. As the content of writing becomes more complex, writers invent writing features when they need them (see Manning & Ransom, Chapter 7). Shoshana's inventions demonstrated her knowledge of orthographic (how the writing looks) and phonological (how the language sounds to each individual) features of writing.

Although her word spacing was conventional from her earliest writing examples, in this letter she didn't yet use periods as punctuation. Her four sentences were grammatically conventional. She began her letter with a salutation and ended with a closing followed by a line of kisses (asterisks), including one surrounded by a heart. She reversed the letter *p* in hope and grandpa; she had only one reversal in any of her subsequent writing.

Shoshana's spelling of "will like" as *wiae llik* shows her knowledge of both phonology and orthography. In oral English the phrase "will like" blends two words together, but Shoshana knew it was two words. She represented the liquid sound at the end of "will" with the vowels letters "ae". Knowing there should be two "lls" in this phrase, but not sure where they go, she invented their placement. She knew most words in English have at least three letters (Ferreiro & Teberosky, 1982) but was not yet sure that each English word includes at least one vowel when she invented *ffr* (for). She decided to use capital letters on important words *Badre* (Better) and *Love*. In this letter, she experimented with inventions that dropped out of her writing even within a few weeks.

## Writing From Experience

At 13 years 4 months, Shoshana wrote a letter with 375 words to *Dear Grandma, and Grandpa*. The letter was the first piece Shoshana wrote on the computer. Its three conventional paragraphs related appropriately to different topics: (1) *Mom, and I are starting a book about me in elimentry* (elementary) *school*; (2) *I'm reading the gratest* (greatest) *book that I'v* (I've) *ever read in my life!*; (3) *My mom is reading me a book called Jerney (Journey) of the Sperows (Sparrows)*. Her language reflected her excitement and she made clear that we would be interested: *I can't wate* (wait) *to see you. I have a lot of things to tell, and showe* (show) *you*. Her sentence structure was conventional, as was her complex and stylistic syntax.

Most of Shoshana's punctuation was conventional; however, as she worked with more complex ideas, she had more complex punctuation possibilities, which led to more sophisticated inventions. She used a comma at the end of an independent clause connecting to following independent clauses that were closely related. For example, she ended the independent clause for her third paragraph (see 3 above) followed by: *its* (it's) *based on familys* (families) *that snik* (sneak) *across the border, its* (it's) *also a good book, its* (it's) *very sad and sereos* (serious) *but its* (it's) *good*.

Eighty-five percent of her words were conventionally spelled, including seven approximated uses of *its*. She invented spellings for *elimentry* (elementary), *perints* (parents), *consitrashon* (concentration), and *recamended* (recommended), which represented her personal phonology and show that she was comfortable using words she did not write often. In this letter, she used a spelling strategy which she used other times: she wrote possible alternative spellings in parentheses and left them to check for conventions later. She obviously knew when she did not know (Duckworth, 1987) but decided not to spend time with accurate spelling while she engaged in writing.

## New Contexts, New Genre

> *Pes entr to*
> *the porde. I will*
> *be tigrlile and noah*
> *will be a indein.*
> *Shoshana*
> *Castro*

When Shoshana was 7 years 2 months, she and Noah planned a Halloween party. Karen suggested they put an announcement on the front door to welcome their guests. Shoshana, an accomplished artist as an adult, always loved to draw, but she selected which writing pieces to illustrate depending on the purpose of her message. In this case, illustration was integral to her announcement as she showed a girl connected to a written message in a speech balloon. Shoshana wrote: *Pes* (please) *entr* (enter) *to the porde* (party). She demonstrated her understanding of context of situation when she did not use illustrations in her letters, lists, menus, or essays.

In this announcement, she used two conventional sentences followed by periods. As in the first example, she spelled function words conventionally (to, the, will, be, and a). She didn't know to use *an* before *indein* (Indian) nor did she capitalize it. However, first person *I* was now capitalized when just a few weeks previously she used small case *i*. She also followed the social convention of including her last name. She ended all of her letters with only her first name but chose in this less personal announcement to use both.

At 7 years 4 months, Shoshana numbered and listed *10 presents I woda* (would) *like* in phrases such as: *1. bord* (board) *game* and *10. a racrd of moyousic* (record of music) without capitalization, punctuation, or illustrations. She repeated the previous strategy she used when she was unsure of spelling: *6. an a erasr* (eraser)/ *a erasr/an erasr/8. Swit pas* (sweat pants)/*swit pants*. She demonstrated that even when she was not in a school setting, she was concerned about conventional spelling.

## Shoshana's Narratives: Invention to Convention

Shoshana wrote a fairy tale when she was 7 years 5 months that included nine sentences with conventional structure and ending punctuation, although no commas. The fairy tale genre was easily recognizable in the language of the opening and closing sentences:

> *Ons* (once) *upon a time thar* (there) *was an old man and his dodre* (daughter). *He becam much yungre and lived happyule* (happily) *aver* (ever) *aftr* (after).

And in her use of magic:

> *One day wen* (when) *the dodre* (daughter) *was wocking* (walking) *throe* (through) *the forist* (forest) *she fawnd* (found) *a magic lefe* (leaf).

She ended her fairy tale with an illustration of a young male with a soccer ball and a caption: *This yunge* (young) *man yost* (used) *toe be a old man.*

The plausible plot, with appropriate details and literary language, revealed once again Shoshana's sensitivity and awareness of social context as it was written for a favorite aunt who was dying of cancer.

This story provides good examples of our concept of the interplay between invention and convention (Goodman & Goodman, 1990). Shoshana used conventional spellings when she knew them. But she was not afraid to write even when she didn't know the conventional spelling and she invented spellings based on her personal phonics. She explored punctuation and other linguistic features to express new possible meanings and she added interesting illustrations when she thought they enhanced her meaning making. Writers use inventions to focus on making sense rather than worrying about "what is correct."

During the same month that Shoshana wrote *Dear Grandma and Grandpa*, she also wrote a narrative called, *A Weird and Funny Dream*, thus providing an opportunity to compare two narratives across time as well as two different genres written within the same month. The letter was a first draft, written on a computer, which she chose not to edit. However, in the dream narrative, also written on the computer, all linguistic features were conventional, including spelling, punctuation, capitalization, paragraphing, and sentence structure. Shoshana sensed when to be concerned about conventional aspects of writing and what could remain in draft. Shoshana remembers she was comfortable with spell check by this time. She even used a colon properly. *We were going to meet Noah and some other characters from the book: Mama, Maria, and Julia.*

Like her fairy tale, this narrative, which had a Disneyland setting, related her dream in detailed action sequences with literary language:

> It was funny because the ride was still on and working, and the people on it saw us and ignored us like it was the most normal thing to see a bunch of people chasing through the ride with a bunch of soldiers chasing them.

**FIGURE 2.1** Mother's Day card.

## Other Personal Genres

Shoshana designed a Mother's Day card for Karen at 7 years 9 months. She used many devices so her mother knew she was sending her love. She wrote her card in first person and signed it with her first name. Her sophisticated invention of the use of a key: *the hart* (heart) *stans* (stands) *for lawde* (loud) was placed separately in the lower right-hand corner and showed her awareness that her mother was unfamiliar with the meaning of a heart with a period under it.

Shoshana's card highlights and extends the idea that children invent more than spellings as they learn to write. Shoshana invented hearts, kisses, font variations, a creative range of exclamation marks, and a key to represent the mood and the tenor of her relations with her mother. Whenever she used language she was not only learning language but at the same time learning about language (Halliday, 2004b). Authentic writing highlights writing development and the control learners have over conventional use of language as they confront authentic needs for their writing.

We went to visit Shoshana when she was 9 years old living in Pasto, Colombia. When we got home from a restaurant (where Shoshana read the menu in

Spanish), she and Noah played restaurant. Shoshana designed a menu, which was her first writing in Spanish.

> 1 *Lengwa de bake con enselatha*
> 2 *Corna con tamtes*
> 3 *Poyoe con arse*
> 4 *poto con salsa*
> 5 *Amdargsa con papse*
> 6 *Aros con pescato*
>   *y pod tomre*
>   1 *modaky*
>   2 *pena*
>   3 *nadanha*
>   4 *cokola*
>   5 *choklata*
>   6 *lamanatha*

Shoshana centered and numbered the entrees: *Lengwa de bake con enselatha* (Lengua de vaca con ensalada – Cow's tongue with salad), which her grandfather had for dinner, as well as *Amdargsa con papse* (Hamburguesa con papas – Hamburger and fries). She separated drinks, *y pod tomre* (and for drinking), on the right side of the menu and numbered them. She drew on English and Spanish phonology, orthography and grammar, and used conventional spelling especially for Spanish function words: *de* (of); *con* (with); and *y* (and). She spelled *por* ("for" in Spanish) as *pod* where *para* would have been grammatically appropriate.

Some of her inventions showed English spelling for Spanish words, as in *lemonatha* and *ensalatha* with *th* where Spanish uses a *d*. She continued to explore the silent "e" rule. She used "y" in *poyoe* for the sound usually represented by "ll" in Spanish (as in pollo/chicken). Her spellings of words like *pescato* (pescado/fish), *nadanha* (naranja/orange) and *pod* (por, for) were inventions native speakers of Spanish might make when writing English. Sometimes she tried more than one spelling for the same word. For example, she first wrote *arse* (arroz) in *poyoe con arse* (chicken with rice) and later *aros* in *pescato con aros* (fish and rice).

Writers solve problems in their writing systems by adapting the knowledge they already have to new situations. Learners' knowledge is revealed in their writing inventions, and in play, young writers experiment because they are less concerned with convention. Opportunities to explore written language in a wide range of contexts and purposes are significant in learning to write. Careful analysis reveals the tensions that exist between conventions and invention as well as the learners' language knowledge (Goodman & Goodman, 1990).

The last genre we examine is an essay Shoshana wrote about teenage pregnancy when she was 13 years 8 months just before high school. Shoshana's middle-school teacher encouraged students to select topics. Shoshana listed her ideas, edited them in handwriting and expanded them on the computer. Her handwritten draft showed many cross-outs, clause-level insertions written in the margins with appropriate arrows leading to specific places within the text, and phrases substituted above crossed out ones.

Parts of the first and last paragraphs of the final two page computerized copy follow:

First paragraph: *Adolescence is one of the toughest times in your life. You are undergoing great changes. Not just physically but emotionally as well. New experience pours itself over you, while at the same time pressure pushes you toward usually the wrong choices. Imagine peer pressure on the right, parent pressure on the left both closing in on you. This pressure is usually the main reason why teens tend to give in to things like drugs and sex. ... But there are ways to prevent this.*

Last paragraph: *Kids need to stop having kids. Teenagers need to find other ways than sex or drugs to cope with pressure. No one is stopping parents from just talking with kids about their problems. People need to be more open. An open and expressive family is definitely a healthy one. But it's not just the parents who need to be open. Teachers, aunts, uncles or any other type of mentor would be helpful. ... Help them, give your attention, show that you care. It won't stop teen pregnancy all together but it will definitely help.*

In the middle paragraphs, Shoshana explained: *Find out how they feel, talk with them, try to understand their point of view* and she suggested causes for the various pressures teenagers face. She was sensitive to *A sixteen year old girl who is raising a one year old child* and she reminded her reader that they need to take *Not just the girls, but the boys,* into consideration. She then provided specific information about organizations and programs *that help get teens back in school, get them health insurance, child care and counseling.*

She used both second and third person voices in this piece. In the first paragraph she seems to talk directly to a teen audience but it is also possible to read this piece with a universal *you* throughout as she addressed adults as well as her peers as she did in the last paragraph. This is also evident in the first sentence in her second paragraph: *First ask yourself, how do you stop teens from having sex?* In addition to her complex topic, syntax, and voice, Shoshana's final copy, which she edited herself, was conventional in spelling and syntax. This essay is an example of Smorgorinsky's (2013) ideas about exploratory written language. "The notion of exploratory speech is central to the *writing to learn* approach in which writers are granted the opportunity to *think through writing* no matter what writing looks like at first glance" (p. 194).

## Shoshana's Agency

As Shoshana learned to write, she made decisions about how and what to write for personal purposes. She expanded her knowledge of the conventions of genre, grammar, spelling, wording, and how to express her meanings to communicate with her intended audience appropriate to her purpose. In each context, she used a genre that included social conventions with which her audience identified. Shoshana became aware of the interpersonal language necessary in a particular piece in a particular setting. She knew she was successful based on authentic responses she received from her audiences. Authentic writing is initiated by the writer to communicate in a particular way for a particular audience in a unique context of situation.

It is impossible in a discussion of reclaiming learning about writing to ignore the significance of teachers and other members of Shoshana's social community on her writing development (Genishi & Dyson, 2009). When teachers, family members or peers were supportive and provided opportunities and diverse contexts for authentic writing experiences, Shoshana's writing and use of language developed in positive ways. She invented forms to fit the purposes of her writing.

There were many aspects of her writing that were not testable by standardized tests. Shoshana's poem written at age 16 is a tribute to her sense of self and better than any final exam in demonstrating her competence as a writer:

> Open the windows, look outside
>    a green eyed girl dances on the shore.
> Her heat driven steps pulse through the sand,
>    her gestures and movements possess wild self-control.
> She glances upward beholding her spirit and soul,
>    the moon … full, glistening, silver and gold.
> Its rich reflection kisses the sea.
> Its audacious snow-white color contrasts against the
>    blankets of the night…
>    just as she…
> She, the green eyed girl,
>    the girl inside me.

## References

Bissex, G. (1985). *Gnys at wrk: A child learns to write and read.* Cambridge, MA: Harvard University Press.

Duckworth, E. (1987). *The having of wonderful ideas and other essays on teaching and learning.* New York: Teachers College Press.

Ferreiro, E., & Teberosky, A. (1982). *Literacy before schooling.* Portsmouth, NH: Heinemann.

Genishi, C., & Dyson, A. (2009). *Children, language and literacy: Diverse learners in diverse times.* New York: Teachers College Press.

Goodman, Y. (1985). Kidwatching: Observing children in the classroom. In A. Jaggar, & M. Smith-Burke (Eds.), *Observing the language learner* (pp. 9–18). Newark, DE & Urbana IL: International Reading Association and the National Council of Teachers of English.

Goodman, Y. M., & Goodman, K. S. (1990). Vygotsky in a whole-language perspective. In L. C. Moll (Ed.), *Vygotsky and education: Instructional implications and applications of sociohistorical psychology* (pp. 223–250). New York: Cambridge University Press.

Halliday, M. (1975). *Learning how to mean.* London: Edward Arnold.

Halliday, M. (2004a). Meaning and the construction of reality in early childhood. In M. Halliday & J. Webster (Eds.), *The language of early childhood* (pp. 113–143). London: Continuum. (Original work published in 1978).

Halliday, M. (2004b). Three aspects of children's language development: Learning language, learning through language, learning about language. In M. Halliday & J. Webster (Eds.), *The language of early childhood* (pp. 308–326). London: Continuum. (Original work published in 1980).

Rosen, B. (1988). *And none of it was nonsense.* Portsmouth, NH: Heinemann.

Smorgorinsky, P. (2013). What does Vygotsky provide for the 21st century language arts teacher? *Language Arts, 90,* 190–202.

# 2 Extension

## RECLAIMING IDENTITIES AND LEARNING TO WRITE

*Bobbie Kabuto*

What are children learning when they learn to write? In their chapter, Goodman and Goodman describe how writing is born out of writers' active and meaningful engagements with their social and cultural environments. By participating in purposeful social contexts, children write, first and foremost, to develop relationships with other people, to organize their social worlds, and to have a voice when voices are sometimes suppressed. In the act of writing to create varied and renewed cartographies of their social worlds, children develop theories about writing conventions. In the process of moving towards conventional writing, children become problem-posers and problem-solvers as they negotiate their personal inventions with social conventions. Learning to write also means learning to become a unique person. In other words, learning to write is also an act of identity.

Goodman and Goodman argue that the writing history of Shoshana provides a theory that can be compared to other writers, and I related Shoshana's writing history with that of my daughter, Emma. I studied Emma's early biliteracy when she was between the ages of three and seven by documenting the ways in which she navigated writing in two writing systems – English and Japanese – which involve four written language forms, or scripts: the Roman alphabet, Japanese hiragana and katakana, and Chinese kanji. Like Shoshana, Emma's bilingual writing history evolved out of and was embedded in a variety of social domains that interpreted her writing, including living in the US and Japan. While using writing to become an active participant in various social contexts defined by English and Japanese, Emma too learned the linguistic and pragmatic elements of writing. Emma also learned to navigate two writing systems: the English alphabetic system and the Japanese syllabic system.

Watching, documenting, and analyzing Emma's writing history painted a picture of how she grew as a competent language user of two writing systems – bringing me to the realization that differences in the forms of multiple written languages do not necessarily equate to learning difficulties. When learning to write across English and Japanese, Emma developed a perceptual flexibility linking the forms of one script to the forms of another. Instead of viewing multiple written forms as inherently "different," Emma looked for the similarities and patterns among them.

## Learning to Build Houses

When I think of the connection between writing and identity, I think of the analogy of building a house. In the process of building a house, we need tools. These tools can range from nails to hammers and from pipes to flooring. No matter the type of house (ranch, colonial, cape, etc.) there are customary tools that are needed. Sometimes we can upgrade or downgrade, but without nails we will have a difficult time keeping planks of wood together and without pipes we cannot have plumbing.

Written language as a tool system is a culturally defined means of engaging in the process of writing. As a tool system, we have written language scripts such as the Roman alphabet for English or Kanji for Chinese or abjad for Hebrew. At the same time, there are conventional ways that these parts are put together to create a whole, just like there is a way of running floorboards together to construct an entire floor. The English language uses periods, commas, exclamation marks, and quotations as punctuation markers. In American English, rule-governed spellings and sentence structures define the cohesiveness of English writing.

As soon as Emma put pencil to paper, she rapidly packed her tool box, and by the time Emma was 5 years old, she was a beginning writer using four scripts related to English and Japanese. Between the ages of three and four, Emma's written artifacts consisted of English and images. A small number consisted of markings made up of wavy lines or letter-like symbols that demonstrated her movement into conventional written language. By the time Emma was between the ages of four and five, written Japanese appeared as a script choice in her writings. During this time, Emma wrote her name in both English and hiragana, and wrote her Japanese friends' names in hiragana.

During her kindergarten years, English and Japanese as script choices increased and Emma wrote her name in English and in hiragana on her school papers. One night, when I observed Emma writing her name in English and Japanese on a phonics homework sheet, I questioned her actions. She replied, "I am the only one who knows Japanese so no one will know what I am writing but me." Emma's comment opens the door into thinking about how the tools that compose writing tool kits are not isolated objects with only one meaning, but in fact are loaded with meanings that assist writers in understanding who they are in relation to other people and social structures as they employ writing tools to navigate their surroundings. Writers, therefore, not only have to understand how to employ the tools but also how they are interpreted within various social contexts.

While we may use the same hammer or the same brand of pipe or the same color and style of tile as another person, how we employ, organize, and/or display these tools is unique to each one of us, making our individual houses different from the next person's. The house in this analogy is our identity: our sense of who we are in relation to other people and social structures. To illustrate, Emma (5 years, 6 months) created a birthday card for Erika, her friend from Japanese school. Erika's birthday party was on Valentine's Day, which caused Emma to write "Happy Valentine's Day" (with my assistance on spelling) on the front of the card. Emma then wrote *From Emma (to) Erika* in hiragana. When I asked Emma why she wrote in Japanese and English, she replied that she needed to write Happy Valentine's Day in English because she "lives in America" and the greeting in Japanese because Erika is Japanese. Through the use of two scripts, Emma was able to make language, social, and cultural boundaries permeable, and in the process was able to identify with her English-language identity as well as her Japanese-language identity. In essence, she was able to have varied linguistic identities as she entered into different participatory structures organized around language.

Consequently, Emma's writing became a means of addressing different audiences for different purposes. While she wrote a card in Japanese hiragana to her Japanese grandmother, she also wrote her name in the same script alongside her name in the Roman alphabet on her kindergarten homework. In spite of the fact that she wrote in hiragana across the two artifacts, the ways in which they were interpreted by the audience who read the artifacts were different and led to different results. For instance, the card written in hiragana provided access for Emma into her grandmother's communicative domains, but Emma's name written in hiragana on her kindergarten homework challenged the language practices of her classroom. Writing, therefore, not only served cognitive and linguistic functions; it was also a tool for constructing her identity as a bilingual and biliterate child.

## Reclaiming Writing, Reclaiming Identities

While both Emma and Shoshana used some of the same writing tools, their houses look very different, and they will continue to evolve and change their houses over time. I saw many of Shoshana's theories of writing in Emma's, but the uniqueness of each child evolved out of each one negotiating the ways in which writing provided access, power and agency in the home, school, and community. Reclaiming writing becomes synonymous with allowing writers to reclaim who they are and who they can become. Typically, language separation is assumed to lead to language competence within the classroom so that language and script switching are generally forbidden practices. Taking this view of writing situates writing as sterile and unrelated to writers' developing identities. If we ignore the meaning potentials of writing tools and limit the tools to which writers have access, we limit the identities they construct in the process of writing.

## Note

To read more about Emma and how she became biliterate at the crossroads of home and school, please see Kabuto, B. (2010). *Becoming biliterate: Identity, ideology, and learning to read and write in two languages.* New York: Routledge.

# 3

# ARTFUL BOOKMAKING

## Learning by Design

*Kathryn F. Whitmore and Marie Gernes*

This chapter considers the role of design in reclaiming learning about writing. While today's writers (adults and children) are immersed in multimodal texts, and clamor for more interactive and innovative digital formats for play and learning, we describe what happened when a class of second graders was afforded the opportunity to learn about print books in a new way – as objects of art they could design. Our observations and analysis of these events led us to think about the role of design in the writing process and how *learning to design* helped children reclaim their voices as writers.

## The Context

This study took place in the lowest performing elementary school in a small city where the children represented a diverse mix of low-income and working-class families and varied cultural and linguistic backgrounds. Stacey Medd, the teacher with whom we worked, felt pressure to raise scores and to demonstrate account-ability to increasingly demanding standards, yet she found numerous ways to immerse her second graders in published children's literature as part of her goal to teach them about purposeful writing. She read aloud to the children several times a day and offered creative ways to respond that brought outside-of-school life into the classroom and attended to the many conventions of print that children encountered. Stacey's students learned about writing from children's literature when they explicitly attended to text features, explored relationships between illustrated and written texts, discussed how they transacted actively in the spaces that authors create for readers to "fill in" personal meaning, and more.

The project we describe engaged children in *artmaking as bookmaking*: from experiencing or imagining content, to drafting, to composing written and illustrated texts, to learning from an artist whose medium is handmade books, to binding their own handmade books. The project culminated when the books were artistically displayed in the school foyer and the children presented public readings of their work at a local independent bookstore and at the public library (where it was recorded and televised). Islam Aly, an artist at the Center for the Book at The University of Iowa, visited the classroom and showed the children a variety of materials and types of handmade books across history as well as his own art. He led the children on a tour of the Center for the Book where they learned about papermaking, binding, and printing. Once the children's written texts were drafted, the children returned to the Center for the Book to bind blank books (see Figure 3.1) into which we eventually glued their written and illustrated texts according to the children's design decisions.

## Some Assumptions That Ground Our Work

Our planning for artful bookmaking assumed that writing is a recursive process in which writers have a great deal of control. We assumed a view of the writing process to include: planning (conceptualizing ideas and selecting topics), shaping ideas into drafts, revising (focused on meaning) and editing (focused on conventions and decisions about presentation), and sharing (including some form of publishing).

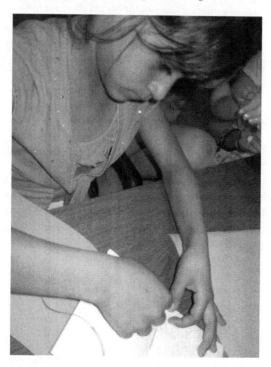

**FIGURE 3.1** Ana binding her book with a wrap-around cover.

We expanded these concepts about the writing process to emphasize the roles of transmediation, aesthetic choices, and voice as children designed. We remained mindful that the goal for a design curriculum is to be generative, iterative, and circular, rather than dictating a single, dominant path or form (New London Group, 2000). Moreover, given that we valued the resources in the local community, we drew on the Center for the Book as inspiration for the children's learning.

Design highlights combinations and limitations of chosen semiotic systems. To Kress and Van Leeuwen (2006), design is part of a visual grammar, showing particular patterns of representation and experience that are culturally specific and socially produced. Design involves the intentional use of this structure as well as agency; it demands an awareness of the rules and social norms that govern each modality to create new meaning. As a social practice and an iterative process, all meaning making uses multiple modes that are situated in and bounded by particular contexts and semiotic conventions (New London Group, 2000). This chapter is a blend of visual and linguistic signs: we played with photographs and words (from audio- and video-recorded interviews and classroom discussions) and their complementary meanings to design it.

We use arts-based (Barone & Eisner, 2011) and ethnographic (Sunstein & Chiseri-Strater, 2011) research methods to document children's bookmaking in the context of all language arts teaching over the course of one academic year. We were directly involved in the production of the books the children made, and pre-service teacher education students from our methods course provided one-on-one and small group support as the children composed and illustrated. In this chapter, we explain how emphasizing design reclaimed children's purposes and identities as writers.

## Learning About Transmediation

School is an increasingly verbocentric space where children's meaning making is confined to expressing meaning through language as well as authors are able, and as well as words are able, whether orally or in writing. This is true even though, as Bezemer and Kress (2008) note, "writing [i.e. print] is being displaced by image as the central mode of communication" (p. 166). In reality, images and visual design carry just as much meaning as words (see Martens, Martens, Doyle, & Loomis, Chapter 9; Schmidt, Chapter 9a Extension). Design's abject focus on the metalanguage of multiliteracies allows teachers and students to study how writers imbue every aspect of text with intentionality and participation to communicate meaning.

Like in all classrooms, Stacey's class included a variety of personalities. Aaron presented a challenge to two teacher education students who were his buddies during the year because he was one of the more verbally astute children in the class and yet the most reluctant child to write. Aaron often refused to put the sophisticated vocabulary and vibrant details in his oral English and Spanish narratives on paper. In a writing conference, Aaron told Kathy a layered and lengthy story about his brother getting a dog at the flea market. Imbedded were a plethora of complaints why he couldn't write his story: "But my hand hurts too much." "I don't know what to write." "My arm hurts." "I don't write in cursive." When Aaron said yet again, "I'm not good at writing," Kathy responded, "You know what Aaron? I don't want you to tell me that anymore." When it came time to decide on content for Aaron's bookmaking project, perhaps because of the rehearsal he had experienced in the conference, he quickly chose his story about the flea market. Once again, however, Aaron was reluctant to write. He selected a comic book style for his format, which we assumed was because he thought the genre would require less writing due to the minimal amount of text in its design.

We offered three basic book designs for children to modify: accordion, dos-a-dos (two stories in one), or pamphlet. Covers could fold over, binding strings could wrap around the book (the children thought this made it a treasure to unwrap), and individual pages or covers could pop out. Aaron was drawn immediately to the accordion format and was emphatic that it have a plain green 4″ × 6″ cover. Interestingly, Aaron's book became the only accordion design in the class, which garnered him a fair amount of positive attention (see Figure 3.2).

Transmediation is the purposeful translation of meaning between and among multiple sign systems, in order to elucidate aspects of intended meaning (Siegel, 1995; Suhor, 1984). When children write, transmediation seems natural, like a playful but purposeful conversation with themselves and the semiotic world. They talk, gesture, and sing, using words and images from the world around them, and select elements that communicate their intentions (Pahl, 2009). Much of Aaron's narrative was composed in these ways. As Kress (2013) describes, representations are always partial and incomplete carriers of meaning. Transmediating among multiple sign systems afforded Aaron more places to represent meaning while designing a text.

**FIGURE 3.2** Aaron's accordion-style design.

## Learning About Aesthetic Choices

Designing is never just reproducing available designs, but is the transformation of these elements into a new iteration of language, image, sound, or movement in particular social situations (New London Group, 2000). Whenever the children made aesthetic choices, they transformed meaning and strengthened their multi-modal voices.

Aesthetic choices included the paper children selected for their covers, which corresponded beautifully to their intentions as writers. Maddy chose fancy and glittering paper for her "Princess vs. Witch" story, which initially looked "girly," but cleverly belied her intention, as reflected in her *about the author* note: "Maddy wants others to be inspired to be tough and not let anyone get in their way." Carlos chose different cover papers for each side of "Super vs. Evil" wherein he told two superhero escapades. His aesthetic choice of a dos-a-dos design, in which the cover paper creates a "Z" so two stories can be written back-to-back, in turn shifted his ideas as an author. He loved the design so much he was inspired to write two stories to fit his characters and their adventures.

Other aesthetic choices included the placement and design of illustrations and written texts on the page. Repetition in image in Mariana's colorful borders (see Figure 3.3) accomplished her intention to communicate a happy mood and gave

I love my Abuela because when I get hungry she makes me cookies and chocolate milk.

I love my Abuela because she was the b

**FIGURE 3.3** Mariana's page designs with colorful happy borders.

her book a traditional, grounded design. Mariana titled her personal narrative "Mi Abuela," and often described it as nonfiction "because it really happened;" it was a love letter to her grandmother who had died recently. A scrolling, italics font in Maddy's book meant "princess" to her and resulted in her exclamation, "I loved the pages because they're so beautiful." Maddy also exhibited design choices for color and texture; filmy yellow paper with sparkles glued onto a page represented a "poof" of magic, for example.

Brady's aesthetic choices were imbedded in the design process, which began with writing and revising. When interviewed about the process he followed when he created a personal narrative called "The Crack in My Head," he said revision made him happier with the outcome. He also said he "got the name of the book by the end" and made intentional decisions about illustrations, including leaving some pages void of artwork. In contrast, the last page (see Figure 3.4) was filled with details. "I did a lot of squares to show you that my head can't break any more. It happened so many times in different colors and actions."

FIGURE 3.4  Brady's last page.

## Voice

We agree with Weedon (1997) that in language

> we learn to give voice – meaning – to our experience and to understand it according to particular ways of thinking, particular discourses, which pre-date our entry into language. These ways of thinking constitute our consciousness, and the positions with which we identify [or] structure our sense of ourselves, our subjectivity (p. 32).

Thus, language is a place that holds promise for constructing identities of power for young children in school (Dudley-Marling & Paugh, 2004). Stacey draws on the potential of voice often while teaching her students to actively structure their senses of themselves. She intentionally creates experiences for children to experience, explain, and appreciate their multiple identities.

> I really want the kids to realize that they … aren't just one thing. They're not just a second grade student. They don't need to talk in a way that you would just talk on the playground. You can also speak like a scientist. You can always write like a scientist…

The curriculum Stacey offers children includes the expressive (Juzwik & Sherry, 2007) and poetic (Eisner, 2002) potential of voice, in written and verbal modes, and in relation to audience. Tannen (1989) argues that the details in poetic language, and their resulting images, create intimacy and cause the listener/reader to experience the feelings of the speaker/writer. Such language seeks, "not merely to convince audiences (a purportedly logical process), but also to move them (an emotional one)" (p. 33).

Stacey says voice means "you can tell something about the author, and the writing reveals thinking and a unique perspective. Writing without voice is distant and writing with voice is close and intimate." She uses the word "voice" with children right away in a new year, defining with them thereafter what it means to speak and write with voice. Stacey equates voice with power, intending to hand power to her students by teaching voice. And she recognizes that as a teacher her voice has a lot of power. "I have control over how I talk about something to the children, how I present it, what I do before and after it."

The children eagerly rose to Stacey's invitations to imbue their book designs with powerful voices, in genres ranging from fairy tales to personal narratives to scary stories and poetry. They readily drew, often literally, on multiple voices as writers. Leticia designed a dos-a-dos bilingual collection of poetry, "Poems of Laticia/Los Poemas de Laticia," that moved from concrete poems ("I am a spoon") to poems about real relationships with friends and her university buddy, to poems that soared with her voice ("Swirl, Twirl, Dancing Girl").

*I am a spoon*

If I were a spoon
I would be cold
if I got dipped in ice cream.
I would be hot
if I got twirled in tea.
I would like spaghetti
if I got twirled in it.

*Swirl, Twirl, Dancing Girl*

Swirl, twirl, dancing girl.
When you are happy you dance fast,
When you are sad you dance slow,
When you are in love you dance gracefully.
Swirl, twirl, dancing girl.
Some ballerinas wear tutus that are pink.
They sparkle the lights with a great smile.
They wear shiny shoes to make them tiptoe.
Swirl, twirl, dancing girl.

"Quick! Get me some water and dirt and soap and a book and Cesar Chavez!" shouted Bella.

"Why do we need Cesar Chavez?"

"Because he is magical!" explained Bella.

**FIGURE 3.5**   Ana includes Cesar Chavez in her design.

Ana designed one of the smallest books for a story about tiny fairies, to fit in a pocket or to be nearly fairy-sized. Cesar Chavez appeared in her fantasy, called on by the fairies to heal a broken flower, because Ana saw his historic social justice contributions as "magic." As the author, she made Chavez willingly appear to "whisper something to the flower" to help it recover (see Figure 3.5). She clarified in her author's note: "[Ana] knows Cesar Chavez is not magical but was pretending because he talks in Spanish like Ana can!" The design blended her impressions of Chavez as an historical and cultural figure with contemporary fairy characters, remixing these symbols (Dyson, 2003) to create a story filled with her particular voice.

## The Important Things About Design

Our artful bookmaking became public when the children's objects of art were displayed and the children presented public readings. The children also spent significant joyful time reading each other's books in the classroom (see Figure 3.6).

Stacey drew the celebration of the bookmaking process to closure by borrowing the design of *The Important Book*, by Margaret Wise Brown (1990). Some children thought "the important thing" was that others liked their books; some thought it was the content or the genre of their books. Some focused on design and their books as objects. Aaron said, "The important thing about my book is it is the only accordion-style book," and Brady said, "The important thing about my book is the protection" (referring to the way his cover wrapped around the pages to protect them). Several children, including Carlos and Laticia, referenced the hard work they devoted. And Maddy described her voice, "The important thing about my book is it has my ideas and my creation in the book."

**FIGURE 3.6** Delight when reading the objects of art.

We discovered three important things about design in artful bookmaking with young writers – transmediation, aesthetic choices, and voice. These elements engaged second graders and their teacher in learning about writing in new ways. In the process, we all reclaimed the beauty of books as objects of art and the joy that accompanies composing with intention.

## Authors' note:

This research was funded by the Arts and Humanities Initiative at The University of Iowa and the Iowa Arts Council.

## References

Barone, T., & Eisner, E. W. (2011). *Arts-based research*. New York: Sage.

Bezemer, J., & Kress, G. (2008). Writing in multimodal texts: A social semiotic account of designs for learning. *Written Communication, 25*(2), 166–195.

Brown, M. W. (1990). *The important book*. New York: Harper & Row.

Dudley-Marling, C. & Paugh, P. (2004). Tapping the power of student voice through whole language practices. *Reading & Writing Quarterly, 20*(4), 385–399.

Dyson, A. H. (2003). *The brothers and sisters learn to write*. New York: Teachers College Press.

Eisner, E. W. (2002). *The educational imagination*. Upper Saddle River, NJ: Prentice Hall.

Juzwik, M. M., & Sherry, M. B. (2007). Expressive language and the art of English teaching: Theorizing the relationship between literature and oral narrative. *English Education, 39*(3), 226–259.

Kress, G. (2013). *Multimodality: A social semiotic approach to contemporary communication*. New York: Routledge.

Kress, G., & Van Leeuwen, T. (2006). *Reading images: The grammar of visual design* (2nd ed.). New York: Routledge.

New London Group. (2000). A pedagogy of multiliteracies: Designing social futures. In W. Cope & M. Kalantzis (Eds.), *Multiliteracies: Literacy learning and the design of social futures* (pp. 9–37). London: Routledge.

Pahl, K. (2009). Interactions, intersections and improvisations: Studying the multimodal texts and classroom talk of six- to seven-year-olds. *Journal of Early Childhood Literacy, 9*(2), 188–210.

Siegel, M. (1995). More than words: The generative power of transmediation for learning. *Canadian Journal of Education, 20*(4), 455–475. doi:10.2307/1495082

Suhor, C. (1984). Towards a semiotics-based curriculum. *Journal of Curriculum Studies, 16*(3), 247–257.

Sunstein, B. S., & Chiseri-Strater, E. (2011). *Fieldworking: Reading and writing research*. New York: Bedford Books.

Tannen, D. (1989). *Talking voices*. Cambridge: Cambridge University Press.

Weedon, C. (1997). *Feminist practice and poststructuralist theory* (2nd ed.). Cambridge, MA: Blackwell Publishers.

# 3 Extension

## THE CIRCUS OF DESIGN

*S. Rebecca Leigh*

When I was six years old living in Brighton, England, the circus came to town. Thirty-six of my classmates and I wrote about it and drew pictures to accompany our stories from animals to acrobats, candy floss to clowns. Each story was glued into a book and, drawing a lucky number, I got to keep it. With the kindness of tape, I still have this wilted book, which has survived two countries, thirteen moves, and a flood. The book housed my earliest written story, contained a few illustrations I had done, and included the names of classmates I remembered and missed. But I mostly attribute the long shelf life of this rectangular book to a reason sure to surprise: it served as a reminder to me of the frustration I felt as a six-year-old author, illustrator, and publisher. I never want to forget how I felt about putting this book together for my teacher. As a child, I never liked the design of the book.

> I never liked the title, "The Circus by Yellow and Turquoise Classes."
> I never liked that we all had to write our stories on the same size paper.
> I never liked the hard crayon we had to work with or the little space for drawings.
> I never liked the construction paper with its rough texture and dull appearance.
> I never liked that there was one end page rather than two.
> I never liked that the teacher glued in the stories. She, not us, determined their position.
> I never liked the gloomy green cover, either.

None of these design decisions were ours and, more notably, none were representative of the vibrant day we had experienced at the circus. Unlike the experience of Maddy, the second grader in Whitmore and Gernes' study in which she shared that the important thing about her book was that it included her "ideas and creation," the circus book for me was representative of someone else's ideas.

As a researcher interested in how access to art serves as a pathway to literacy learning and its impact on students as writers, I honor the frustration I felt so many years ago by raising the question: What book could we have created, what meaning could we have constructed and shared, if given the opportunity to think about design and learn how it is used to communicate visual and verbal ideas? For me, the circus book serves as a reminder of the verbocentric circus we continue to see in some schools today where children are relegated to create and express meaning, oftentimes exclusively verbally, in spite of living in a world that is growing more visually oriented. There is a mismatch between the visual world children experience daily and the verbocentric classroom that puts a premium on language. Learning about the role of design in reclaiming students' voices as writers highlights what can happen when we disrupt the curricular circus of privileging language over other ways of knowing and encourage, instead, a mindful curriculum where language *and art* are valued, complementary modes of communication. As Eisner (2002) maintains, not all knowledge can be reduced to what can be said. The expression of particular ideas sometimes lends itself better to modes of knowing beyond the limits of language.

## Illustrating the Connection

No one student has made me revisit the circus book more than Diane (pseudonym), a high school student in grade 10 who participated in two of my research studies on how artmaking supports students as writers. In interviews, Diane talked about how she grew as a writer from the aesthetic choices she made in her sketchbooks (Leigh, 2012). The more she shared about how visual design decisions she made affected her writing, the more I thought about what the circus book could have been and the "circus books" we still create today. I was motivated to continue conversations with students about the relationship between artmaking and writing.

Disinterested in writing throughout middle school and grade 9, Diane turned to artmaking where she discovered, quite serendipitously, that her generative, iterative, and circular ways with sketchbooks influenced what and how she wrote. Like Aaron and Maddy, and Mariana and Brady, Diane made intentional design decisions. She considered choice of paper (e.g., "Does it reflect the message I want to convey?"), space (e.g., "What message can I create with the size of my drawing and where I put it on the page?"), and thickness of line (e.g. "What mood or tone can I create from how I draw lines?") as having an impact on her writing.

When Diane was in grade 11, she actively explored her love of watercolor as an aesthetic pathway for thinking about how to develop story. In a poem entitled "Twenty Fireflies," Diane painted two whimsical sketches of fireflies in pale blue. Flitting across the page, the fireflies created a sense of movement and complemented the airiness of the writing. In the bottom left-hand corner of the page, a pond sketch captured a serene setting.

> I miss the twenty fireflies.
> The ones that used to turn the river into a Glowing World of Light.
>
> I know it's the Man that came to town.
> The one with the Dark Aura.
>
> He drove away the jeweled birds, the lizards and the swans.
> And even now,
> The twenty fireflies have failed to return.

"Visual details," she explained, "help me think of what to write. I think you're just trying to get the real focus and emotion of the picture and like the story behind it" (Leigh, 2012, p. 545). I agree with Eisner (1998) and McLuhan (1967) who say that the tools we use influence what we think about. For Diane, sketching and watercolor painting influenced her writing. The generative process of sketching and painting allowed her to think about the story she wanted to tell about the fireflies. "Ideas always come to me when I create and experiment in my book," she said.

In my last interview with her, Diane described with clarity the importance of having access to the aesthetic:

> When I'm given an assignment to write a short story, essay, or even a poem, I see it as just a piece of homework. After going through years of this style of thinking, I decided to try and create a way to make these assignments more enjoyable. I started to create pieces that I felt had more character, meaning, and body to them. When I started to incorporate visuals (and even audio and scents) to go with the writing, I began to care more about the development of the piece. The way words looked on the page. The way the story sounded to me. It became its own entity rather than just another essay or poem. The whole process was more fun and engaging once art was involved.

My circus book, now cracked and peeling, flakes like dandruff. But even from a weathered book, lessons can be drawn. The confetti corners serve as a reminder of the kind of literacy experiences we do not want for our children. I agree with Diane that we must help students discover ways to care more about the development of their written narratives. Access to design is one such way. Our conception of literacy continues to undergo a metamorphosis, where constructing meaning involves not just reading and writing, listening and speaking, but also critically viewing and visually representing our ideas through visual and verbal texts to reclaim writing.

## References

Eisner, E. (1998). *The enlightened eye.* Upper Saddle River, NJ: Merrill Prentice Hall.

Eisner, E. (2002). *The arts and the creation of mind.* New Haven, CT: Yale University Press.

Leigh, S. R. (2012). The power of the sketch (book): Reflections from high school English students. *Journal of Adolescent and Adult Literacy, 55*(6), 539–549.

McLuhan, M. (1967). *The medium is the message.* New York: Bantam Books.

# 4

# LEARNING TO RESPOND IN WRITERS' WORKSHOP

*Allen Koshewa*

I like to find out what people in the class think about my story before I finish it, because they're going to read the final story in the class book. (Alison, fourth grade student)

Alison has learned several things in my classroom. She has learned that we periodically produce class anthologies, and therefore there is a potential audience for her best writing. She has learned that the members of our class community are interested in each other's writing. Most importantly, she has learned that considering responders' points of view can strengthen her own writing.

In order to fully understand the role that peer response can play in the writing process, teachers must attend to the roles of trust and communication strategies in the classroom. We know that "literate practices are embedded in complicated social relationships" (National Council of Teachers of English, 2005); therefore, building trusting relationships within a classroom helps students value each other's reactions to their writing. If the community does not have strong norms of listening and respect, the opinions of any given peer about a piece of writing will not be seriously considered. In addition, providing specific response strategies is key in helping students give robust feedback.

In this chapter, I present my classroom as a place in which students engage in effective critique as authentic responders to each other's writing. My students learn the importance of choice and inquiry, and how response can affirm strengths as well as critique shortcomings. The students learn to use a four-step guide to improving peer response.

## The Roles of Choice and Inquiry

Inquiry-based curriculum springs from learner interest, which is why self-selected topics constitute an important element of a writers' workshop model. As state writing tests increasingly guide teaching practices, classroom writing based on prompts has increased, and the emphasis on writing to prompts is certainly evident in the proliferation of professional publications on this topic. Yet the motivational factor behind free topic choice cannot be discarded; indeed, it is at the heart of writers' workshop.

Like Graves (1994), I focus on personal narrative as a starting point, since one's own stories provide built-in authenticity. I usually begin the school year by providing guided imagery that will help students remember key experiences to write about. I might begin by saying, "What do your family members say about your years as a baby or infant? What is your earliest memory? What problems did you have when you were little? Do you remember being confused? Embarrassed? Afraid? Surprised?" The children engage in a chronological exploration of experiences, writing about topics such as moving, losing a family member, friend, or pet, discovering something new, or getting angry about something. The students take notes for an idea bank that serves as a reservoir of topics for later writing.

English language learners are included in this early writing in a variety of ways. If students are literate in their primary language, they write in their own language. If interpreters are available, publishing in the original language as well as English broadens audience appreciation of the work. If students are composing in English, starting with "yes/no" questions and "either/or" prompts help them create enough material to generate response. The following exchange I had with ten-year-old Hasti, an Iranian student with only a few months of English under her belt, shows how she got started on a personal narrative:

AK: Did you ever have a problem with your brother? [I help Hasti find the Farsi word for problem in a dictionary.]
HASTI: Yes, problem. Brother playing car. I do homework.
AK: Was the car a problem, or the homework?
HASTI: Homework. I sit in chair and brother pull chair.
AK: Then what happened?
HASTI: I fall down.

After Hasti keyboarded some of these phrases and shared her draft with classmates, peer questions prompted her to add that she fell on her elbow and screamed when the chair fell down. Their request for an ending led her to add a final sentence: "I said to my friend, 'My brother's a bad boy.'" Although I spurred Hasti's choice of topic within our inquiry model of writing, it was her peers' responses to her skeletal first draft that encouraged her to further develop her story.

Similarly, keeping track of students' questions that arise in the classroom provides individual topics for nonfiction writing. During a recent school year, teaching a fourth/fifth grade blend in a Title I school, learners' questions about such diverse topics as fog, DNA, food coloring, opera, blood cells, video-game procedures, wolves, and Lamborghinis all led to compositions, many of them published in our monthly newsletter, read by all elementary students in our school. Students knew that their writing could be published, and this knowledge provided the motivation for students to seek response to these pieces.

Topic choice expanded when the children learned a variety of genres and purposes for real audiences. A chart paper solution to a class problem, a thank-you note, or a letter to a pen pal all laid foundations for intentional drafting and revision. When I assigned topics, I tried to make them broad and provocative enough to invite more than one genre of writing. When given the topic "The Cat," for example, my fifth grade students produced both fiction and nonfiction, and the topic "Pollution" generated personal narrative, poetry, fiction, and expository and persuasive writing.

Teachers can still provide student choice within a prescribed genre. After I had students create their own artwork based on portraits by famous artists, I asked them to write a piece of historical fiction based on a portrait. I expected students to create a conflict that could have happened during the period of the portrait and to refer to at least one artifact that existed during that era. Peer response groups to early drafts of these historical narratives focused on whether or not the event could have happened or on why the event happened. Supporting writers' choices, encouraging them to publish, and allowing time for peer responses made my students eager to revise their work.

## Considering Both Strengths and Shortcomings

> You don't always have to chop with the sword of truth. You can point with it, too. (Lamott, 1994, p. 156)

Components of a Writers' Workshop model are typically construed as prewriting, drafting, responding, revising, editing, and publishing, though these elements are recursive and often not linear or sequential. Responding, however, is a phase of the cycle that is frequently shortchanged, confined to a teacher conference or even omitted. During our regular peer response groups the children rely upon three guidelines: (1) every participant should have a draft of writing to discuss; (2) the author should like the piece yet want to improve it; and (3) each author should be prepared to seek critique and accept responses as valid despite any response's departure from the authors' intent. [Guidelines 1 and 2 are adopted from Short, Harste, & Burke's (1996) notion of an Author's Circle.]

Looking for strengths or potential strengths in writing supports and encourages the writer. If we only criticize or condemn without recognizing the value or potential value a writer has to offer, we are unlikely to build the trust and confidence that induces others to revise or to seek our help. This delicate balance between support and critique is evident in peer responses to Dion's story in my 2011–12 fifth grade class.

> VANESSA: When the hunter comes, it's very exciting. I feel like I'm the wolf trying to be completely still. But then the problem goes away so fast. I wanted more.
>
> MARIA: Yes, if the moment lasted a little longer, or if there was more action, like a chase, it wouldn't end so quickly. And I wanted to know what happened next.

Vanessa first affirmed an exciting aspect of the writing; it established point of view effectively. Then, she explained what she, as a reader, wanted more of, rather than what the writer "should" do. She suggested that the climax of the piece wasn't fully developed. Maria affirmed Vanessa's analysis, also wanting more details about the climactic encounter between the hunter and the wolf. Dion responded well to the feedback. She drew out the climax, added a resolution, and even brought the draft back to her colleagues to see what they felt about the new ending.

Peer response groups have been shown to help students assess the quality of their own writing, to allow students to better understand the role of audience in writing, and to produce improved drafts of a written piece (Cramer, 2001). Young learners, however, need demonstrations for the clear, direct, yet diplomatic communication that will obtain these results. Writers learn to find the "gems" (Bomer, 2010) in a piece of writing, while at the same time raising questions concerning possible alterations that will enrich meaning. Following my demonstrations, the students learn to state the message they hear most clearly, point out what they liked, and ask questions concerning content that could be clarified, expanded, or deleted. They learn to support and critique in order to provide appreciative comments and recommendations for revision in response groups.

## Using the FRIA Guidelines to Peer Response

> [Writers need] to construct personal visions of the world around them, but then they also [need] to submit those unique versions to peers for response, negotiation, and confirmation. (Kirby & Crovitz, 2013, p. 13)

When conferring with each other, my students are expected to: provide Feedback (say what they heard to be the essence of the piece), Respond (describe reactions, beginning with a positive one, and then raise questions and offer suggestions), Invite (ask the author to raise questions or seek responses to a specific section or concern), and Advise (prioritize one or two suggestions for revision). I refer to these as the FRIA response guidelines, which I developed with Elly Tobin. The FRIA Response

Guidelines set up the expectations that all responders participate, that authors accept all responses, and that authors later demonstrate changes in a subsequent draft that can be linked to response group suggestions. Responders are also expected to take notes during an initial reading to remember content and reactions, and authors are expected to take notes in order to remember peers' suggestions.

Encouraging the responders to speak before the author does (Feedback step) forces the author to hear how readers react to what was written without the dilution or expansion that frequently emerges in author conversations about his or her own text. Many writers, especially young children, tend to explain their writing when they are the first speaker in a response group; such an explanation doesn't allow the writing to speak for itself, may lead the responder to see a message that isn't actually in the writing, or may obscure a "gut-level" reaction to what the piece is all about.

Like any good guidelines, the FRIA sequence should be adapted to the needs of the users. Straying from the FRIA sequence by starting with an author's questions or concerns before the rest of the group has responded can be helpful as well, as a preliminary solicitation of the author's response forces the author to come to the group with particular revision concerns in mind. Graves's (2003) recommendation that a response session begin with the author identifying the "heartbeat" of the piece requires author reflection and immediately allows the responders to hone in on the author's primary intention.

A fishbowl session during the first writing cycle of a school year sets the tone for later response group sessions. I involve the first two or three students who have finished a draft, and include my draft as well. I find that the students who finish a draft first are more likely to think of themselves as writers and to enter the response session eager to read and hear responses to a draft. Working with the early finishers also allows the others to have more time to write later and be ready for their own response groups. In an early childhood setting, such a fishbowl may occur later in the year, and can evolve from daily celebrations of and questions about each child's work. A document camera can be used to show each student's work as members of the classroom community talk about what they like about the student's art, story transcriptions, or writing attempts.

One year in my fourth grade classroom, I chose Kaitlynn to lead an early fishbowl session because her empathy as well as her eagerness to ask good questions indicated that she would easily frame critique as questions. For example, when her classmate read a rambling draft about a family vacation, Kaitlynn told her, "I like the way you used dialogue when your mom's boyfriend spoke. In the story, he mentioned that he had a car accident. What happened? That might be very important in your story." After extensive revision of the piece, the accident became the lynchpin of the story, as the author wrote about how her reaction to the accident led her to understand and accept the boyfriend.

There are many alternatives for organizing effective groups. With older students, response groups for all can follow a long (30–60 minutes) drafting session, which encourages students to bring a "meaty" draft to the sessions and provides an opportunity for the teacher to determine membership for each group. Alternatively, groups can form as soon as several students have finished a draft, if they are "stuck" and need help, or if they are seeking specific feedback on a piece in progress. Sometimes giving authors the opportunity to "talk through" an unfinished piece (or even a piece they haven't yet started) prevents the excessive attachment to a first draft that can inhibit extensive revision.

Aldo, a fifth grader, benefitted from seeking a peer response group when he was stuck after writing a few paragraphs. He had begun a story called "Dawn" about a mysterious voice that awoke the protagonist, Alex, at dawn. He wasn't sure about how to develop the story, so he read his beginning to his response group and told about his plan for the rest of the story. His "talk through" mentioned that he wanted the voice to belong to a girl who had died in the house a hundred years earlier. His peer responders were enthusiastic about this, but thought he should focus more on the encounter with the girl rather than a long explanation about why he changed his name to Alex. As a result, he not only abandoned most of his rambling first draft and highlighted Alex's encounters with the ghost, but created a clever ending in which the "ghost girl" inspired Alex to become a successful writer of ghost stories.

Language learners beginning to acquire a second language (in this case English) can also learn to ask genuine questions that spur revision. Framing critique in questions can help those whose cultural background or self-consciousness about current levels of language proficiency may inhibit them from pointing out ineffective passages or offering suggestions. Questions may also help the writer realize that important details are missing from the piece. The following conversation (Koshewa, 2011) occurred when Yuji, a newcomer in first grade, responded to his classmate's two-sentence story about bumping into a pole:

YUJI: Why you bump in pole?
SHU: I fall down. I no look.
YUJI: I fall down. What you look?
SHU: I fall down. Look at girl. Fall down. (p. 51)

When Shu revised his story accordingly, his addition of the distracting glance and the post-bump fall helped the skeletal draft become a simple story.

Reflection about the response group experience is crucial, especially after the first session. Journal entries provide a safe and confidential way for teachers of older students to gauge effectiveness. Based upon student journal reflections, teachers can highlight areas of success or need in subsequent discussion or, if necessary, intervene and arrange new groups for individuals whose needs are not being met by a particular group. If response sessions continue to be unproductive, class discussion or a fishbowl session can help students create their own guidelines for response groups, particularly if sessions are videotaped and can be reviewed.

Viewing videotaped sessions can help students identify the strengths and weaknesses of their responses. One session I taped was dominated by students who wanted the writer to add more about playing video games when the student's piece was mostly about the anticipation of getting the video game. When viewing the taped session, several students realized that the responders had not really asked the writer what he wanted to emphasize. This sort of "debriefing" allows participants to internalize the factors that promote successful response group sessions.

A major asset of the FRIA approach is its insistence that students respond to content before addressing conventions. Once my students are comfortable with the FRIA guidelines, they begin steering away from premature discussion of conventions and technical concerns. Commonly cited concerns about writing, such as organization or word choice often emerge naturally, but without the negative potential of ratings or grades. Gradually, generic responses such as "Add more detail" give way to deeper insights.

By using questions and reflections rooted in FRIA, students engage in lofty conversations as writers. They might ask or discuss, "What did you hear?" (Feedback), "What did you like?" (Respond), "What help do you need?" (Invite), or "What should be revised?" (Advise). For example, eleven-year-old Rachel's peers responded to a draft of her story, "Genetic Angel," showing how important writing criteria can emerge naturally within FRIA. The response session started out with enthusiastic praise for her lead: "While experimenting with different attempts at a cure for cancer, Aperture Laboratories came across a brew with an odd color." (Later, a discussion of "brew" as a word choice came up.) Kaeden, one of Rachel's peer responders, gave this feedback: "It seems you are showing that the successful cancer experiment with mice led to genetic defects." Kaeden then pointed out that we didn't know what the defects were, and the actual characters were not experiencing a conflict. Rachel then said that she could have a scientist give the "brew" to his pregnant wife, knowing that attempting to cure her cancer would risk mutation of their child. The story then evolved into one in which the development of wings, a genetic mutation caused by the cancer cure, began to transform society. Kaeden's response, and Rachel's subsequent development of a conflict, could not have happened if the critique session had been confined to discussion of conventions.

## A Culture of Critique

Bradley (2001), in her study of three first grade classrooms, confirms that the ways in which students respond to each other's writing is greatly influenced by what teachers' writing instruction emphasizes. Thus, a teacher who highlights the importance of revision and demonstrates how peer response can lead to good revision is more likely to hear students talking about revision concerns during peer response sessions rather than talking about conventions and other editing concerns. We need to monitor response groups and point out the distinction when the violation of spelling, grammar, or punctuation rules becomes the topic of peer response group sessions prior to a focus on content.

A culture of critique demands safety so that all members of a writing community view each other as capable learners, readers, and writers. A child may need transcription or translation to support her own perception of self as writer, yet the teacher and students need to see the child as a writer from the very beginning. If a teacher does not presume meaning in text, and does not see each child as a reader and writer, it is unlikely that a "culture of critique" will emerge.

## Other Considerations

> Good writing takes not only doggedness, but also a willingness to expose oneself and be ... vulnerable to criticism. (Siu-Runyan, 2011, p. 24)

There are three other aspects of peer response in the twenty-first century that are significant within writers' workshop. Within my teaching, I am increasingly aware of the social realities (especially relationships between students), the influences of digital media, and the potentials of writing for action.

### Social Realities

Ultimately, peer response is about relationships amongst learners supported by teachers periodically taking the "pulse" of the class. Class meetings that address how response groups are going can lead to deeper issues of communication and respect. Social realities affect learning, and if students can articulate how certain practices enhance rather than hinder response groups, they may be more prepared to take responsibility for the response group's outcomes. These social realities, coupled with peer responses and providing sufficient time to draft, revise, and edit writing, mean that time is precious as we work to strike a balance between flexible timelines and deadlines (see Pierce, Chapter 8).

### Digital Media

The increasing fluidity of audience and purpose within social media, such as blogs, texts, and Internet chats require new views of response (see Blady & Henkin, Chapter 6; Vasquez, Albers, & Harste, Chapter 15). Van Sluys (2011) reports reflections of an upper-elementary student who maintained that blogs allow for topic switching, immediate responses, and expected reader response, that is, "rhetorical moves that would cause readers and responders to engage with her thinking in particular ways" (p. 43). Another student she observed mentioned how the immediacy of blog responses spurred his motivation to write. Norms and protocols within new literacies evolve; how they might be responded to and critiqued by peers in classrooms is in the same state of evolution.

In a recent conversation about Facebook with my fifth grade students during a class meeting, I discovered that some fifth graders thought it was acceptable to present fictional Facebook profiles and posts as fact. (I had only recently discovered that a number of my students had their own Facebook accounts, pretending to be older than they really were.) This led to a fascinating discussion about the ethics of Facebook writing and the writers' desires to be creative, hide identity, or be viewed as older. Although we could not all agree about what was ethical within this relatively new writing medium, the discussion prompted several students to close their Facebook accounts and several others deleted false information about their ages.

## *Writing for Action*

The potentially wide audience of the Internet expands the possibilities of action that can result from writing. Critical literacy takes on new power when it can be transformed into a way to stop racist advertising or to raise funds for a well in rural Senegal. How we guide students through persuasive writing in our classrooms may have an impact on later, wider applications of writing. Hansen (2012) asks his third grade students the following questions to guide their writing: "Is this an issue that affects a lot of people or just a few? How much do you know about this topic? Would you have a lot of smart ideas to share about this or just a few?" (p. 22). Writing to change the world is central to reclaiming writing because the cultivation of voice is essential to democracy. Social realities, digital media, and writing for action generate questions and issues that may need to be incorporated into peer response work in order to keep writers' workshop relevant to our students' lives.

## Learning to Critique in a Community of Writers

An individual perception of self as writer is inextricably linked to a perception of self as reader (McCarthey, 2001), and students' willingness to revise a piece of writing is dependent upon seeing themselves as able to critically read the piece during the revision process. How reading is approached in a classroom shapes the view of writing in many ways. I try to create a "culture of miscue" (Davenport, 2002; Goodman, 1973; Goodman, Watson, & Burke, 2005) in which unexpected language that is produced is a source of interest and analysis rather than a reason for alarm or derision. Within our culture of critique, the learners realize that written miscues are likely to be the result of thoughtful attempts to make meaning as an author. A case in point is the word "brew" in Rachel's "Genetic Angel" story, which, as a result of peer discussion about its meaning, she later changed to "concoction." The "match" between author intention and reader response becomes closer when author intention is questioned and discussed during peer conferences. When an author realizes, for example, that the feedback about the main message of his or her work is not the intended message, a "culture of miscue" leads that author to probe the cause of the disjunction, rather than to reject the reader's interpretation. Thus, our classroom is a collective of readers and writers who share their processes, concerns, successes, and more in an effort to push the limits of what they might do as writers and as consumers of writing.

Creating a community of writers is ultimately about every member of the community believing that the other members have something important to contribute. Peer response groups can contribute to the building of such a community. Just as taking the risk to share a piece of writing in progress represents an author's trust in his or her responders, thoughtful responders show that they see the author as a capable writer and trust the author to seriously consider and act upon their reflections. Students who are genuinely committed to respectfully helping each other improve their writing are the foundation of a productive writers' workshop that can reclaim writing as relevant, social, and at the heart of a robust and active literacy curriculum that serves all learners.

## References

Bomer, K. (2010). *Hidden gems: Naming and teaching from the brilliance in every student's writing.* Portsmouth, NH: Heinemann.

Bradley, D. H. (2001). How beginning writers articulate and demonstrate their understanding of the act of writing. *Reading Research and Instruction, 40*(4), 273–296.

Cramer, R. (2001). *Creative power: The nature and nurture of children's writing.* New York: Addison Wesley Longman.

Davenport, M. R. (2002). *Miscues not mistakes: Reading assessment in the classroom.* Portsmouth, NH: Heinemann.

Goodman, K. S. (1973). Miscues: Windows on the reading process. In K. S. Goodman (Ed.) *Miscue analysis: Applications to reading instruction.* Urbana, IL: ERIC Clearinghouse on Reading and Communication Skills and the National Council of Teachers of English.

Goodman, Y., Watson, D., & Burke, C. (Eds.). (2005). *Reading miscue inventory: From evaluation to instruction.* Katonah, NY: Richard C. Owen, Inc.

Graves, D. (1994). *A fresh look at writing.* Portsmouth, NH: Heinemann.

Hansen, M. (2012). Writing for justice: Persuasion from the inside out. *Rethinking Schools, 26*(3), 19–24.

Kirby, D. L., & Crovitz, D. (2013). *Inside out: Strategies for teaching writing.* Portsmouth, NH: Heinemann.

Koshewa, A. (2011). Finding the heartbeat: Applying Donald Graves's approaches and theories. *Language Arts, 89*(1), 48–56.

Lamott, A. (1994). *Bird by bird: Some instructions on writing and life.* New York: Random House.

McCarthey, S. J. (2001). Identity construction in elementary readers and writers. *Reading Research Quarterly, 36*(2), 122–151.

National Council of Teachers of English (NCTE). (2005). NCTE beliefs about the teaching of writing. Retrieved from http://www.ncte.org/positions/statements/writingbeliefs

Short, K. G., Harste, J. C., & Burke, C. (1996). *Creating classrooms for authors and inquirers.* Portsmouth, NH: Heinemann.

Siu-Runyan, Y. (2011). My journey as a writer – a dozen rewrites later: Insights to share with students. *The Council Chronicle, 21*(2), 24–25.

Van Sluys, K. (2011). *Becoming writers in the elementary classroom.* Urbana, IL: National Council of Teachers of English.

# 4 Extension

## LEARNING AUTHENTIC GENRES IN A COMMUNITY OF WRITERS

*Michael L. Shaw*

As I read Allen Koshewa's chapter, I found myself thinking about the many communities of writers with whom I've worked and the ways in which they engaged in authentic writing. Since Koshewa focuses on personal narrative, I chose to focus on three other genres of authentic writing: letter writing, persuasive essays, and class magazines.

### Letter Writing

I have observed too many lessons on letter writing that have focused on form and structure rather than content and voice. How sad! In contrast, letter writing for real reasons to real people establishes potential for real response to students. When I taught in elementary school, my students began each year writing a letter to themselves. I taught and modeled friendly letters and how to address envelopes. Students generated a list of spelling words they might use which became a word wall. We began by brainstorming what we could say to ourselves. They mailed the letters to themselves and you can imagine the excitement when they brought these treasures into class. Throughout the year they wrote friendly letters to their classmates and to authors to give response to books. They sent letters to veterans in the local VA Hospital on Valentine's Day and wrote letters to celebrities. They wrote complimentary letters to companies that manufactured products they loved and complaint letters to companies of products that failed to meet their standards (and in each case they got coupons for lots of free "goodies"). They wrote to government leaders including the president, governor, and mayor, and letters to the editor of the local newspaper about issues relevant to their lives.

In 1973 my first grade students chose to write letters to Coretta Scott King as the culmination of our study of Dr. Martin Luther King, Jr. Of course, I told the children that I could not guarantee that she would respond, but late in June we received a letter from her. Below is an excerpt:

> My Dear Young Friends,
>     Thank you for your kind letters. They made me very happy.
>     I, too, am sorry that my husband died. The children and I miss him very much. But he was a man who wanted to make life better for all people. He died so that all of us might have a better life. He loved all people and refused to hate anyone.
>     My husband wanted justice, freedom and love for all people. He wanted them so badly that he was willing to die to help people be treated justly, be free, and be loved.

She then went on to answer their questions about her children and the cost of living. "Yes, I will be glad when prices go down. I have four children and it costs a lot of money to feed them and buy their clothes."

## Persuasive Essays

A number of years ago in my graduate-level writing course, teachers challenged my statement that children as young as first grade could learn to write powerful persuasive essays. Teachers at all levels, including middle school and high school, contended that their students could not write powerful persuasive essays. What they really meant was that they had not created an authentic context to teach students how to use their writing voices to persuade a real audience to take real actions.

In response, I shared essays fourth graders wrote in my writing lab to improve the school lunchroom rules after I was continually hearing gripes. I first approached the lunchroom teacher to inform her of their complaints and asked if she would be willing to set up a Lunchroom Leadership team to work with students to improve the conditions they did not like. She agreed, so I extended an invitation to any fourth grader who wanted to apply to serve on the team. I established a process where they first had to explain the things they liked in the lunchroom and why, and then explain the things they did not like and why, and detail proposed changes. Below are excerpts from two of their essays.

> I like the food they serve because the way they're made… I don't think it's fair that people get in fights and then we all get in trouble. I think that the people that get in fights are the ones that should get in trouble and write a sorry letter to the lunchroom teacher.

> I like when the lunchroom is playful and fun and when the food comes out fast. I don't like when the bathroom smells and nobody flushes. I think you should make an automatic flush.

While the students did not get everything they wanted, the lunchroom teacher worked with them to make some of the proposed changes. Their essays empowered them to have a voice in improving the quality of their school lives.

## Class Magazines

One great motivator to continue writing is getting published. It is easy to establish an ongoing classroom magazine center where students can sign up to work together on a magazine of their choice. My students, grades 1–6, studied mentor magazine texts to establish standards and then collaboratively planned content. Students created magazines focusing on the environment, Martin Luther King Day, Women's History Month, Families from Around the World, and other topics that were decided as a class or initiated by small groups of students. One example of a small group decision occurred when a group of fourth grade boys decided that they wanted to create a sports magazine. We reviewed *Sports Illustrated* as a mentor text, analyzed the content, and examined the writing styles. They wanted to call their magazine "Sports Illustrated" and I explained that this name was already copyrighted. They decided on "Sports Only." This is their Volume 1, Number 1 front page introduction:

> There will be a new magazine coming out in P.S. 108. It will only have sports so we call it Sports Only. It will have activities, stories and cartoons all about sports. It will be for sports lovers like us. We hope everyone will enjoy it.

The first issue included an article on Jackie Robinson during Black history month, baseball predictions, the "Patrick Ewing Report," and more. Their first editorial had the headline, "Sports People Using Drugs" and it focused on famous athletes who admitted using drugs. They editorialized:

> We hope that no sports players use drugs so sports can be respected by everyone. We think players should have drug tests every month, and if they use drugs they should be fined $500. If they use drugs again they should be suspended for two years and fined the thousands dollars. We want no one to use drugs.

These fourth graders certainly foreshadowed the work of some sports commentators of our present time.

In their second issue, their editorial focused on, "Wrestling and Boxing (The Vile Sports)". They wrote:

> The reason we don't put wrestling or boxing in our magazine is because they are vile sports! We think that if you wrestle or box the only thing you get is hurt. We know that you can get hurt in other sports but not as

seriously as in boxing or wrestling. And in the other sports the object is not fighting ...

Shortly after publication, another group of boys approached me; they wanted to begin a magazine called "Wrestling Only." Their first editorial had the headline, "Why We Decided to Make Wrestling Only:"

We decided to make Wrestling Only magazine because we like wrestling very much and Sports Only does not have wrestling in it. Wrestling is very funny. We think that people want a wrestling magazine. We like wrestling because it's exciting ... Wrestling is fresh!

Koshewa strongly demonstrated the importance of creating a community of writers with opportunities to share personal stories. This extension is intended to highlight other writing initiatives that focus on developing student voice within a community of writers through a variety of authentic genres intended for a variety of real audiences.

# PILLAR II
# Teaching

# 5

# WHEN THE WATER GOES BAD AND OTHER ESSENTIAL REASONS TO ARGUE AND WRITE ABOUT SCIENCE IN ELEMENTARY CLASSROOMS

*Lori Norton-Meier and Brian Hand*

> So, in conclusion … all I can say is … to quote Woody from the movie, "Toy Story" – SOMEONE HAS POISONED THE WATER HOLE! (Anthony, age 11. Emphasis in original utterance; pseudonyms used throughout.)

## Questioning Water Quality: An Introduction

Anthony was a student in Ms Margaret's classroom. Over the past three years, Ms Margaret participated in a professional development initiative to put science back into the elementary curriculum by connecting it to what teachers already know about excellent literacy instruction using an approach called "argument-based inquiry." Argument-based inquiry can be defined as an investigation that is intended to build students' grasp of scientific practices while motivating an understanding of disciplinary big ideas. Construction and critique of knowledge are centrally located through an emphasis on posing questions, gathering data, and generating claims supported by evidence. The argument approach was intended to be structured around the way scientists do their work; they ask questions, carry out investigations, make claims, gather evidence, and present findings to others for argument and debate. Rarely do they complete a traditional laboratory report.

Anthony's quote above was spoken as he presented the evidence from a recent investigation of water. When they tested water samples in their small rural community, Ms Margaret's group of intermediate grade students discovered there was a problem with its quality. The class began a three-week investigation that involved the work of scientists to make claims, gather evidence, keep notes to document their findings, present their research to their peers for critique, rethink and revise their research methods, and compare their findings with other scientists (through text, interviews, and other media). Finally, the students communicated their results and suggestions to the audience that most needed to hear their findings; in this case, their report went to the city council, which found, through their own independent investigation, that the fifth grade scientists were correct and the nitrates in the city water were beyond suggested guidelines for safe water.

Ms Margaret was part of a three-year research study and examples in this chapter represent the findings from 32 teachers and approximately 1500 students in elementary classrooms (K-6; the majority lived in rural, economically poor areas). Our study focused on the research question: How does the use of argument-based inquiry support children's literacy and science learning in elementary classrooms? Data collected included videotaped classroom observations, interviews with teachers, pre-/post-unit thinking from students, a collection of writing samples and other artifacts (e.g. lesson plans, photographs, group concept maps, and group brainstorming notes). For the purposes of this discussion, we focus on what we learned from the action of teachers while facilitating argument-based inquiry and the evidence of this teaching approach in the writing samples collected throughout this study as students engaged in argument-based inquiry.

## Why Do Scientists Write?

When teachers in our research study asked their elementary students at the very beginning of the school year, "Why do scientists write?," we heard a variety of responses.

> "They write to remember stuff." (Avery, age 6)

> "They have to write down what they see, hear, smell, taste, and touch so they can think about it and try to see if they can figure out what is happening." (Tristan, age 9)

> "To tell moms and dads and other people about important science things." (Abigail, age 7)

> "They write to plan for the debate, you have to present your thinking to other scientists so they can challenge you, you need to have your points written down and in charts so you are ready to answer with your evidence." (Brianna, age 11)

In their words, the students illuminated key aspects of writing in science: to document, to think, to organize, to ideate, to present, to share, and to critique. The basic underlying philosophy of this work is this: *There is no science without language* (Lemke, 1990). It is impossible to think, question, wonder, make claims, describe evidence, present findings, and critique others' work in science without some form of language. In recent years, science education has focused on the need to engage students in the real work of scientists, that is, to experience natural phenomenon through the approach of scientific argumentation (Cavagnetto, 2010).

Argument-based inquiry leads to an alternative format for laboratory reports, as well as an enhancement of learning possibilities of this science genre (Hand & Keys, 1999). Instead of responding to the five traditional sections (purpose, methods, observations, results, and conclusions), students respond through questioning, knowledge claims, evidence, description of data and observations, and methods. Then they reflect on changes to their own thinking. Key to this approach is the summary writing experience when students present their thinking using a variety of different genres to a variety of different audiences. The structure of argument-based inquiry writing is as follows.

1. Beginning ideas: What are my questions?
2. Tests: What did I do?
3. Observations: What did I see?
4. Claims: What can I claim?
5. Evidence: How do I know? Why am I making these claims?
6. Reading: How do my ideas compare with other ideas?
7. Reflection: How have my ideas changed?

The approach is structured so that students engage in reasoning and writing that parallels scientists' reasoning and writing. Because argument-based inquiry focuses on canonical forms of scientific thinking, such as the development of links between claims and evidence, it also has the potential to build learners' understanding of the nature of science, strengthen their conceptual understanding, and engage them in the authentic argumentation process of science. Ultimately, the argument approach emphasizes the collaborative nature of scientific activity, specifically scientific argumentation, whereby learners are expected to engage in a continuous cycle of negotiating and clarifying meanings and explanations with their peers and teacher. The teacher promotes classroom discussion in which students' personal explanations and observations are tested against the perceptions and contributions of the broader group. Learners are taught to make explicit and defensible connections among questions, observations, data, claims, and evidence. The important element is that they engage in the real work of scientists, both writing for self and others within and beyond their immediate classroom setting.

## What We Learned from Students and Teachers Writing Like Scientists

For three years we learned many lessons about writing from the young scientists and their teachers who participated in our research project. To describe what we learned from the analysis of their writing, we draw upon the work of linguists Halliday (1975) and Halliday and Martin (1993), who explain that individuals are continually learning about language, while they learn through language, while living language. We expand on this thinking (Norton-Meier, 2008) and use it to analyze the writing of the K-6th grade students in this study. In the following paragraphs we describe our findings using Caleb and Aubrey's notebooks; they were two intermediate grade students who were engaged in an investigation of the water cycle. The examples illustrate the complexities of their writing while learning about writing and through writing, all while they lived the writing of scientists. Finally, we conclude with three key teacher actions and beliefs that enabled Caleb and Aubrey to learn and write in an argument-based classroom.

## Living Writing

Children are born into a world where they engage in a variety of literacy practices both in and out of school. They live language when they write for pleasure and as part of play, write letters to communicate, and experience a variety of daily events that include meaningful print. In Ms Margaret's intermediate grade classroom, the students were able to live as writers and scientists by keeping a notebook of their developing thinking about water. Figure 5.1 shows Caleb's intricate initial design for an experiment to explore condensation. He used text, images, labels, and procedural language to show his initial thinking and planning. At the completion of this design phase, Caleb met with his classmates to debate and negotiate his thinking. This feedback and questioning helped Caleb live the

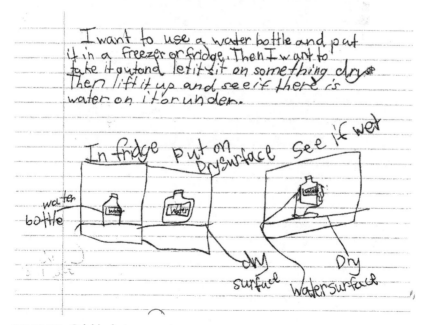

**FIGURE 5.1** Caleb's design experiment.

writing of scientists; as a result, he redesigned his study in order to collect data specifically relevant to his question.

## Learning About Writing

In Figure 5.2, an interesting convention developed in Caleb's notebook. His writing shifted from his initial design in Figure 5.1 to a more procedural design in Figure 5.2. After Ms Margaret held a class discussion on how scientists can write about procedures so other scientists can replicate tests and see if they can get the same results, the class designed a template so that they would all have similar procedures. In Figure 5.2, Caleb described his procedures step by step with

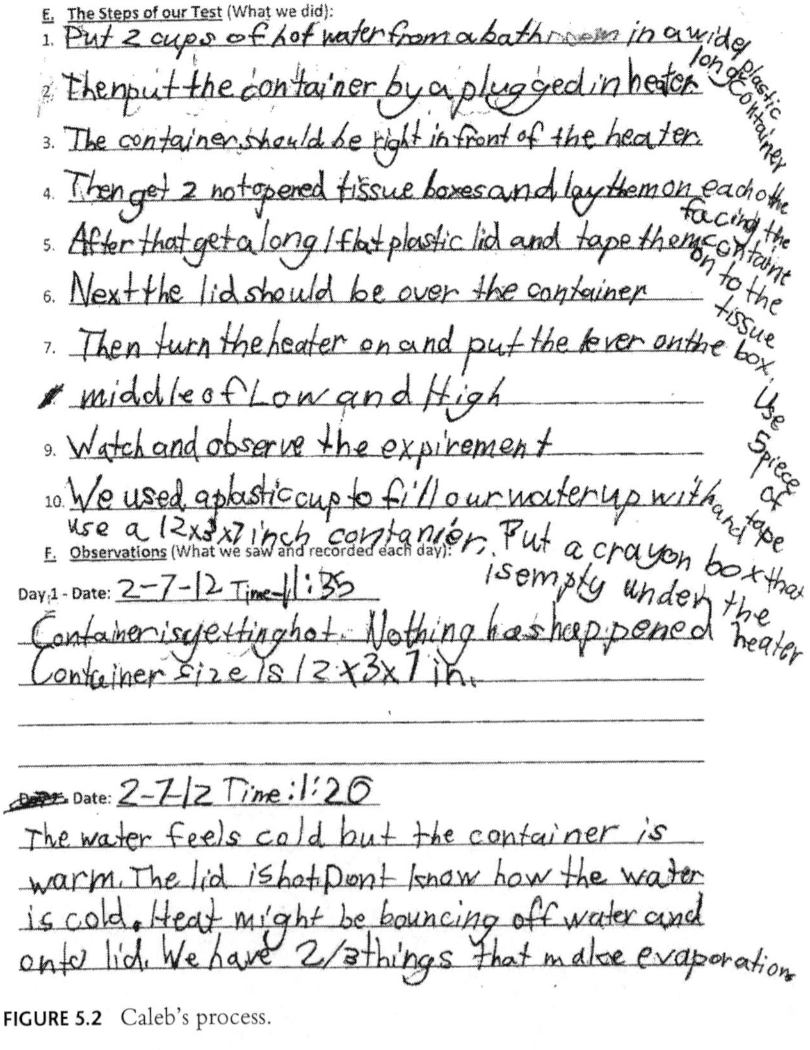

E. The Steps of our Test (What we did):

1. Put 2 cups of hot water from a bathroom in a wide lon plastic container
2. then put the container by a plugged in heater
3. The container should be right in front of the heater.
4. Then get 2 not opened tissue boxes and lay them on each of facing the container
5. After that get a long/flat plastic lid and tape them on to the
6. Next the lid should be over the container tissue box.
7. Then turn the heater on and put the lever on the Use
8. middle of Low and High
9. Watch and observe the expirement
10. We used a plastic cup to fill our water up with a piece of tape and crayon box that is empty under the

use a 12x3x7 inch container. Put a crayon box that is empty under the heater

F. Observations (What we saw and recorded each day):

Day 1 - Date: 2-7-12 Time 11:35

Container is getting hot. Nothing has happened
Container Size is 12x3x7 in.

Date: 2-7-12 Time: 1:26
The water feels cold but the container is warm. The lid is hot Dont know how the water is cold. Heat might be bouncing off water and onto lid. We have 2/3 things that make evaporation

FIGURE 5.2 Caleb's process.

procedural language and with specific word choice to help other scientists know how to replicate the study. In step 4, he wrote, "Then get 2 not opened tissue boxes and lay them on each other facing the container." The detail in "then" (as a procedural indicator as to what to do next) and in "not opened" (to ensure details of the experiment are specific and the selection of materials is consistent) and "lay them on each other facing the container" (to indicate position, direction, and spatial relations) all indicate Caleb was learning *about* how scientists use writing to communicate procedures, details, and essential elements of their tests and observations. At the bottom of this page, Caleb demonstrated he had learned the language of observation and wrote the details and questions of a scientist who is collecting data. He recorded the date and time as well as the details about his container, including initially that "nothing has happened." In his next observation, he put a wondering, "The water feels cold but the container is warm. The lid is hot. Don't know how the water is cold. Heat might be bouncing off water and onto lid." Caleb recorded his observations and then used text to wonder about why he was getting certain results. Using writing to think, he may have framed the beginning of a new experiment. These literacy processes allowed Caleb and the other intermediate grade students the opportunity to be language detectives and to wonder about language while developing their own personal understandings and theories about how language works in writing, orally, and visually.

## Learning Through Writing

One way Ms Margaret supported her students in this argument-based inquiry classroom setting to learn through language was during a group argumentation time, when all students gathered together to "go public" with their claims and supporting evidence. Typically, a group created a poster or put their thinking on a white board so others could examine their question, claim, and supporting evidence. In Figure 5.3, Caleb's recording sheet shows how he learned from (and questioned) each group's presentation. This is an example of Caleb learning through writing. As he created his chart, he was able to see how his research connected, questioned, or refuted those from the other group. He couldn't simply put "I agree" or "I disagree." Rather, he had to reason and negotiate new understandings, question others' findings, and revisit his own study for possible revisions. In this case, Caleb used writing as a tool for ideating (Goodman, 2003), meaning that writing became a tool for thinking through and negotiating meaning.

## In the Overlaps Between Living Writing, Learning About Writing, and Learning Through Writing

The overlaps between living writing, learning about writing, and learning through writing are key spaces that emphasize language uses can't exist in isolation in the classroom. Continually, the action of the argument-based inquiry

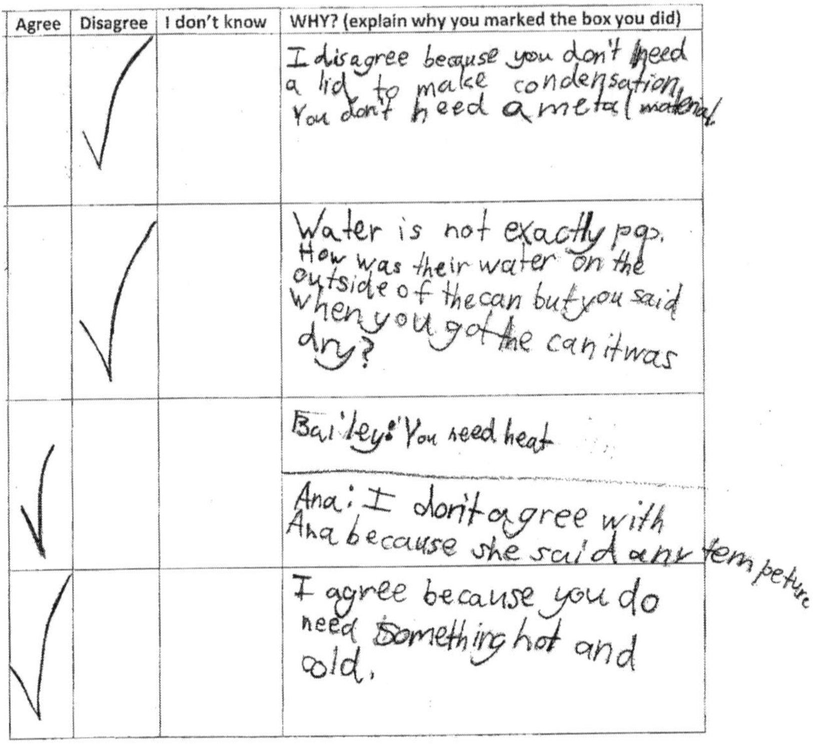

| Agree | Disagree | I don't know | WHY? (explain why you marked the box you did) |
|---|---|---|---|
| | ✓ | | I disagree because you don't need a lid to make condensation. You don't need a metal material |
| | ✓ | | Water is not exactly pop. How was their water on the outside of the can but you said when you got the can it was dry? |
| ✓ | | | Bailey: You need heat<br><br>Ana: I don't agree with Ana because she said any temperture |
| ✓ | | | I agree because you do need something hot and cold. |

FIGURE 5.3 Caleb's argument chart.

community offers up new opportunities to write, argue, and use language to make sense of the natural world. A few examples from Ms Margaret's classroom and Caleb's notebook illuminate writing in the overlap.

## Learning About Writing and Learning Through Writing

When he wrote the list in Figure 5.4, Caleb had now gone to a variety of different types of texts and taken notes about what he learned from other scientists that could inform his own work. He learned key facts through his writing, while at the same time he was just beginning to understand how to take notes from text. Note that he did not cite his sources (most likely a focus of a future mini-lesson by Ms Margaret) but he did sketch an image/model in the margin to help fuel this thinking when he went back to his own experiment and future investigations.

## Living Writing and Learning About Writing

Essential to the work of any scientist is to continually make claims and be willing to revise those claims based on new negotiated understandings. Ms Margaret

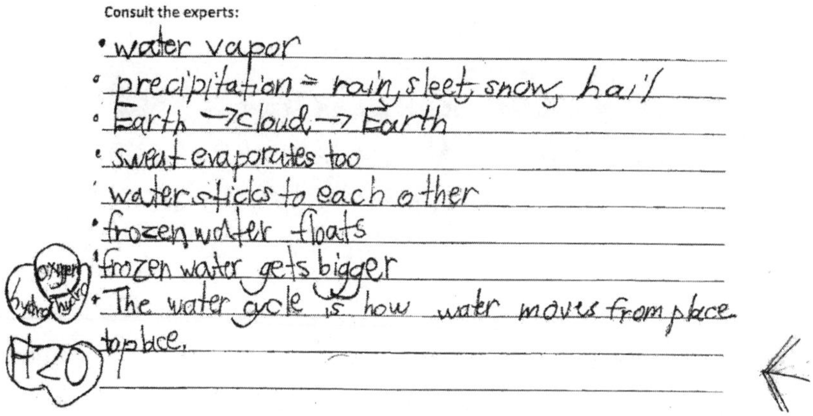

Consult the experts:

- water vapor
- precipitation = rain, sleet, snow, hail
- Earth →cloud →Earth
- sweat evaporates too
- water sticks to each other
- frozen water floats
- frozen water gets bigger
- The water cycle is how water moves from place to place.

**FIGURE 5.4**  Caleb's connection to what others say about water – going to text.

asked Caleb to make a "final claim" based on "everything we have learned," which is presented in Figure 5.5. Caleb lived the writerly life of a scientist by designing a claim, "I think …" and backing it up with evidence, "I know this because …" This demonstrated his understanding of his proficiency by using the language of science to structure a claim and back it up with evidence to support his new thinking.

## Living Writing and Learning Through Writing

Finally, a key point in the argument-based inquiry approach is to reflect and to consider: "How have my ideas changed?" The work of scientists means that every investigation ends with new questions and reflections about procedures, new vocabulary, new discoveries, and frustrations about investigations that failed to answer an initial question. In the example at the bottom of Figure 5.5, Caleb lived the writing of a scientist who has reflected on current understandings yet is thinking to the future. He recorded in writing that he learned through the work of others. He thereby documented in his notebook important findings to use in future research and inquiries.

## Where Learning About, Learning Through, and Living Writing Come Together

Finally, in the space where learning about, learning through, and living writing come together, we look to Aubrey who created a book about the learning she experienced during the same water inquiry that was described through Caleb's science notebook. Key to the argument-based inquiry approach is to end with a summary writing experience – a moment at the end of the unit when learners are asked to look back over all that they learned and create a piece of summary

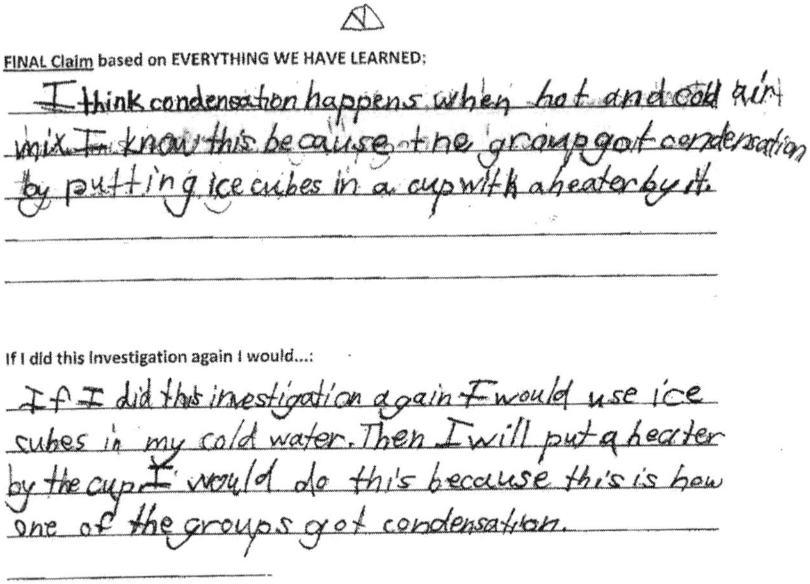

FINAL Claim based on EVERYTHING WE HAVE LEARNED:

I think condensation happens when hot and cold air mix. I know this because the group got condensation by putting ice cubes in a cup with a heater by it.

If I did this Investigation again I would...:

If I did this investigation again I would use ice cubes in my cold water. Then I will put a heater by the cup. I would do this because this is how one of the groups got condensation.

FIGURE 5.5   Caleb's final thoughts.

writing – typically a creative piece of writing for an authentic audience. We have also learned from the work of scientists that they need to write for many different audiences to report their findings. In this case, Aubrey wrote a book to share with her first grade buddies (an authentic audience outside of her immediate classroom) to explain the water cycle (see Figure 5.6). She created a character (Harry, the water droplet), whose voice she used to systematically share what she learned through her science inquiry about the water cycle. She demonstrated what she knew about writing by writing in a narrative voice using text and image to tell her story to a younger audience. Through writing, she articulated the water cycle and, ultimately, she engaged in the work of scientists by presenting her findings through writing to an appropriate audience.

## Key Teaching Actions

It is important to consider what teacher actions enabled this type of writing classroom. The data revealed three key teaching actions that demonstrate the complex relationship between language, inquiry, and pedagogical practices.

### Collective Zone of Proximal Development

We understand that learning is an act of personal and social negotiation of meaning. Vygotsky (1962, 1978) originally presented the notion of an individual zone of proximal development. "But to understand what children know developmentally,

**The Water Cycle**

Hi my name is Harry and I am a water droplet. I am going to take you through the water cycle. Follow me! Let's go!

**FIGURE 5.6** Aubrey's book.

we need to understand what children can do with the assistance of others: such demonstrations are more indicative of their mental development than what they can do alone" (Whitmore, Martens, Goodman, & Owocki, 2004, p. 295). Moll and Whitmore (1996) extended the concept when they presented the role of a *collective* zone of proximal development in classrooms: the space between where learners can go alone and where learners can go together when learning as a group and mediating for one another. In Caleb and Aubrey's classroom, Ms Margaret created a space or a zone of functioning for a group of individuals in which learning was supported through guidance and participation in the community through partner, small group, whole group, and individual experiences. It was through this participation and engagement in the community that students developed the knowledge and skills of science and literacy as well as a sense of self-efficacy that motivated them to learn (Dyson, 1989). Also, it is important to note that Ms Margaret saw herself within this collective zone of proximal development as she engaged as an active investigator of her practice as well as in relation to argument-based science and literacy learning.

## Symmetric Power and Trust Relationships

Ms Margaret knew that her students controlled learning. She validated their questions, supported them in their own inquiry, and gave them opportunities to write their developing thinking. In turn, students took risks and trusted Ms Margaret as she pushed them to dig deeper. This act of creating symmetric power and trust relationships between teachers and students was described by Whitmore and Crowell (1994) as a space where conditions exist for students to engage in writing based on their current intellectual and literate activity, thereby supporting children to make connections between the known and new, and providing thoughtful opportunities for negotiation in a non-threatening learning environment. Ms Margaret gave her students time to read and write, time to wonder, and time to explore their questions about the world. She invited them to try out thinking and to make approximations as they made claims and gathered evidence to support their thinking.

## Teacher as Decision Maker

Ms Margaret was trusted as a curricular decision maker to decide what to do next based on her students' learning needs as well as their questions. The school and administration provided support for her and other teachers to continually question their practices and created school communities where they were allowed to enact a teaching philosophy consistent with how children learn.

## When the Water Goes Bad …

Before this project began, many of the teachers in this study told us they had no time to teach science. Since the No Child Left Behind Act (2002) called for the testing of literacy and mathematics, they just couldn't "waste school time on content that wasn't going to be tested," or they "taught science on Fridays if we had time." We continue to learn from this group of teachers and students who put science back into the curriculum. Within the context of argument-based science inquiry, students can not only learn science concepts but also develop understandings about writing and through writing while they live the writing lives of scientists. Perhaps it was Malia (age 7) who put it best:

> Ya' know, when I write, I think, and when I think, then I have to write more, and if I write more, then I think more and wow, my brain is just going to keep growing and growing – it just goes round and round: write, think, write, think, think, write.

Malia intuited that central to the life of young scientists in our classrooms is reclaiming science writing, reclaiming thinking, and reclaiming joy as we learn about writing, learn through writing, while living as writers.

## References

Cavagnetto, A.R. (2010). Argument to foster scientific literacy: A review of argument interventions in K–12 science contexts. *Review of Educational Research, 80*(3), 336–371. doi:10.3102/0034654310376953

Dyson, A. H. (1989). *Multiple worlds of child writers: Friends learning to write.* New York: Teachers College Press.

Goodman, Y. M. (2003). *Valuing language study: Inquiry into language for elementary and middle schools.* Urbana, IL: National Council of Teachers of English.

Halliday, M. A. K. (1975). *Learning how to mean.* London: Arnold Press.

Halliday, M. A. K., & Martin, J. R. (1993). *Writing science: Literacy and discursive power.* Pittsburgh, PA: University of Pittsburgh Press.

Hand, B., & Keys, C. (1999). Inquiry investigation. *The Science Teacher, 66*(4), 27–29.

Lemke, J. (1990). *Talking science: Language, learning, and values.* Norwood, NJ: Ablex.

Moll, L. C., & Whitmore, K. F. (1996). Vygotsky in classroom practice: Moving from individual transmission to social transmission. In E. A. Forman, N. Minick, & C. A. Stone (Eds.), *Contexts for learning: Sociocultural dynamics in children's development* (pp. 19–42). New York: Oxford University Press.

No Child Left Behind (NCLB) Act of 2001, Pub. L. No. 107-110, § 115, Stat. 1425 (2002).

Norton-Meier, L. (2008). Creating border convergence between science and language: A case for the Science Writing Heuristic. In B. Hand (Ed.), *Science inquiry, argument and language: The case for the Science Writing Heuristic (SWH).* Rotterdam, the Netherlands: Sense Publishers.

Vygotsky, L. (1962). *Thought and language.* Cambridge, MA: The MIT Press.

Vygotsky, L. (1978). *The mind in society.* Cambridge, MA: Harvard University Press.

Whitmore, K. F., & Crowell, C. (1994). *Inventing a classroom, Life in a bilingual, whole language learning community.* York, ME: Stenhouse.

Whitmore, K. F., Martens, P., Goodman, Y. M., & Owocki, G. (2004). Critical lessons from the transactional perspective on early literacy research. *Journal of Early Childhood Literacy, 4*(3), 291–325.

# 5 Extension

## YOUNG MATHEMATICIANS WRITING FOR REAL REASONS

*Elisa Waingort*

Norton-Meier and Hand defined "argument-based inquiry" as an

> investigation that is intended to build students' grasp of scientific practices while motivating an understanding of disciplinary big ideas. Construction and critique of knowledge are centrally located through an emphasis on posing questions, gathering data, and generating claims supported by evidence. (p. 58)

Generally speaking, the goal is always to gain conceptual understandings through an inquiry approach. And, just as real-world scientists "rarely complete a traditional laboratory report" (p. 58), real-world mathematicians rarely fill in pages and pages of computation problems or take mad minute quizzes. It is important to get beyond these and similar ineffective practices to teaching and learning mathematics – a difficult task in the current climate of high-stakes testing that condones and applauds memorization as evidence of mathematical prowess.

Throughout my teaching career, my goal has been to kindle a passion and an appreciation for the power of writing and reading. I found this easy to do through a writing and reading workshop approach but much more challenging when dealing with content area topics in science and math. However, whether we were studying the water cycle or the concept of multiplication, I made sure students used writing as one way to work out their understandings.

In the ideal math classroom (one that focuses on deep understandings rather than superficial skills), student-mathematicians, like student-scientists and other inquirers, ask questions, pose problems, experiment with possible solutions, and provide explanations for their results. They look for proof or evidence that their answers make sense. They discuss their results with other student-mathematicians and are open to different ways of arriving at an answer. The beauty of math is that, although there may be only one acceptable response to a problem, there are many ways to get there. Listening to how others solved the same problem allows children to experience complex ideas such as perspective and flexibility. And, it allows children to assess their learning by responding to the questions that Norton-Meier, Hand, and Ms Margaret asked students in this chapter: "How have my ideas changed?" and "What have I learned?" In other words, "What do I know *now* (about math and/or myself as a learner) that I didn't know before?"

The statement "There is no science without language," (p. 59) is just as true for math as it is for science. Language is the basis of communication and any learning that we do. Without language, particularly socially constructed language, we are bereft of our knowledge and stripped of our humanity. Language – communication – is the essence of understanding. Conversation, writing, drawing, and (mathematical) symbols allow understandings to surface. Yet, the process and products of thinking are often messy. This simple truth needs to be honored in the classroom.

If you were to walk into my classroom during math time, you might see clusters of children exploring with a variety of manipulatives in different areas of the classroom. You might also see other children constructing and solving math problems resulting from self-selected investigations, some of these originating outside the math block. You may find me winding my way around the classroom guiding students to articulate the math in what they're doing or simply encouraging them to persevere, an important math disposition for students to develop. Or I may simply be standing back to observe the flow of the work my students are engaged in, allowing me to determine which students to approach next and who may need my help. At the end of this exploration period, we will gather on the rug to discuss what we did, what we discovered, and what we learned. Who we learned with and from is also an important element of this discussion.

John (a pseudonym) was a highly able child identified with Autism Spectrum Disorder in my Spanish bilingual early childhood class. In this school, math was taught in Spanish, and students, all native English speakers, were expected to speak and write in Spanish during this time. In addition to being irritated by the demands of his second language, John was easily frustrated whenever any task necessitated some form of writing. In fact, if he wasn't certain of the spelling of a word, he refused to write. I worked closely with the educational assistant assigned to John to ensure that she used a variety of strategies to support and extend his learning, rather than take the easy way out and provide the spelling of every single word he requested. In arithmetic, John was a whiz! He did complex math computations in his head quickly and sometimes he willingly explained how he arrived at his answer. However, when asked to write about his process he often shut down. No amount of cajoling could convince him of the importance of writing about how he solved a problem or how he knew he had the correct answer. If I pressed too hard, John responded with survival behavior: hiding under a table or in a corner or ripping up his paper, which often resulted in frustration on both our parts; I had failed to get him to write in the ways I thought were appropriate. John's resistance made me doubt my practices and I started asking myself some hard questions: What does writing in math *look like*? How is writing in math the same and different from writing in other content areas and in the writing workshop? If writing is a way to discover new ideas and deepen one's thinking, then how can I reconceptualize writing in math to be more than words on a page?

In order to revise my thinking from writing as primarily "words on the page" to writing as "communication," I had to let go of conventional notions of writing. This new way of thinking allowed me to re-vision John's notes, some scribbled quickly while I was teaching and others written hours or days after the lesson had been completed, as his unique way of thinking through math ideas. I began to see that, although using words, pictures, and symbols was important for writing in math, what had been missing was the student-mathematician's voice, literally and figuratively speaking, to complete the story. Therefore, in order for our classroom math community to extend and expand on members' ideas, we needed to write and discuss in order to revise or cement our thinking. Sometimes these discussions took place in Spanish. At other times, I made the decision that we needed to temporarily abandon learning a language for learning math and so our discussions were carried out in English.

Any attempts on my part to organize John's writing into my adult idea of what writing was supposed to look like met with failure. So I stopped expecting a particular kind of writing in math and instead helped students to use their written explanations as a way to clarify their thinking. These one-on-one discussions often revealed much more than any formal writing or test could have yielded and became an important cornerstone of our math time.

Thinking, discussing, writing (in all its forms), and revising our notions about mathematical ideas became how we did math in our classroom. Unbeknownst to him, my attempts to get John to adopt conventional forms of writing were the catalyst that turned my thinking on its head and allowed our classroom to deviate from traditional forms of writing about and learning in math. John's resistance to what I was asking him to do broke through my own reluctance to listen carefully to my students in order to continually design literal and figurative spaces where real mathematical learning could take place. So, I closed the door to my classroom in order to open my students and myself to alternate ways of doing math. My students and I discovered that young mathematicians can reclaim writing in much the same way that young scientists reclaimed writing in Norton-Meier and Hand's study; we did it through thinking, living as writers and mathematicians, and sharing the joys that authentic writing brings.

# 6

# TEACHING THE JOY OF WRITING THROUGH WIKIS

*Shannon Blady and Roxanne Henkin*

## Roxanne

When I visited Shannon's classroom one day, I found it inviting and comfortable. There were couches, tables, and areas for quiet reading and working together. There were also long tables, some of them low to the floor where students worked on laptops and desktops. Students worked individually or in pairs or small groups. On that particular afternoon, three girls sat together with one laptop completing their book review from their book club, preparing to post it on Amazon.com. A boy and a girl were creating a glog, an interactive web poster, for their book report and adding video and web links to it. One boy sat in the corner and worked on the class wiki. He experimented with the font size and chose to highlight his responses in green, so that his responses stood out. Another boy sat next to me for ten minutes, showing me the class wiki. He explained that a wiki is a space where multiple authors can work together. They read each other's contributions and can even edit what others have written. He proudly told me how often he posts to the wiki. This was just another day in the fourth grade class of Shannon Blady. I asked her to share her amazing journey to reclaiming the joy of writing through wikis.

I first met Shannon shortly after she had relocated to San Antonio, Texas, from New Orleans, Louisiana. She was a teacher consultant for the Greater New Orleans Writing Project and we adopted her into the San Antonio Writing Project (SAWP), which I direct. Shannon and I quickly became friends because we both loved writing, writing research, and writing practice, and we both had a passion to share this love with our students, whether it is with elementary students (Shannon) or with adults (Roxanne). We were also fascinated with digital and multimodal literacies and were eager to bring them into our classrooms.

We teach in Texas, where high-stakes writing tests are taken very seriously. We have watched the joy of writing fade from children across San Antonio as writing instruction has narrowed to teaching what is needed to pass the tests. Too often in classrooms when teachers announce that it is time to write, children groan. The joy that children felt during writing workshops of the past seemed to be missing in too many classrooms. Shannon and I felt that teaching digital and multimodal writing could restore some of the love for writing that children in writing-process classrooms formerly had.

## San Antonio Writing Project

Shannon joined the SAWP 2010 Summer Institute, even though she had previously participated in a Summer Institute in New Orleans. The SAWP is part of the National Writing Project (NWP), with over 200 affiliated sites. Operating for almost 40 years, NWP provides high-quality teacher professional development by having teachers share their best practices in writing with each other, including demonstrations of specific strategies, ideas, units, and more. Teachers also write across genres and participate in writing and research groups.

Although Shannon had participated in a previous writing institute and had gone through the key elements of a summer institute, there were differences in her second experience. In the intervening years, digital literacy came to the forefront of writing instruction, and by the 2010 summer institute, SAWP had gone entirely digital. No longer did we have notebooks filled with handouts; instead we had computers and jump-drives. Most of the teacher demonstrations incorporated digital resources and literacies. Shannon was at the forefront of this movement, and shared her insight and understandings with us. We were working to demonstrate the possibilities of teaching writing with renewed joy via digital avenues.

Shannon returned to the 2011 SAWP summer institute as a co-director. Her incredible teaching skills with children were evident in her work with adults, too. She gently supported teachers with less technological skill and inspired them to incorporate technology in their demonstrations and their classrooms. She inspired teachers to use wikis as a tool for collaboration, and as a place to gain multiple audiences for our writing. The teacher-to-teacher connection in this type of work is central to the idea of reclaiming. We want to reclaim writing instruction that is collaborative, involves all participants in thoughtful conversations, and is sensitive to and reflective of the diversities in our world.

## Shannon

As a teacher of elementary students, I feel that it is my responsibility to teach students to understand the power of writing as a means to communicate and to express themselves. As a teacher in a high-stakes testing grade, I feel the pressure of making sure they learn every strategy to make their writing more effective and to help them learn all of the grammar and spelling standards set forth by our state. As an educator, doctoral student, and researcher in an interdisciplinary program, I was able to apply or reflect upon the newly learned theories and concepts in the context of my own students. I considered their sociocultural contexts and their funds of knowledge (González, Moll, & Amanti, 2005) as we approached new writing topics. I also considered their zones of proximal development (Vygotsky, 1978) as their peers and I guided them through the writing process. And because one intense area of my study is literacy, I also considered the rapidly changing landscape of literacy given the influx of digital tools.

Within these complex learning and teaching roles, it was crucial for me to be reflective in my practice to make sure I was meeting the needs of all of my students. Part of this reflective process included receiving feedback from Roxanne. We asked ourselves about our own literacy and the tools that we were using. Roxanne and I wondered if our experiences and teaching philosophies were meeting the needs of our students. As Grabill and Hicks (2005) stated, "If we want to teach writing or help students learn how to write more effectively, then we have to see writing in the same ways that they do and be with them where they write" (p. 306).

Many Web 2.0 tools have dramatically altered the way users communicate and share information (Brunsell & Horejsi, 2010). Web 2.0 is based on more socially collaborative engagement, where teachers support learners in building upon each other's knowledge as they interact (Brunsell & Horejsi, 2010) through a relatively new generation of Internet-based services, including blogs, glogs, wikis, and Prezis. Rather than passively read a web page constructed by someone else, these resources allow the user to actively create the content.

If implemented effectively, Web 2.0 resources meet the National Educational Standards provided by the International Society for Technology in Education (2007), which hold that technology should be used for creativity and innovation. Students are to apply existing knowledge to generate new ideas, products, or processes. They are also expected to use digital media to communicate and work collaboratively to support individual learning and contribute to the learning of others.

In a recent study on the professional development of pre-service teachers and new literacies (Ajayi, 2010), the participants report that they are aware of the impact of the new communication technologies on literacy learning and instruction, and also that they are affected by constraints coming from schools, parents, and administrators. These constraints include a lack of computers, a fear of what the Internet may reveal to students in the way of uncensored photos and unfiltered information, and the ever-present pressure to get students to pass state-mandated tests. These pre-service teachers also express concerns regarding the adequacy of their preparation to teach new literacies. During the SAWP summer institute, however, we encouraged each other to start small by choosing one technological tool at a time to integrate into our literacy instruction, whether it was strictly for English/Language Arts or writing across the curriculum. We asked that participants use the tool that worked for them and their students, and to assume a stance of genuine inquiry and curiosity by learning as their students learn with the ultimate goal of reclaiming their teaching of writing.

## Starting the Project

Although I was an avid user and consumer of blogs, I decided that wikis might better serve the ways in which I wanted to teach my students to compose digitally. I had learned about wikis for the first time during the summer, and I was immediately intrigued. I wondered if my students would feel the excitement of working on web pages that groups could edit together, using the same simple editing tools provided by word-processing programs. I imagined them adding videos and links and graphics to support their learning.

After informally assessing my students' experiences with new literacies through class discussions, I discovered that they were quite familiar with texting, communicating on social network sites, and blogging. It was what their parents, their older siblings, and their favorite television and movie characters were doing. Clearly they were part of the sixty percent of America's children, more than 43 million children under 18, who use the Internet (Levin, Arafeh, Lenhart, & Rainie, 2002). I knew I could capitalize on my students' experiences to engage them as writers, and to build a bridge from their personal digital experiences to activities that integrate technology in the classroom. Understanding their digital literacies through a sociocultural context helped me to reach their "third space," which is described as an integration of their funds of knowledge and Discourses that merge from the first space of home, community, and peers with the Discourse that students find in more formal settings, like church, school, or work (Moje et al., 2004). "Discourse" refers to the ways of being in the world, our identity kits that include the way we speak, act, dress, shaped by our beliefs, values, and attitudes (Gee, 1990). So often students feel that school does not connect to their real lives, that it is not relevant. When we recognize that students bring knowledge with them, we honor their experiences and backgrounds. When we understand their knowledge and Discourse, we can begin to examine how students interact with literacy in and out of school. It became clear that we needed to make the wiki relevant, a place that bridged academic writing to the kind of writing the fourth graders were doing already out of school.

## Introducing the Class Wiki

Once I realized that integrating a class wiki could help to meet many of my students where they were technologically, I had to figure out how to foster its effective use, and how to integrate it for communicative purposes (Grabill & Hicks,

2005). For my first year, I modeled my classroom activity after Roxanne's use of Web 2.0. She integrates Google sites as a repository for assignments, as a discussion board, and as a place to encourage discussions-in-writing on readings and current events.

To introduce our class wiki, I gave a general overview of how the wiki would operate, but did not provide specific directions for using the wiki. I knew they would explore it and eventually teach me some of the available affordances. I did, however, demonstrate responses to help them get started if necessary and how to cite sources appropriately when posting a photo or text on a page. For that first year, each student had his or her own page, and I posed questions or prompts on our home page. I added a few content area pages as well. For example, on our *Weathering and Erosion* page, I posted pictures of examples of particular kinds of weathering and asked students to identity them, and challenged them to write metaphors based on the pictures. We also had a page of favorite videos that highlighted community building or interesting science inventions.

Over time, for a majority of students, the wiki became a place to read and write even without assigned prompts. This was important work as they truly claimed themselves as authentic writers, writing for true purposes and audiences. Candace wrote:

> Hey y'all!!!! I can't belive I'm up at .... let's see ... 7:03 AM!!! Yes, I'm the only one awake! (Well at least I don't here anyone else awake) Anyway, my mom told me that I should try to go back to sleep but that obviously didn't really work out. Then I just hug around our living room thinkin' about my day and what I was going to wear. (It's St. Patrick's Day!!! To all of y'all out there who won't wear GREEN today: PINCH!!! If you don't understand what I just typed then you could look it up or ask your parents.) Then I got tired of that so I went back into my mom & dad's room where they were both sleeping. I did it in a very "sneaky" way: I "tiptoed", The floor creaked a little and- Hey! I hear something!!!! I think it's my mom! Well, It sounded like it came from my parents' room. ANYWAY, I went into my parents' room and tapped on my mom's shoulder and she finally told me I could use her laptop to write on the wiki. So here I am! Wow! I've been typing for 24 minutes!!! Happy St. Patrick's Day!!! [Typed as original.]

Candace was clearly thrilled to have an audience and an avenue to express herself and to communicate. The wiki allowed for transactive writing, writing for an audience beyond teacher-as-examiner; this is the kind of writing that students need for effective communication (Berryman & Russell, 2001). Students were reading each other's responses, responding in writing, or arriving at school the next day to respond in person, further building a sense of community: "Did you win the game?" "Did your cousin have her baby?" "I'm going to see that movie, too." Each afternoon, we met as a classroom community to reflect on the learning that occurred that day and to share any big news. Often, we ran out of time, and as we scrambled to pack up at the dismissal bell, I would announce, "If you didn't get to share today, post it on the wiki." And they did!

Of course, not all students were as eager as Candace to write. Understanding their behaviors and assessing fully their funds of knowledge (González et al., 2005) helped me to develop differentiated tasks, to scaffold their learning, to engage their interests, or to address other barriers. A few of my students just needed time before and after school and during lunch because they did not have Internet access at home. In addition, the occasional sharing of the wiki in a whole group setting, using our class projector, prompted those who did not share to start participating more. Thus, teaching writing digitally involved many of the pedagogical decisions that are part of thoughtful teaching, including facing resistant students, such as Ronald.

Ronald did not show an interest in the wiki at first. He was a hesitant writer and often did not sit still for very long periods of time. Ronald did not choose writing, but would complete assigned writing. After I integrated the wiki into a class rotation, making it mandatory for them to respond to a science question as part of their science lesson that week, Ronald began to see how his classmates were communicating and enjoying the wiki. He figured out on his own how to post photos of his dog, who eventually became the unwitting protagonist of a spy story. When students gave him feedback (either in person on via the wiki), Ronald started to talk about his writing process. His classmates called him a funny or a good writer. He was a writer! His perception of his literacy abilities completely shifted and as he joined the literacy club (Smith, 1988) that was becoming part of the writing culture of our classroom.

The following school year, I wanted to increase the academic content on our class wiki. I had seen its potential, and I knew I could foster more learning and writing in the content areas. Among others, I created the following pages: *Science, Math, Social Studies, Homonyms, Roald Dahl* (our first author study). The math page included pictures of geometric art and links to the artists' web pages. When children completed their projects on fractions in the real world, those who chose to represent their knowledge in a PowerPoint presentation requested to have their projects uploaded to our math wiki page to share with their classmates. I also added links to sites for practicing multiplication facts or other math games. On the social studies and science pages, in response to our mixtures and solution lessons, one student created a short video of an experiment that he conducted at home. Another completed an iMovie about the US Constitution.

## Reflecting With Roxanne

When Roxanne visited my classroom, she encouraged me to examine the wiki from my researcher's lens. I began to see the co-creation of knowledge, through the sharing of thoughts and ideas. The wiki appeared as a tool that highlighted constructivism and socio-constructivism since it encouraged "users to participate, to think and to construct information together" (Gokcearslan & Ozcan, 2011, p. 483). I also observed an increase in agency as evidenced by students being engaged and expressing their own unique opinions. They lived the lives of real writers when they experienced their contributions as valued voices in our growing written (and oral) conversations.

Students determined what kinds of pages we should have on our wiki, including pages on *Random Thoughts, Creepy Crawler Stories,* and *Things to Ponder.* They controlled the 'conversation' and content on each page. There was an opportunity to disrupt traditional power structures and I was no longer a teacher who deposited knowledge into students' minds (Freire, 1970). The wiki was theirs and my role shifted to that of facilitator. They wrote about their feelings of past schools, asked about an upcoming field trip, and discussed books that they were reading. They posted: *Which book will we read next? Why do we have mosquitos? How long is the longest book? Who knows anything about constellations? Who else in the world has my birthday?* Then, there was the anonymous post of: *How are we oneday a kid then we become a gronup?* The students were inventing the many functions of written language that the context of the wiki nurtured.

As students participated on our class wiki, they demonstrated their multiliterate capabilities as well. A multiliterate person must be literate in traditional and new communication technologies and the semiotics, or sign systems, embedded in them (Anstey & Bull, 2006). The class wiki invited students to express themselves in these various modes, which opened sign systems beyond the linguistic (Eisner, 1994; Kress, 2003). Such multimodality plays a pivotal role in students' understanding of language, of images in their communication, and of their learning (Kress, 2003). The class wiki motivated students to share their multigenre and multimodal projects and to communicate with various font colors, sizes, photos, and links. The intertextual connections within their works demonstrated their growing understanding of themselves as part of larger conversations within our classroom and beyond. It allowed them choice, freedom, and a safe place to communicate their ideas with their peers. Students knew that their particular talents and/or interests were being valued, and I knew that they were being exposed to the literacies and modalities they will need to engage and succeed in our increasingly diverse, digital world.

We included the students in our discussions about their experiences and were able to ascertain that much of the appeal seemed to be in the social space that the wiki provided. Students were willing to write so much because it was interactional. Under the links to multiplication practice sites, they posted comments about their scores and their opinions of these sites. When someone posted an assignment, a question, or a video, they quickly discussed it either in writing on the wiki or in person at school.

Each week, I read their responses and offered my own. If a teacher tells her students "just put that on the wiki" but never responds or actively engages on the wiki, she and her students will not develop the fullest potential inherent in a community of practice (Grabill & Hicks, 2005). Communities of practice are created when groups share an interest in an endeavor, use the same resources, and learn together how to improve in that endeavor as they interact regularly (Lave & Wenger, 1991). Not only did I let them know that the wiki was important to me and that I honored their contributions, but I provided a demonstration of lifelong learning. I was not the one with all of the answers.

As far as I could tell, the wiki was never viewed as a chore. Students reminded me that they needed to post on the wiki. On many occasions, students asked if traditional writing activities could be completed on the wiki instead. If these activities were part of individual rotation work (similar to Centers) and there were enough computers, I allowed it. If we were all writing together, there were not enough computers for each person to write via the wiki, so, out of fairness, we would usually stick to pencil and paper. When I wrote "Post to the Wiki" on our home learning assignment board, they told each other, "We don't have any homework tonight." When I reminded them that they were to post to the wiki as their homework, they often replied, "Well, that's not work. That's the wiki."

## Closing Thoughts

Working simultaneously as a doctoral student and a public school teacher in today's classroom environment, I tried very hard to integrate my new learning into my teaching and to conduct action research, but I must admit that I fell prey to the ubiquitous deadlines and pressures that come with being a teacher today. I found myself cramming in "combining sentences" lessons right before our standardized testing, despite knowing better. I even assigned a few revising and editing worksheets. Because so much of our literacy practices were taking place on the wiki, I also felt pressure to make it "count" in the traditional manner. I feared, however, that it would become another assignment that they dreaded where the content had to be revised, edited, and evaluated. Therefore, in the past two years, I have given only two grades on the wiki for participation, not on content.

But because of my philosophy of education and my theoretical lens, I continue to reflect on my practices, to check in on my students, and to remain abreast of the latest research. I know the importance of new literacies in today's digital age. I know my teaching of new literacies supports my students in feeling that their voices are honored as they work from within their diverse cultures and multiple identities using their own languages and experiences to create new knowledge (Hocks, 2003). They also learn all the conventions that twentieth-century writing demanded as well as the skills and strategies of twenty-first-century composing.

The experience with the wiki points out the urgent need for a change in assessment that will be concomitant with the authentic writing that occurs in digitally conscious classrooms. Assessment issues may be the next area that I explore as I work to enhance my teaching.

Roxanne and I continue to research, reflect, and write together, always interrogating the whats, whys, and hows of our teaching. Individually, we explore Web 2.0 tools in our classrooms, but together we work to understand the deeper implications that these tools have on writing. The wiki has proven to be a tool that fosters all six Language Arts: reading, writing, listening, speaking, viewing, and visually representing. Students find it an engaging, safe place to communicate, collaborate, and create. It is a place just to be a kid in an increasingly pressurized climate. These kids will be 'gronups' in a blink of an eye. Engaging in web tools now can prepare them to participate in an increasingly complex, global, multicultural society as writers who communicate effectively and who, we hope, have reclaimed the joy of writing.

## References

Ajayi, L. (2010). Preservice teachers' knowledge, attitudes, and perception of their preparation to teach multiliteracies/multimodality. *The Teacher Educator, 46*(1), 6–31.

Anstey, M., & Bull, G. (2006). *Teaching and learning multiliteracies: Changing times, changing literacies.* Newark, DE: International Reading Association.

Berryman, L., & Russell, D. R. (2001). Portfolios across the curriculum: Whole school assessment in Kentucky. *English Journal, 90*(6), 76–83.

Brunsell, E., & Horejsi, M. (2010). Science 2.0. *The Science Teacher, 77*(1), 12–13.

Eisner, E. (1994). *Cognition and curriculum reconsidered* (2nd ed.). New York: Teachers College Press.

Freire, P. (1970). *Pedagogy of the oppressed.* New York: Continuum.

Gee, J. P. (1990). *Social linguistics and literacies: Ideology in discourses. Critical perspectives on literacy and education.* London: Falmer Press.

Gokcearslan, S., & Ozcan, S. (2011). Places of wikis in learning and teaching processes. *Procedia–Social and Behavioral Sciences, 28*, 481–485.

González, N., Moll, L., & Amanti, C. (2005). *Funds of knowledge.* Mahwah: Erlbaum.

Grabill, J. T., & Hicks, T. (2005). Multiliteracies meet methods: The case for digital writing in English education. *English Education, 37*(4), 301–311.

Hocks, M. E. (2003). Understanding visual rhetoric in digital writing environments. *College Composition and Communication, 54*(4), 629–656.

International Society for Technology in Education. (2007). National educational technology standards. Retrieved from http://www.iste.org/standards.aspx

Kress, G. (2003). *Literacy in the new media age.* London: Routledge.

Lave, J., & Wenger, E. (1991). *Situated learning: Legitimate peripheral participation.* New York: Cambridge University Press.

Levin, D., Arafeh, S., Lenhart, A., & Rainie, L. (2002). *The digital disconnect: The widening gap between Internet-savvy students and their schools.* Washington, DC: Pew Internet and American Life Project. Retrieved from http://www.pewinternet.org/PPF/r/67/report_display.asp

Moje, E. B., Ciechanowski, K. M., Kramer, K., Ellis, L., Carrillo, R., & Collazo, T. (2004). Working toward third space in content area literacy: An examination of everyday funds of knowledge and discourse. *Reading Research Quarterly, 39*(1), 38–71.

Smith, F. (1988). *Joining the literacy club: Further essays into education.* Portsmouth, NH: Heinemann.

Vygotsky, L. (1978). *Mind in society: The development of higher psychological processes.* Cambridge, MA: Harvard University Press.

# 6 Extension

## AFTER-SCHOOL TECHNOLOGY POSSIBILITIES

*Lindsay Laurich and Kathryn F. Whitmore*

Blady and Henkin describe how sometimes "children groan" in classrooms in response to writing time. They write of the "increasingly pressurized climate" of schools and the temptation of "cramming" decontextualized skills lessons before high-stakes testing. They show how incorporating wikis afforded Blady's students a chance to reclaim the joy of writing as they collaborated and wrote for real purposes and audiences. Their story is one of young literacy learners exploring their identities as writers in a classroom space.

While we certainly advocate for the valuable writing that Blady and Henkin describe, we also consider writing in spaces outside of the classroom walls, in a search for spaces that are not constrained by standards, administrators, political will, classroom management considerations, time, and resources. We have previously considered how literacy learning and teaching happen in video arcades (Whitmore & Laurich, 2010) and family literacy programs (Whitmore, 2007). Here we describe an after-school space where Lindsay designed and facilitated a "Technology Think Tank," where fourth and fifth grade boys and girls gathered to share how they used technology both in and outside of school and to explore new possibilities for technology in these spaces. The Think Tank was consistent with Blady and Henkin's belief that "[e]ngaging in web tools now can prepare [students] to participate in an increasingly complex, global, multicultural society as writers who communicate effectively" (p. 81). Although it was not a requisite for participation, most of the Technology Think Tank children had difficulties in their classroom settings. Many were considered "struggling" writers by their teachers and according to classroom and standardized assessments. Yet they wrote prolifically after school on paper and online.

## After-School Spaces

> I like the Think Tank. 'Cause I can just be me. (Matt, age 11)

Seven fourth and fifth grade students gathered quietly in the doorway of their school's computer lab after the dismissal bell. It was the first of eleven meetings of the after-school Technology Think Tank and the last time they would be this quiet. "What are we going to do here?" Kassandra, a fifth grade participant asked. "We're going to do what you decide," Lindsay responded.

### Shifts of Power

Although she had meticulously planned almost every minute of instruction as a fourth grade and middle-school classroom teacher, Lindsay wanted the Technology Think Tank to be student-led. She knew that her plans and intentions for the group would sabotage this goal, so she created a *loose framework*, leaving out many of the objectives, questions, procedures, etc. that are expected in a classroom lesson plan. Lindsay describes how this decision played out:

> Although the notion of leaving the direction of our weekly time together less structured was terrifying, it was also liberating. There were initial awkward moments in the Technology Think Tank where I felt we lacked purpose, I thought we were "wasting time," when I felt I had lost control and desperately wanted to seize it back, yet they were outnumbered by the fantastic moments when students taught one another, shared their amazing learning with pride, and talked excitedly about the next time we could gather together.

One of the most amazing outcomes of letting students lead came when Carson, a student who was continually in trouble with his classroom teacher, began to stay after meetings to plan the next week's topics. He volunteered his expertise, and stood comfortably in front of the group or made diagrams on the white board while issuing directions such as these:

> Okay, everyone. If you stand together you can see my blog here, and this is where I update each day. These are pretty easy to make, so, um, I'm going to help you set up one today. Then we can read and post on each other's.

Carson was so enthused by the activities of the Think Tank that he coined the nickname "Think Tankers" to describe the group. One day Lindsay heard Carson reference her to a group of boys, "She's in the Think Tank." They nodded, and after school one of the boys appeared in the doorway and asked if he could join.

As the student participants in the Think Tank came to realize that they were increasingly in charge of our activities, they negotiated new relationships with one another and with Lindsay, played with agentic identities, and mediated one another's learning.

## Redefining and Revaluing Writing and Technology

As Blady and Henkin describe, new technologies have changed what and how we write. Wikis, for instance, allow for multiple authors, collaborative revision, and interesting ways for publication. Many schools now mandate that teachers introduce students to online research sources, use word-processing software, or experience presentation platforms such as PowerPoint. While many students appreciate the opportunity to explore technology (or refine their existing expertise), there are still countless boundaries within classroom settings that define writing in specific ways and value certain experiences over others. For instance, it is not uncommon for schools to prohibit Facebook, which is currently a key part of many students' outside-of-school literacy portfolio. The underlying message is that Facebook is not academic, not safe, and not valuable.

In an after-school setting, Lindsay was able to lift the boundaries of writing, and children were encouraged to share the types of writing they were doing at home. This writing included: back-and-forth communication with other children as they played games online, an online presence where one Think Tank participant was buying and selling sports items, the creation and publication of YouTube videos, communication with extended family members via Facebook and other sites, a memorial to a beloved pet who had recently passed away, and countless stories, pictorials, and short videos.

The combination of positioning the children as leaders of the Think Tank, along with a genuine interest in writing quickly led to students using the after-school time to continue and expand their outside-of-school interests. In one particularly memorable meeting, the children gathered around Daniel, a fourth grade boy, who showed them how he had sold an autographed baseball bat for $30. It was the first time that he had success selling an item and he was elated. The other children looked at his other listings of items for sale, and the conversation turned to how he could improve his advertising to entice more buyers. Together, the group revised his web page. He reported the following week that he had sold a baseball card and the children cheered while he smiled from ear to ear.

## Back to the Classroom

The after-school space is a special one where power relationships can be more easily negotiated and boundaries that constrain school writing are lifted. It is a space of freedom – markedly different from the constraints of the classroom. Still, we know these elements can find their way into classrooms spaces, too.

Teachers are pressured, as Blady and Henkin described, to prepare students to do well on increasing numbers of assessments, more frequently, and with more intensity. Truthfully, in this climate many lessons teachers believe to be thoughtful and purposeful, and crafted carefully so as not to waste time are also designed to control the behavior and performance of the children. Even when teachers offer "choice" in learning, it is on limited terms. It is clear to the students who is in charge.

Teachers worry about losing power: What if the students want to do something we haven't planned? What if what we do isn't purposeful or important (or linked to standards)? What if we don't agree with their decisions? Our answer to all these questions is: these will happen! And, as a result possibilities multiply and joyful language learning emerges!

Lindsay discovered in the Technology Think Tank that children take responsibility and leadership when power is offered to them. Moreover, they need this responsibility if we hope to create independent thinkers and leaders with critical consciousness. One of Lindsay's best moments in the Think Tank came when Carson described her as being "in" the group not "in charge" of it. To be counted as an equal participant in a classroom community of writers is to reclaim the joy of teaching.

## References

Whitmore, K. F. (2007). Bridging the worlds of home and school: Keeping children's identities whole in the classroom. In P. Martens, & Y. M. Goodman (Eds.), *Critical issues in early literacy development: research and pedagogy* (pp. 177–198). Mahwah, NJ: Erlbaum.

Whitmore, K.F., & Laurich, L.N. (2010). What happens in the arcade shouldn't stay in the arcade: Lessons for language arts classroom design. *Language Arts, 88*(1), 21–31.

# 7

# SUPPORTING WRITERS AS THEY LEARN TO SPELL

## A Holistic Approach

*Maryann Manning and Marilee Ransom*

We know a great deal about how children learn to spell and instructional practices that best support the natural progression from early written marks on the page to conventional spelling. We understand that spelling, writing, and reading all develop simultaneously in an inextricably connected process. Common spelling instruction, in which students are forced to memorize word lists, is rooted in misconceptions about how children become conventional spellers. Such practices segregate spelling as a distinct act, when spelling should be learned in its natural context – as children compose. Although many teachers enthusiastically support children's spelling through appropriate instructional techniques, antiquated and ineffective spelling practices persist. This chapter is intended to provide a research-informed call to reclaim spelling instruction from rote memorization to supportive of the overall goal of encouraging children to become involved readers and expressive writers.

## A Brief Historical Perspective

### Behaviorism and Developmental Views

Spelling instruction was long considered a convention to be learned with extreme rigidity in classrooms. Horn (1946), the authority on spelling instruction from the 1940s to 1960s, demanded that students memorize lists and take tests to demonstrate mastery. Horn's assumption was that language is a list (like the unabridged dictionary) that one must memorize word by word in order to write. Such a word-by-word approach is linguistic behaviorism.

During the 1960s through the 1980s, educators began to seriously question behavioristic spelling instruction. Read's (1975a, 1975b, 1971) work described a developmental process, rather than a behavioral one, in which children use what they are learning to invent spellings. The idea that spelling could be developmental was supported by Chomsky (1971), who established the then-novel idea that children associate letters with sounds in the absence of direct instruction. She recommended that even young children be engaged in independent writing and that teachers value invented spelling.

Bissex (1980) chronicled her son's development as a writer and speller from five to ten years old. She suggested classroom practice based on what children naturally do, including inquiry-based teaching. Henderson (1981, 1985) focused on developmental and cognitive aspects of learning to read and spell, studying the ways in which young spellers learn patterns and apply that learning to other words. His stage models for spelling development are well known and inform some teachers' understanding of the stages in which their students are writing. Beers, Beers, and Grant (1977) considered children's logic in their spellings and Zuttell (1978) studied how spelling affects reading development. Remarkably, in spite of the progressive flavor of some of the developmental research on spelling, the behaviorist perspective persisted in classroom instruction as teachers continued to assign and test children on lists of words.

## Constructivism and Spelling

A shift occurred in our understanding of spelling development when Piaget's theories were applied to research into reading and writing. Constructivist spelling researchers view approximated spellings as a natural part of children's construction of knowledge about written language. From a constructivist point of view, learning to spell is a process that occurs within children as they develop; as a result, the teacher's role is to facilitate and guide. In this view, teachers know they must be knowledgeable about spelling learning in order to provide appropriate spelling instruction for groups and individuals.

Emilia Ferreiro, an Argentine developmental psychologist, studied invented spelling and established a constructivist basis for spelling. Ferreiro and Teberosky (1982) informed our understanding of how children become conventional spellers; they described their work as

> an attempt to explain the developmental processes of children learning to read and write. By processes we mean the path that children take to comprehend the characteristics, value, and function of written language, from the time it becomes an object of their attention (and as such, of their knowledge) (p.1).

They explained that children's spelling development is a progression that is logical when viewed through a constructivist lens and within the larger context of how children construct knowledge over time. This research was replicated in

English (Kamii, Long, Manning, & Manning, 1990 ; Kamii & Manning, 1999) and Japanese (Kato & Kamii, 1997).

Next we describe the likely progression of spelling development as represented by one young writer. Although we present this progression in "levels" because we recognize the common features of children's development, we also recognize that each child is unique, that specific features may not occur or be visible in every child's development, and that what is important here is the progression, not the stages per se. The rest of this chapter is devoted to strategies teachers can use to support children's spelling development, thereby reclaiming spelling as an essential facet of meaningful writing.

## Constructivist Spelling Levels

When preschool and primary teachers have a working knowledge of spelling levels, they are equipped to meet students where they are and offer them the kind of support they need to continue to move toward conventional spelling. Spelling levels are determined by observing the writing that a child does or by asking the child to spell a few words. By observing, informed teachers can tell if a child is using letter strings (Level 1), writing short words with no sound-symbol correspondence (Level 2), inventing spelling with conventional and/or approximated letters to represent sounds (Level 3), or is spelling conventionally for the most part, with only some vowel and consonant approximations (Level 4). Eventually, children's spelling becomes conventional for most words (Level 5), although invented spelling continues, less and less frequently, of course, throughout life. These levels are useful in understanding children's written production, planning for instruction, and explaining early spelling development to others.

### Level 1

Children at this level write representations in strings with the intention of producing different meanings, including words, phrases, names, labels, sentences, and even stories. Adults generally discern no differences between the symbol strings at this level. The written shapes may or may not look like letters until drawing and writing become more differentiated.

In Figure 7.1, we see that three-year-old Tori purposefully used her own notions about how written language works when she wrote a string of shapes. Although there is no visible correspondence between conventional English letters

FIGURE 7.1  Three-year-old Tori's string of shapes.

and Tori's symbols, there is definite variation in the shapes. Tori wrote from left to right and we can assume that she had an intended meaning for what she wrote.

## Level 2

Representations at this level are more recognizable to adults as writing, and the characters often resemble conventional letters. Children begin to understand that words have a minimum and maximum number of letters, and that words are made up of different combinations of letters in varied order. Children follow personal and common patterns and rules for written language that reveal their unique individual thinking.

Tori composed the text in Figure 7.2 about eight months after the first sample. Now she clearly understands that words have letter-like shapes and are three or four shapes in length. The letters look more like conventional letters, but there is no letter-sound correspondence yet. Although Tori may have known what she meant at the time, most adults cannot read invented messages like this one.

## Level 3

Children at this level begin to write with an understanding that symbols (letters) are related to the sounds in oral language. They sometimes use only one symbol to represent a syllable, which is termed syllabication. Further, children learning to write in English begin to represent sounds with long vowels and consonants, typically moving from prominent initial, to final, to medial sounds in words.

In the sample in Figure 7.3, adults can read Tori's ideas: "I went to a sleepover at Ava's house. We had lots of fun." Tori composed this piece about a year after the

**FIGURE 7.2**  Tori (3 years 8 months) writes with invented and conventional letters.

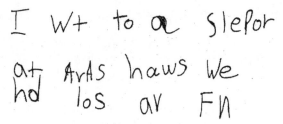

**FIGURE 7.3** Tori (4 years 8 months) demonstrates increasingly conventional (and readable) spelling.

sample in Figure 7.2, and it demonstrates that she now understands the concept of word and represents the sounds of language with letters that make sense, even though they approximate convention.

## Level 4

Short vowels become more frequent and consistent at Level 4. The spellings are almost conventional, and are easily read by an adult. Young writers may not control all vowel choices conventionally, but most consonants and long vowels are conventional. In the sample in Figure 7.4, Tori wrote, "If I had a garden, I would plant strawberries and grapes and oranges and lettuce and carrots and tomatoes."

## Level 5

Level 5 occurs when the majority of a child's writing presents conventional spellings. Students at this level are less likely to invent spellings, although inventions are still evident when children write words they encounter less frequently in their writing and reading.

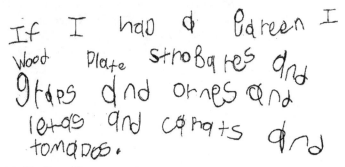

**FIGURE 7.4** Tori's spelling approaches convention.

## Classroom Practices – Preschool and Kindergarten

All classrooms have students with a wide range of spelling levels, thus making it impossible and undesirable to create a single instructional plan that is appropriate for all children. Preschool and kindergarten teachers will likely enjoy observing students experimenting at Levels 1, 2, and 3. As a general rule, rather than formal spelling instruction, the early childhood classroom should immerse children in engaging reasons to write, create real audiences to write to, and excite children about writing as part of play (see Wohlwend & Medina, Chapter 14). During early preschool, most children do a great deal of "scribbling" to represent what they want to write. Rather than asking preschool children to practice writing skills out of context, like copying the alphabet, we know concepts about how written language works develop naturally in print-rich environments and through purposeful engagements with real texts and literacy events (e.g. reading aloud, observing writing, etc.). In time, when preschool children have many literacy experiences, they construct relationships with and through written language. Thus, invented spelling should be encouraged through the kinds of experiences we discuss below.

Kindergarten classrooms may have children at Levels 1, 2, or, occasionally, Level 3 and beyond; it is likely that students will invent spellings for the messages they compose. Kindergarten teachers can provide numerous reading and writing experiences to encourage children's natural expressions in lieu of any direct spelling instruction. Understanding the ways that children invent spellings, as opposed to calculating a percentage of accurate spelling, serves teachers' assessment of children's literacy development well because invented spelling reveals so much about children's changing knowledge about written language concepts (Kamii & Manning, 1999).

Here are some instructional practices that strongly support young spellers as they develop while reading and writing.

### Demonstrate Writing Frequently

When teachers write throughout every day in front of their students and occasionally ask, "What letter do you think I might use?" they engage children in thinking aloud about how spelling works. Children have varied opportunities to see adults write for multiple reasons, and their understandings about basic concepts of writing vary accordingly. Every time teachers demonstrate writing for authentic reasons, during classroom brainstorming sessions, calendar times, and so on, they are teaching.

### Label Projects and Create Charts

Many preschool children enjoy labeling their projects. Marilee's three-year-old son makes a series of marks to label the dinosaurs he draws. He occasionally says he is making a letter or asks what letters make up the name of the particular dino-saur, but generally he proceeds with scribbles and shapes. Usually his marks are not conventional letters. It is important to encourage early expressions like these, without correcting. Further, when early childhood teachers use conventional spelling to create similar labels for children's creations, they provide another important demonstration of purposeful writing.

### Invite Journal Writing That Illustrates Drawing

We encourage teachers to offer children bound notebooks and stapled paper that has space for pictures and writing so that children can write before, after, or while they are drawing. When children ask how to spell words in a journal, we encour-age teachers to ask the children what they hear or think and encourage them to represent their thoughts with marks (conventional letters and otherwise). When children ask adults to write words, it is a wonderful opportunity to discuss how spelling works.

### Engage Children in Interactive Writing

Teachers and children can collaboratively write a variety of types of texts during the classroom day. For example, teachers might record daily news from each child's life as they dictate: "Micah has new shoes today. Mary's grandmother came to dinner last night. Monica's daddy brought sweets home for everyone." Or, teach-ers might record classroom events on chart paper, a white board, or a smart board. Field trips, a class guest, or something exciting that happened to the group offer real reasons to write. In these literacy events, the teacher is an active participant, but the students lead the writing. The children might negotiate a title and offer ideas for content. Posting interactive writing for all students to see, while it is being written as well as to be read throughout the day or week, means children can learn about relationships between oral and written language.

### Read Broadly

Texts such as big books, projected songs, and poems on posters, which allow eve-ryone to see the print, also teach children about spelling. Aside from enjoying such varied reading materials together, children can be encouraged to notice how words in these texts are spelled. Other conventions can be brought to discussion by asking children, "What do you notice about the writing in the song we just sang?"

## Classroom Practices – Primary and Intermediate

Primary and intermediate teachers teach students with a wide range of spelling development in their classrooms. A second grade classroom might include a Level

5 student with exceptional visual memory who spells almost all words conventionally, but the same class is likely to have other students who are at Levels 2 or 3. Further, children who express themselves well verbally may spell in less developed ways than adults expect. In Maryann's research, she found that there are usually three spelling levels in primary classrooms and two levels in intermediate classrooms (Manning, 2004). Knowledgeable primary and intermediate teachers identify such a range of development in order to provide individually appropriate instruction. Meaningful and effective instructional practices, particularly writing workshop, keep the focus on spelling development as part of learning about writing.

Most children in primary and intermediate grades write in invented spelling (Level 3) and are becoming increasingly conventional spellers. These students' texts can be read because their inventions are consistent with the alphabetic principle, meaning they are phonetic but perhaps different from conventional spelling. Students who are inventing spelling should have as much exposure to writing – and to reading – as possible. Some spelling instruction benefits all students; some is appropriate for individuals who are currently learning about specific concepts. Because spelling and reading are so interrelated and develop in tandem, practices that support one generally support the other.

Formal spelling instruction becomes more appropriate for primary and intermediate students who have already moved beyond Level 3 and are spelling some words conventionally, but offering formal spelling instruction too soon can undermine children's confidence because they cannot yet make sense of the information. Presenting spelling rules before a child is ready can have a frustrating effect.

Students who are in Level 5 are uncommon even in intermediate grades, but some teachers may have many students who are intuitively exceptional spellers. Level 5 students, who are likely to spell with more automaticity than younger children, benefit greatly from all forms of writing practice as they explore the craft of writing. These students, as well as students whose spelling is less conventional, are excited to create their own plays, poetry, fiction, or nonfiction and to explore a variety of forms for their writing (see Blady & Henkin, Chapter 6, and Jurich & Meyer, Chapter 16, for examples).

The following instructional ideas will support primary and intermediate grade spelling learning.

## Center Instruction in a Writing Workshop

Writing workshop is the best forum for spelling development. The writing workshop refers to the time set aside for children and teachers to write and interact in meaningful ways to focus on the writing process (Fletcher & Portalupi, 2001). Students write individually and in small groups as a community of writers, complemented by group and one-on-one instruction with the teacher. The benefit of writing workshop for spelling development is that it invites children to use invented and conventional spelling to engage in large volumes of writing for many different purposes. Every kind of writing that has purpose gives children the opportunity to develop as spellers, especially when the social nature of workshop is encouraged.

Mini-lessons, one typical component of the writing workshop, can easily focus on spelling, including topics like word families and letter patterns. The texts referred to during mini-lessons can be excerpts from a published author or written by students. Spelling can also be a focus for some peer and teacher–student conferences. In mini-lessons and conferences, the teacher relies upon what the students are doing as writers to make informed decisions about what to teach. (See Manning, Morrison, & Camp, 2009, for an extensive discussion of writing workshop.)

## Demonstrate Spelling Decisions

All students profit from teacher demonstrations, and children can learn different things from any given opportunity. Primary and intermediate grade children observe spelling, sentence construction, and mechanics like indentation and punctuation. Whole group demonstrations about spelling need to be planned for such a broad audience according to teachers' knowledge about the needs of their students. Group picture dictionaries, displays of words the children consider interesting, and other environmental print also offer demonstrations of conventional spelling in context.

## Engage Children in Interactive Writing

For primary and intermediate students, as for younger children, interactive writing affords teachers opportunities to tailor instruction to immediate needs. Student collaboration can vary according to the levels of the children; for example, teachers might write ideas that children dictate on paper, white boards, or a smart board, and use these texts to start discussion about the conventions of writing. The texts generated by interactive writing become engaging and ever-changing reading material.

## Recognize That Every Shared Reading is a Spelling Lesson

Every time teachers read published children's literature students become more aware of the many conventions that writers use. As children encounter the same words or patterns over and over while they read literature (particularly literature that plays with language through rhythm, repetition, and rhyme), their visual memory increases; thus, children are able to make more sophisticated decisions about spelling because they increasingly know how words should look.

## Family Education

Although spelling ability is often an indication of visual memory, it is not an indicator of overall intellectual ability. Children (and their parents), however, may become frustrated by a student's spelling approximations; teachers' explanations of spelling development will encourage attitudes that appreciate and celebrate what children know and are learning.

As early as the 1970s, both Read (1975a) and Chomsky (1979) asserted the importance of parental acceptance of their children's invented spelling. Many parents rely primarily on their own early education to assess what happens in their children's schools. They remember weekly spelling quizzes and the painful process of memorizing word upon word for regurgitation; often, they view their personal experiences as the one correct way to learn spelling. Teachers and school administrators need to effectively communicate their reasons for contemporary approaches for spelling instruction. Parents should respond with enthusiasm to their children's invented spelling when they understand it, even if it does not conform to their own notions about how children learn to write. Once parents better understand the wonders of invented spelling, they join teachers in a celebrating what their children know.

## Conclusions

Classroom practices that emphasize purpose allow teachers to help their students become good spellers in a meaningful way. Such practices are rooted in scientific research – and are respectful of children's status as active learners. After all, we believe that the ultimate goal of spelling instruction is to cultivate a love of language and a profound desire to communicate using the written word. Engaging in such work is at the heart of reclaiming writing for the young literate souls coming into their own voices as they cultivate deepening understandings of the workings of written language.

## References

Beers, J. S., Beers, C. S., & Grant, K. (1977). The logic behind children's spelling. *Elementary School Journal, 77*(3), 238–242.

Bissex, G. (1980). *GYNS AT WRK: A child learns to write and read.* Cambridge, MA: Harvard University Press.

Chomsky, C. (1971). Write first, read later. *Childhood Education, 47*(6), 292–299.

Chomsky, C. (1979). Approaching reading through invented spelling. In L. B. Resnick, & P. A. Weaver (Eds.), *Theory and practice of early reading* (Vol. 2, pp. 43–65). Hillsdale, NJ: Erlbaum.

Ferreiro, E., & Teberosky, A. (1982). *Literacy before schooling.* Exeter, NH: Heinemann.

Fletcher, R. & Portalupi, J. (2001). *Writing workshop: The essential guide.* Portsmouth, NH: Heinemann.

Henderson, E. H. (1981). *Learning to read and spell: The child's knowledge of words*. DeKalb, IL: Northern Illinois University Press.

Henderson, E. H. (1985). *Teaching spelling*. Boston, MA: Houghton Mifflin.

Horn, T. (1946). *The effects of the corrected test on learning to spell*. Unpublished master's thesis, University of Iowa, Iowa City.

Kamii, C., Long, R., Manning, M., & Manning, G. (1990). Spelling in kindergarten: A constructivist analysis comparing Spanish-speaking and English-speaking children. *Journal of Research in Childhood Education, 4*(2), 91–97.

Kamii, C., & Manning, M. (1999). Before invented spelling: Kindergarteners' awareness that writing is related to the sounds of speech. *Journal of Research in Childhood Education, 14*(1), 16–25.

Kato, Y., & Kamii, C. (Eds.). (1997). *Young children's reading and writing: A Piagetian, constructivist view*. Tokyo: Child Honsha.

Manning, M. (2004). Invented spelling. *Teaching K-8, 35*(2), 86–88.

Manning, M., Morrison, G., & Camp, D. (2009). *Creating the best literacy block ever*. New York: Scholastic.

Read, C. (1971). Preschool children's knowledge of English phonology. *Harvard Educational Review, 41*(1), 1–34.

Read, C. (1975a). *Children's categorization of speech sounds in English*. Urbana, IL: National Council of Teachers of English.

Read, C. (1975b). *Children's categorizations of speech sounds in English*. Research Report No. 14. Urbana, IL: National Council of Teachers of English.

Zuttell, J. (1978). Some psycholinguistic perspectives on children's spelling. *Language Arts, 55*(7), 844–850.

# 7 Extension

## CONSTRUCTIVIST SPELLING, YES! CONSTRUCTIVIST GRAMMAR, TOO!

*Sandra Wilde*

Just like spelling, grammar (to be defined shortly) is part of the language that children learn before and during their years in school. Just like spelling, grammar is recreated in the mind of every person that acquires it. Just as with spelling, teachers can support the learning of grammar.

When teachers say, "My kids' grammar is terrible," I ask them what they're referring to. Usually it is some combination of writing mechanics ("It's all one big sentence"), usage ("They say *ain't*"), and technical grammar ("They don't even know what a noun is"). You hear the same thing from the general public: "They don't teach grammar anymore, and it shows." Typically, the solution suggested is to bring back the grammar books, even though the same complaints were common when grammar textbooks were universal.

I would like to suggest, instead, a constructivist approach to the topics in the grammar grab bag. Let's start with writing mechanics. An example: Recently I met with some second grade teachers who were concerned that their students did not know how to write sentences. I suspected that the problem was less serious than they realized, and I asked to look at some of the writing. No surprise; the students had written, for the most part, well-organized, interesting pieces about an area of personal expertise ranging from dancing to beatboxing to buying a car. Most sentences read like sentences. The only thing missing was that the sentences were not always punctuated like sentences. Teachers and textbooks have traditionally tried to help students to punctuate sentences by defining them as "a complete thought," "made up of a subject and a predicate," and so on. This never works.

To demonstrate a lesson with second graders I wrote three brief unpunctuated sentences below each other on the white board: "I have a dog/His name is Bash/ He plays with me." I then asked the students how the sentences should be punctuated and why – an easy question for them. Next, I asked how they know when they have come to the end of a sentence when writing. My favorite response was, "I finish writing my idea and then realize it's time for a new sentence, so I put a period." I then told the children that there are two times you can put periods in: when you're first writing the piece, and after you're done, when you can go back and read it over and see where the periods should go. I got them to agree to try to do this.

I added one more piece to the lesson to address a problem I had seen in their writing: long sentences connected with *and*s that weren't run-on because they were connected but just were not very good. I erased the periods at the end of our first two sentences and replaced them with *and*s, and read the result aloud, throwing in a couple more sentences and exaggerating the intonation. We agreed it was just too long. I told them it was still one sentence since the parts were joined together, but that it wasn't a very good one, and suggested that they look out for these long "and sentences" in their writing and break them up.

This description does not reflect the interactivity of the lesson; the children were reacting and commenting throughout. I suggested to the teachers present that they follow up by reminding students to notice where the sentences end when they are writing, and check again when they read their pieces. In second grade, kids will not be able to completely master sentence boundary punctuation (in particular, they'll still have fragments) but they can learn the basics.

What makes this lesson constructivist rather than didactic? First, I based it on what I saw in the students' writing, so that I was building on their present level of development (using periods, but not consistently). Second, I presented them with some written language and asked for their feedback about its punctuation, as well as how they conceptualized when and how to punctuate a sentence. Third, I addressed a pattern in their writing that wasn't incorrect, but infelicitous, to stretch their thinking. Fourth, I left them with a strategy to apply in their writing. Fifth, I suggested the teachers continue to work with them on the strategy.

Didactic lessons, on the other hand, are mainly worksheets or lessons that explain which punctuation mark to choose for the end of a sentence. At best, didactic teaching may inform students that a sentence should start with a capital and end with a period, but not how to determine where the sentences break.

My second example, about parts of speech, involved getting fifth graders to think about prepositional phrases. My stated goal for the lesson was to explore one way of creating longer sentences as part of a larger goal of developing more sophisticated writers. I began with the sentence "We played basketball" written on the smart board. I then added "on the street" and said that it was a prepositional phrase, defining it loosely as a phrase that begins with a word that can help the writer link in more information. The students and I added more prepositional phrases, creating a sentence that worked surprisingly well even as it got fairly long (along the lines of "We played basketball on the street around the corner with our friends in Harlem until 6 PM," to which I then added a new clause: "and then we went home and had dinner with our families"). I pointed out that we had gone from a three-word sentence to a coherent twenty-eight-word sentence, and that they could use prepositional phrases to add more information to their own sentences and make them more interesting. I did not try to define prepositional phrases but might have chosen to give them a list of prepositions. Again, this was a constructivist lesson because I identified a possible area of growth for their writing and explored it interactively with them, demonstrating and suggesting a strategy rather than teaching them terminology didactically.

My third example covered the more contentious topic of usage. I had been asked by a sixth grade teacher to help students master subject–verb agreement for the upcoming state tests. In the present tense in Standard English, only the third-person singular is inflected, that is, has a suffix: I/you/we/they walk, but he walks. In the language of these students' community, present-tense verbs are often uninflected regardless of person: I/you/he/we/they walk. Note that subject–verb agreement is expected on standardized tests at this grade level primarily to catch our students whose home language varies slightly from Standard English. (Such testing could also affect English language learners, of course.)

After establishing that "I walk to the store" is the verb form we would all use, I asked the students whether they would say "He walk to the store" or "He walks to the store." Some raised their hands for each, some said they might use either, and some were confused by the whole thing. I asked which they had heard people in the neighborhood say, and they agreed that they heard both. I then asked the important question: Why are there two ways of saying it? What's the difference between them? Silence. After a minute or so, one student raised his hand and said "'He walk to the store' sounds a little more 'street.'" Bingo. They were aware of the distinction between formal and informal language from previous discussions, so we spent a little time inventing street and formal ways to express the same idea: "Wassup, bro?" vs. "Hello sir, how are you this fine afternoon?" This also included mentioning the settings where you would use different kinds of language, with a brief mention of being more formal in most writing and on tests.

I was particularly happy that we didn't need to attach any stigma to the community's home language as being considered incorrect in some circles. It was properly considered as a variation, period. We had an earlier discussion about whether *ant* and *aunt* were pronounced the same or not, with two different pronunciations being the norm in their community. (One girl noted, "Why would you call your aunt the same thing as an insect on the ground?") This variation in language, however, is not stigmatized in standards and testing.

As with Manning and Ransom's examples for spelling, these three constructivist lessons support children in their growth of the technical features of language that fall under the umbrella of school "grammar." In all cases, the teacher has a sense of students' present developmental level and builds on it in an active way, connected to goals for their speech and writing. Grammar is considered the most boring of topics, yet students were fully engaged in these three lessons because their thinking was being pushed.

## Note

To read more about teaching grammar, see Wilde, S. (2012). *Funner grammar: Fresh ways to teach usage, language, and writing conventions, grades 3–8*. Portsmouth, NH: Heinemann.

# PILLAR III
# Curriculum

# 8

# REWORKING WRITING WORKSHOP

*Kathryn Mitchell Pierce*

Having had opportunities to create writing workshop environments in elementary, middle school, and college teacher education settings, I found that our writing workshops included the same general components. In this chapter, I'll first describe some of those components and the ways in which they varied across curricular settings. Then I'll present some of the tensions that inform my process as I reclaim an ever-growing and changing writing curriculum.

## General Components of Writing Workshops

Writing workshop is a mainstay curricular framework for process writing in the progressive tradition. It is an organic space in which teachers cultivate a community of writers to support students' growth as writers, thinkers, and citizens of our country and the world. What follows are some of the components that have nurtured the writing workshop for my students.

### Immersion in Reading to Study Different Types of Writing

Elementary students read poetry in advance of writing poetry. Middle-school students read nonfiction picture books and articles in *Cobblestone* magazine, and watched documentaries before writing history reports. College students read lesson plans and teacher narratives in advance of writing their own lesson plans. While studying specific genres, we talked about distinguishing characteristics or traits as well as the strategies authors used in their writing to influence our thinking or feeling. Elementary students decided that good folk tales have a lesson and sometimes a scary part. Middle-school students recognized that immigration stories often include at least two of the following:

- the reason why characters chose to leave their homeland;
- the journey to a new land;
- the arrival and adjustment to life in a new land.

College students identified traits of good lesson plans as including a clear purpose, a list of specific materials to be used, and an easy-to-follow set of directions for teaching the lesson.

## Time to "Muck About" with Topics, Structures, and Elements of Craft

Elementary students tried writing about topics we were studying in science or social studies (space, the human body, ecosystems) as well as their experiences (friends, siblings, family outings) before settling into a topic to pursue in greater depth. They played around with first- and third-person storytelling voices and different formats for organizing nonfiction (including chapters, question and answer, charts and tables). Middle-school students wrote different leads, tried formal and informal tone, and rewrote paragraphs from a positive or negative bias. College students explored different topics related to children's literature in the classroom before settling on an author, genre, or literature response strategy as the focus of a major written assignment. At all three levels, students completed quick-writes in which they tried out different ways of telling their stories or sharing their new learning.

## Conferences to Reflect on Explorations and Emerging Plans

As elementary and middle-school students engaged in "mucking about," I dropped in on them for quick conversations about what they were doing, what they were learning, and what they were struggling to figure out. I did the same with college students. These informal conversations helped students define their final products and helped me understand how they arrived at these decisions and what might be challenging for them as they moved ahead.

## Informal and Formal Sharing

While students were "mucking about" and then working on the final products, I provided formal and informal ways for them to share their learning with one another. Informal sharing included invitations to, "Turn and talk with your neighbor about something you've learned today about your topic or about your writing," or to, "Tell the people in your small group what you plan to do next and then listen while they ask you hard questions." More formal sharing included structured peer response sessions with feedback forms or rubrics. These collaborative conversations supported students at all three levels as they selected topics, tried out ways of writing, and shaped their final products.

## Creation and Celebration of Final Products

One year, all the elementary students wrote about animals living in Australia; some of them focused on animals in the coastal forests while others selected animals in the outback. Some wrote nonfiction reports while others wrote first-person accounts of a day in the life of their animal. The stories and reports, along with murals and artifacts of the learning process, were shared in a family celebration. The narratives, poems, and sketches from Sixth Grade Camp were published in a bound volume, copied for each sixth grader, and shared during our "Camp Night." Students in an online graduate-level children's literature course published on our course website their annotated bibliographies of fiction and nonfiction books about a particular culture, along with interviews with someone representing that culture. These products were later shared in school and public libraries. These phases or components bear striking similarities to the Authoring Cycle (Short, Harste, & Burke, 1996). Short, Harste, and Burke have had a profound impact on my thinking about curriculum and about writing.

## Creating Curriculum

My own learning about writing workshop, across the diverse settings previously described, has been propelled by three powerful tensions: balancing the needs of the individual against the power of learning community; balancing the need for assignments and units against the power of exploration and curriculum as inquiry; and balancing the need to be both mentor and evaluator when responding to and grading student work. While these tensions appear to be based on dichotomies, they are more nuanced than that. The choices are not mutually exclusive. Talented and experienced teachers find ways to wrestle both into theoretically sound practices (see Atwell & Newkirk, 1987; Bomer, 2010; Christensen, 2000; Graves, 1983; Hindley, 1996). I continue to wrestle with the options, and considering them as dichotomous tensions has been helpful. The remainder of this chapter is focused on how these tensions have helped me to reclaim and rework what happens during writing workshop.

## Individual vs. Community

At the heart of my struggles to define and redefine the writers' workshop is the tension between the needs of the individual learner and the power of a classroom learning community. Consider, first, the example of reading. When students engage in individual or independent reading, the focus is on individual choice. Book selection and conferences focus on the individual reader's needs. This is different from a whole class reading a shared title in which we discuss what *we* made of this text collectively or how each of our ideas connect to the ideas of others. When independent reading is the focus, the reader is the center. When the community is the focus, the center becomes the shared space within which the reading takes place. Ideally, classrooms include space for individual reading, small-group shared reading, and whole-class shared reading.

In much the same way, I struggle to balance space for individual writers to pursue their own topics and interests, time for small groups of writers to pursue shared interests, and time for the entire class to pursue particular authors, genres, or writing topics. If writers are all pursuing their own writing projects, then the focus is on the individual writer and the individual project. Writers gather input and responses from other writers, but this process is more "self" centered. If a community of learners is working collaboratively on writing, say, fictional journals in the context of immigration studies, then writers come together to discuss not just the individual writing pieces, but how the writing reflects and contributes to their growing understanding of the immigrant experience. At the same time, the sharing contributes to a growing understanding of the genre of journals as well as the broader category of creative nonfiction. In this scenario, the process is more "community" centered. Students bring their writing to the community not only for feedback on craft and content, but to challenge and contribute to the collective understanding of the broader inquiry. Even when individual writers are working on different pieces or in different genres, the focus on a shared inquiry can provide authentic reasons for sharing their work with one another.

Since moving to teach middle-school level ten years ago, I have structured our writing workshop time around shared inquiries into topics such as *Immigration Stories*, *The Harlem Renaissance*, *The Civil Rights Era*, *Living a Writerly Life*, and *Borders, Boundaries, Lines, and Fences*. These inquiries generally begin with shared experiences in which all students are completing similar, informal writing tasks. From this base of shared writing, students select their individual areas of focus. Throughout the writing inquiry, students bring their work back to the larger group for feedback and as a source of ideas for the other writers.

In our recent study of *Borders, Boundaries, Lines, and Fences*, I began by reading aloud the picture book, *The Other Side* by Jacqueline Woodson (2001). Students recognized the fence in E. B. Lewis's illustrations as both a literal fence and as a powerful metaphor for the fences we build to separate ourselves from others. Next students completed a series of quick-writes in response to other picture books as well as images, political cartoons, quotes, poems, and excerpts from longer writing pieces. These "prompts" offered different perspectives on the literal and figurative borders, boundaries, lines, and fences that hold us together or separate us from one another. The prompts and our follow-up discussions served to expand students' ideas about borders as literal elements. Later, students selected their own "border" to explore through writing, and worked with two or three different genres to help them "see" their idea from different perspectives. Each time students brought their drafts back to the larger group, we all saw "borders" in new ways while also learning writing strategies from one another.

I like this unit because it seems to combine both individual choice and collaborative inquiry. In addition, the structure of the unit supports students in developing their voices as writers, in shaping powerful thesis statements, and in recognizing how shifting genres can shift perspectives. By the end of the unit, students seemed to have a better understanding of the connection between rethinking ideas and revision in writing.

In the richness of a generative, collaborative inquiry, I still wonder if some of my writers' needs are being fully addressed. I think about Maggie who loves to write horse stories, *Cinderella* variants, and fan letters to Taylor Swift. Certainly she can "adjust" these personal passions in order to squeeze them into a shared inquiry, but I don't think she should always have to do this. In an expanding curriculum with decreasing time, I struggled with how to make room for Phoebe's entry in a writing contest with a deadline that falls in the midst of our exploration of *Borders* or Cameron's passion for writing the action/adventure stories he lives through vicariously as he plays his video games. Dorothy Watson (1980) stated it eloquently over 30 years ago when she said that our curriculum should include "yours, mine, and ours." She was referring to student reading selections: *your* books, *my* books that I choose for you, and *our* books that we select together. I've adapted this perspective to my own thinking about writing curriculum – time to work on *your* stuff, time to work on *my* stuff that I selected for or assigned you, and time to work on *our* stuff that we are doing as a class, that we negotiate together: yours, mine, and ours. It's taken me an embarrassingly long period of time to fully grasp the power of this quick phrase and how it influences curriculum. Now I'm struggling to create the balance – how much time we devote to or preserve for each component.

Currently, I believe that the broader classroom writing community requires that significant time be devoted to "collective" writing – writing that is designed intentionally to contribute to each individual writer's growth as well as to an inquiry pursued by the classroom community. I don't think it matters whether this inquiry is focused on genre, content, or both. What matters is that individuals bring their work to the larger group for the benefit of all, and that the learning of the larger group is used to support the work of the individual.

## Assignments vs. Explorations

Throughout my teaching I've struggled with the balance between preparing broad, open-ended assignments that allow for choice and yet still have some sort of end-point in mind vs. creating an environment that allows students to engage in their own explorations. On the surface this may seem like another way of looking at "individual vs. community," but it's more about how much control I exercise in planning our curricular experiences. In a writing workshop, for example, I have assigned students to write an ode, a memoir, or a personal narrative. Within that genre, students had lots of "wiggle room" to make choices about topic, focus, or tone. Other times, I tried creating an even broader assignment, an Identity Unit, within which odes, memoirs, and personal narratives were options.

When teaching at the early elementary level, my primary goal was for students to engage in the process of writing and to view themselves as writers. I was comfortable with a writing workshop structure that allowed students to explore the craft of writing. At the college level, in education courses, our workshop structure was designed to support students in completing the written documents associated with teaching: philosophy statements, lesson plans, or reflections on practicum experiences. At the middle-school level I still want students to engage in the process of writing and to view themselves as writers. However, I now also want them to encounter certain genres and certain elements of craft – often the ones assigned to a particular grade level by a district curriculum plan or a set of state standards. With the challenges of time created by the schedule of a middle-school or college class, I find myself using "assignments" more often. The very existence of a syllabus at the college level requires advance decision-making on my part regarding the work we will do during the course. Working with middle-school colleagues at the same grade level to create common assessments leads me to design assignments that will prepare students for the learning expected in these common assessments. However, I don't want the schedule of the day, the syllabus, or the common assessments to threaten my commitment to inquiry and choice.

I found it helpful to list out the key features of a curriculum perspective driven by assignments vs. a curriculum grounded in exploration, or inquiry. The process of creating the list in Figure 8.1 helped me clarify my thinking and confirmed for me that these are not mutually exclusive. The list also helped me identify which components were contributing to my sense of disequilibrium. Arguably, I can move back and forth between the two perspectives within a given unit or experience. I can also act deliberately to balance the pros and cons of one perspective while operating from another.

Currently, I try to approach curriculum planning by dividing the course or unit into three chunks.

1.  *Frontloading*: Immersing students in lots of sample texts that highlight the focus I've selected (a genre, an element of craft, a topic or issue in a content area), including mini-lessons and quick-writes. Everyone is "assigned" to do these bits.
2.  *Workshop*: Allowing students time to "muck around" with the ideas and possibilities generated through the *Frontloading*, including drafts that may never be completed or revised. Generally, this chunk is characterized by a menu of options and may include both "required" and "optional" items. Everyone is assigned to work on the menu, but they have choices about which items they select, and choices about how they address the menu item. Most of this work is done together, while we are in the same room.
3.  *Focused Writing*: Producing a final piece or collection of pieces that demonstrate what the student has learned. Generally, these focused pieces are shaped through conferences held during the *Workshop* portion of our work. Students talk about the ideas stimulated through the *Frontloading* and about the possibilities that emerge during the *Workshop*; together we develop a plan for this *Focused Writing*. Ideally, the *Focused Writing* reflects the students' interests and goals, as well as the goals I have identified for the unit and the individual student. More of this work is done outside the classroom setting, with class time devoted to conferences, sharing with others, and peer response events.

Figure 8.2 provides an overview of these elements, with examples from each.

| ASSIGNMENT | EXPLORATION |
|---|---|
| I can plan ahead, as a teacher, and even map out where we will be on the calendar. An assignment provides me with a clear sense of direction and the dubious comfort of "control." | I can plan large "chunks" of our work – the frontloading, the "mucking about" time, the drafting/revising time. However, I am more likely to misjudge the amount of time students will need for any given component – because the work is organic. |
| I can focus on a particular writing task or skill or genre, while also allowing students to function at various levels of proficiency. | I can focus on "writers" rather than on the "writing" itself. |
| I can develop rubrics, scoring guides, or other "common assessments" based on this assignment. | I can create assessment tools based on process (did students complete each component of the exploration), but my culminating assessments must be very broad, making it more difficult to provide specific feedback relative to standards or learning targets. |
| I can collaborate with other teachers at my grade level: planning, sharing resources, reflecting on the teaching/learning during the experience, etc. | I can collaborate with other teachers at my grade level; however, our students may take their work in different directions making it more difficult to see the connections across classrooms. |
| I can determine, up front, which standards, learner outcomes, and critical skills students are most likely going to work with/demonstrate in the process of completing the assignment. | I can determine, after the fact, which standards, learner outcomes, and critical skills students ended up wrestling with as part of the exploration. These will not be the same for all students. |
| I can enter something in the online gradebook that applies to all students. | The "descriptor" of the assignment in the grade book must be very broad in order to apply to all students. |

**FIGURE 8.1** Comparison of writing as assignment vs. writing as exploration.

Comparing my work now to my work earlier in my career, I can see how grades, standardized assessments, and state/national standards are influencing my thinking. When designing a unit or individual assignment, I am now more likely to wonder how I will capture it in a rubric or grade-book entry and whether it will also lead students to engage with concepts specified in state grade-level expectations. I don't start out thinking about the standards, but I do use them as one filter for critiquing and revising my plans. If I'm not careful, I can let the limitations of an online grading program begin to shape my curriculum, instead of my beliefs about teaching and learning, and about writing. If I'm not deliberate in how I use standards to *inform* my work, I can let the standards *define* my work.

| FRONTLOADING | WORKSHOP | FOCUSED WRITING |
|---|---|---|
| *Mini-lessons, Read-Alouds, and other shared experiences that provide a foundation for the work to follow. All students complete these experiences.* | *Explorations of craft, quick-writes, brainstorming and other experiences designed to help students select an area of focus and develop the craft skills necessary to carry out the writing. Students have choices within limits as they explore options for the Focused Writing.* | *Final writing piece or collection of writings that provide evidence of individual students' learning, and growth as writers. These pieces are negotiated between student and teacher.* |
| ▪ Discussing political cartoons about Mexican Immigration and U.S./Mexico border disputes<br>▪ Reading poems and picture books with literal and symbolic fences<br>▪ Reading first-person accounts of crossing political borders, and of being discriminated against based on race, gender, or national origin<br>▪ Discussing photographs and maps depicting various fences and boundaries<br>▪ Reviewing the history of such barriers as the Berlin Wall and the Great Wall of China<br>▪ Studying Fria Kahlo's self-portrait, *The Two Fridas* (1939) | ▪ Brainstorming political, social, economic and physical boundaries<br>▪ Quick writes about personal experiences with borders and boundaries<br>▪ Rewriting picture books to change the ways characters respond to societal borders and boundaries<br>▪ Crafting thesis statements that represent personal ideas about borders that need to be torn down<br>▪ Creating sketches that represent various thesis statements as well as characters facing boundaries<br>▪ Writing first-draft poems,mini-dialogues, fictional journal entries, quick-skits, and short short stories depicting perspectives on borders | ▪ Crafting a final writing piece based on one of the draft thesis statements and reflecting some element of social critique or action<br>▪ Building a portfolio of artifacts tracing the evolution of ideas from *Frontloading,* to *Workshop,* to *Focused Writing* and including personal reflections on the collection |

**FIGURE 8.2** Frontloading, workshop, and focused writing elements in a reclaimed writing curriculum.

## Mentor vs. Evaluator

One strategy or technique that I have used throughout my career to respond to new questions is to use my experiences in another setting as a starting point. For example, when I wanted to learn how to engage students in small group discussions about mathematical ideas, I used what I knew about supporting literature discussion groups to help me get started. When I wanted to transform my university teaching from "covering content" to inquiring into the topics and issues of our profession, I used what I knew about constructing curriculum as inquiry in an elementary classroom setting. When I wanted to tease out the issues involved in grading student work at the middle-school level, I referred back to what I had learned about teacher professional development and mentoring new teachers.

Initially, I titled this section "grading vs. mentoring." The use of "mentoring" to describe my interactions with writers helped me to recall my study of mentoring programs for newer teachers. The consensus among those writing about mentoring teachers (Lipton, Wellman, & Humbard, 2001) is that the person who evaluates a teacher cannot also be the primary mentor for that teacher. Teachers need someone they can turn to for help, particularly when they are feeling at their most vulnerable and least effective point. The role of the mentor is to coach and support that teacher so that the teacher can grow professionally. The best models of teacher evaluation also contribute to teacher professional growth, but the primary function of teacher evaluation is to pass judgment on the performance of that teacher relative to a set of expectations.

Teaching writing in a context that also requires grades (i.e. most schools) puts teachers in the awkward position of being both writing mentor *and* writing evaluator. Once I made the connection between my angst over grading and my insights into teacher professional development, I had named the problem: being mentor *and* evaluator is difficult to reconcile. Bomer (2010) inspired me and added depth to my role as writing mentor. She demonstrates how we can support writers by pointing out the ways they are beginning to use the craft of writing like specific, well-known published authors. To engage in such a supportive conversation with a young writer, and then to assign a grade to that writing piece seems counter-productive. Yet grades are a reality in school. Grades currently serve an important communication function in our society; however, they rarely meet the needs of communicating with the writer.

I have struggled as a classroom teacher to balance my role as nurturer and supporter of growth in writing while also sitting in judgment on grading day. I know that student self-evaluations are crucial, that growth and effort can be addressed in the context of standards and benchmarks, and that multiple sources of data are essential in determining a student's level of achievement. I also know that grading – whether on an individual assignment or for a complete marking period – is challenging work. Goodman, Goodman, and Hood (1988) remind us that "evaluation" has, at its core, the idea of "value." I worry whether my assignments and assessments reflect values I am proud to hold up for others to see as indicators of the true nature of my writing curriculum.

Students in the classes I teach quickly learn not to ask, "Is this good?," because that's not a question I'm willing to answer. In an effort to avoid passing judgment on the "goodness" of a final assignment, I have shifted my grading practices at the middle-school level to focus on the "process" of writing. I give students credit for engaging in the writing process, for exploring different versions of a piece, and for making meaningful revisions rather than just surface level edits. I ask students to submit artifacts of their work to document their efforts to play with a particular element of craft (e.g. multiple leads), evidence of their use of classroom resources to strengthen their writing (e.g. a peer response form they received with notes by the suggestions they accepted), and evidence that they contributed to the writing growth of their classmates (e.g. a peer response form they provided for another writer). I ask them to submit multiple drafts so that we can look at their drafting and revising processes, and "process" cover letters in which they discuss their revisions.

I'm not satisfied with my grading practices. As I focus on process, I wonder if I am being honest with students about the level of their work. As standards-based grading practices pick up steam, I question whether my grading practices effectively communicate to students if their essay meets the "standard" for an essay at that grade level. (And then I tie myself up in knots trying to figure out if I really *know* what the standard is for an essay at that grade level.)

As I struggle to balance the tensions outlined here, and as I develop a plan for teaching in a time of externally imposed standards and excessive testing, I am more determined than ever to reclaim the writing workshop for its intended purpose: to provide time and support for students to grow as writers. For support, I refer back to my experiences teaching at the elementary and college levels, my work with teacher professional development, and my own experiences as a writer and a writing student. I turn to voices I trust and value in the professional literature and engage with my colleagues in thought-provoking discussions (see Meyer & Whitmore, Chapter 17). I've learned to anticipate the critical event that will disrupt whatever tenuous balance I have created. Each time one of these tensions returns to disturb my sleep or my work in the garden, my practice grows.

## References

Atwell, N., & Newkirk, T. (1987). *Understanding writing*. Portsmouth, NH: Heinemann.

Bomer, K. (2010). *Hidden gems*. Portsmouth, NH: Heinemann.

Christensen, L. (2000). *Reading, writing and rising up*. Milwaukee, WI: Rethinking Schools.

Goodman, K. S., Goodman, Y. M., & Hood, W. (Eds.) (1988). *The whole language evaluation book*. Portsmouth, NH: Heinemann.

Graves, D. (1983). *Writing: Teachers and children at work*. Portsmouth, NH: Heinemann.

Hindley, J. (1996). *In the company of children*. Portland, ME: Stenhouse.

Lipton, L., Wellman, B., & Humbard, C. (2001). *Mentoring matters: A practical guide to learning-focused relationships*. Arlington, VA: MiraVia.

Short, K., Harste, J., & Burke, C. (1996). *Creating classrooms for authors and inquirers* (2nd ed.). Portsmouth, NH: Heinemann.

Watson, D. (1980). *Class presentation*. Columbia, MO: University of Missouri.

Woodson, J. (2001). *The other side* (E. B. Lewis, illustrator). New York: Putnam Juvenile.

# 8 Extension

## CREATING GEMS OF WRITING

*Dick Koblitz*

I love writers' workshop! When I first started teaching, writing always seemed to be a chore and I didn't have my second graders do much authentic writing. Once or twice a week I might have them write a few sentences from a prompt I assigned. It was always difficult for some students and there was never much enthusiasm. But what a joy writing became when a number of years later I implemented a writers' workshop in my classroom. My students' writing fluency increased immediately and dramatically, and I noticed that they developed more confidence in themselves as writers and enjoyed writing more. But it was when I began teaching a multiage/multiyear classroom that I realized how powerful a writing workshop was as a structure for empowering students to become more prolific and sophisticated writers.

The journey was not all smooth sailing, however. The tensions that Pierce described in Chapter 8 became very real for me. As I gave my students more choice in topic selection and focused on supporting them as writers in more contextualized ways through individual conferencing, I struggled with the notion of teaching *writing* or teaching *writers*. I had not yet realized how both pedagogical stances work together.

### Process and Product

One summer a number of years ago I participated in a study tour with other American teachers to visit schools, many with multiage/multiyear classrooms, in Auckland, New Zealand. Our tour leader and mentor was Don Holdaway, teacher, researcher, and author of *The Foundations of Literacy* (1979) and *Independence in Reading* (1980). In our debriefing one evening, I remember Don saying in response to our queries about student achievement, "If the process is right, the product will be good." He went on to explain that the reverse was seldom true, that is, if teachers first or only focus on expecting students to produce good products, this does not guarantee children will automatically understand the process or develop self-efficacy as a learner. Those words were very powerful to me. When I returned to my classroom in the fall, I began to view everything I taught from a process perspective. As I did so over a period of time, my students led more literate lives both inside and outside our classroom.

## Multiage Education

Teaching a multiage classroom as a single learning community and working with children for two years instead of only one forced me to stop using grade-level materials and develop a more holistic, child-centered, literature-based curriculum. A literacy workshop, as well as math and inquiry workshops, worked beautifully in accommodating the greater range of ages, interests, prior knowledge and skill development of my students. I was able to place greater emphasis and time on process as well as differentiation, and my students' products greatly improved compared to what I experienced in a single grade classroom. As my older students modeled and collaborated with their younger classmates (and often vice versa), the quality of all of their writing and their level of engagement in writing significantly increased. The greater range of ages led to less competition to perform at the same level and shifted their focus to pursuing their own goals. A sophisticated community of writers developed which allowed my students' passion and joy for writing to naturally emerge. Many wrote at home in the evening and brought first drafts to school each morning to work on in the writers' workshop. I began to experience in greater depth the truth of what Don Holdaway had told our study group in New Zealand.

## Exploring Poetry

One writing genre that I encouraged my students to explore throughout their two years in my classroom was poetry. My intent was always that they discover the writing process organically. I exposed them to a lot of poetry each week during the entire year through read-alouds and shared reading. We talked about poetry and poets, studied poetry by noticing and naming what poets do, and memorized poetry. And we wrote poetry *all year long*, not just during Poetry Month in April. The writing of poetry during our writers' workshop was always an invitation, never an assignment. As a few students began to write poems, I provided opportunities to share and critique. Throughout the course of the school year more and more students explored writing poetry. Over a two-year period, my students wrote numerous poems for sharing and publication, and I often discovered, like Bomer (2010), wonderful "gems" in their writers' notebooks and journals.

## Writing Poetry

The following two poems illustrate the quality of writing that is possible when students are first engaged in the process of writing poetry in a multiage/multiyear classroom. The first was written at home in a small 3 × 5 inch spiral notebook by a first grader named Adam Jaffe. He brought it to school one morning and asked to share his "peace story" with the class. He read it several times and a few students commented that it sounded more like a poem than a story. After some thought, Adam agreed. Over the next several days, the class and I helped him revise and edit his poem. These are Adam's first draft and final copy of *Peace*, retaining his original formatting and spelling.

First draft:

When the birds
chirp. And when people
chake hands it is peace.
And peace gos by one
And othr it is peace.
And when peace trans
in to love it is my
darm of the wolde

Final copy:

*Peace*

When the birds chirp
And when people shake hands
It is peace.

And when peace goes by
From one to another
It is wonderful.

And when peace turns into love
That is my dream of the world.

Adam, who is now in fourth grade, recalls writing the first draft of his poem at home right before bedtime. He remembers that in our classroom he learned to write whenever the words came into his mind.

Another student, Charles Wolford, was a third grader when he wrote the following poem. He became a prolific writer in our multiage classroom and his favorite genre was always poetry. Here are Charles's first draft and final copy of *Butterflies*.

First draft:

What I feel when I see a butterfly,

I feel like a bright picture came by,
Swiftly cutting through the air,
Flying North, South, East, or West,
As if a pice of the sun broke off,
Or butter was smeared over it,
It tickles trees when it flies by there
     leaves,
     Zinging through the clouds,
     As if hitting the surface
     of melted salt or a soft
     puffy blanket,

Final copy:

*Butterflies*

I feel like a bright picture came by,
Swiftly cutting through the air,
Flying north, south, east, or west,
As if a piece of the sun broke off,
It tickles trees when it flies by their leaves,
Zinging through the clouds,
As if hitting the surface of melted salt,
Or a soft, puffy blanket.

When I recently spoke to Charles, who is now a graduate student studying writing in London, he vividly recalled writing *Butterflies* fifteen years ago and remembered that the poem wrote itself as he sat on his knees by his bed at home late one afternoon. He said that clouds always seemed like piles of salt to him and he knew from reading and listening to the poetry of Shel Silverstein that poems did not have to be expansive. They could be powerful in a few lines. I love the fact that both Adam and Charles wrote their first drafts at home when the muse hit them. They were learning that written literacy (both were also prolific readers) could be a meaningful part of their everyday lives – so meaningful that they remembered these events years later.

## Process First

These poems represent the many "gems" of writing in multiple genres that frequently emerged in my multiage classrooms over the years. They demonstrate the quality of writing that is possible when students are encouraged to lead literate writing lives, are mentored as writers by their classmates and teachers, and are allowed to explore the writing process within a developing community of writers.

I have learned that process and product, as Pierce has written, are not mutually exclusive. *But process must always come first.* When it does, not only are the products always better, but the tensions that exist between showing fidelity to the writer or showing fidelity to the writing are greatly lessened. We can reclaim authentic writing curriculum when we trust our individual and collective knowledge and experience, when we trust children to learn, and when we create the conditions in our classrooms for that to occur. Don Holdaway had it right many years ago.

## References

Bomer, K. (2010). *Hidden gems.* Portsmouth, NH: Heinemann.

Holdaway, D. (1979). *The foundations of literacy.* Gosford, New South Wales, Australia: Ashton Scholastic.

Holdaway, D. (1980). *Independence in reading* (2nd ed.). Gosford, New South Wales, Australia: Ashton Scholastic.

# 9

# WRITING PICTURES, DRAWING STORIES

## Reclaiming Multimodal Composing in First Grade

*Prisca Martens, Ray Martens, Michelle Hassay Doyle, and Jenna Loomis*

Carrie is reading the picturebook she created titled *A Good Memory*. It's the story of a young girl who wants to help clean the water for animals in an aquarium tank. On page three Carrie reads, "The manager said yes. We went in and some animals had trash in their mouths. We had to take it out. We found shredded up paper, long bracelet strings, and big coffee cans" (see Figure 9.1).

When asked about her art, Carrie explained:

> I put a turtle with gloomy colors [blue, green] for its shell because it's sad ... The jellyfish is angry. It's stinging the coffee can because it doesn't like having trash in its tank. I showed it's mad with emotions [on its face] and hot mad colors [red, orange, yellow] ... The manager is nodding his head yes and I put lines by his head to show it's moving ... The scuba equipment on the wall is for Zoe and Christy to use when they go in to clean the tank.

Carrie composed her intricate multimodal text by making a series of deliberate decisions. To create her written text, like all authors, she decided on how to represent her meanings (semantic system) in grammatical structures (syntactic system) using graphic/sound symbols (graphophonic system), similar to how she integrates these same language cueing systems when she reads (Goodman, 2003). She also decided when and how the writing, art, or both would carry the meaning. Her written text included information available only in her writing (i.e. "We had to take it") as well as information provided in both her writing ("The manager said yes.") and art (a speech bubble indicating the manager said, "Yes.").

Carrie's comments revealed that she also made deliberate decisions to compose her art. Like all artists, she decided how to represent her artistic meanings (semantic system) in organizational structures (syntactic system) using graphic

The manager said yes. We went in and some animals had trash in their mouths. We had to take it out. We found shredded up paper, long bracelet strings, and big coffee cans.

**FIGURE 9.1** Page 3 of Carrie's book.

symbols (graphic system). In art, the *elements of art* (EA; i.e. dot, line, value, shape, color, space, form, texture) are the graphic cues and the *principles of design* (PD; i.e. balance, emphasis, pattern, rhythm, movement, variety, harmony, contrast, unity) are the syntactic cues that organize them meaningfully (Piro, 2002; Pumphrey, 1996). Carrie placed small lines (EA) around the manager's head to indicate its movement (PD) and chose specific colors (EA) to reflect the feelings and emotions of the turtle and jellyfish. She also provided information in her art not available in her written text (i.e. scuba equipment).

Just as writers organize graphic/sound symbols (i.e. words) in grammatical structures to create meaning, artists organize the EA using the PD to create meaning. Just as in written language, different wordings have different meanings in different contexts and grammatical structures, in art different EA have different meanings when organized using the PD in different contexts. Through her writing and art, Carrie composed a sophisticated multimodal picturebook with meanings embedded in both her written and pictorial texts.

Carrie's picturebook is like all picturebooks: "text, illustrations, total design; ... As an art form it hinges on the interdependence of pictures and words ..." (Bader, 1976, p. 1). Picturebooks are a type of multimodal text; the meaning of the whole involves the weaving together of multiple modes. All communication occurs through equally valid modes, including linguistic (i.e. written/oral language), visual (i.e. images), spatial (i.e. design, layout), and gestural (i.e. body language) (Bezemer & Kress, 2008). In picturebooks, the art (visual mode) is just as important in telling the story as the written text (linguistic mode) (Bader, 1976; Nodelman, 1988). We intentionally write picturebooks as one word to emphasize the importance and equivalence of these multiple modes (Kiefer, 1995; Sipe, 2008). We also prefer to use "artists"/"art" rather than "illustrators"/"illustrations" to emphasize that illustrators/illustrations are, in fact, artists/art.

In this chapter we reclaim writing by sharing how twenty-seven first graders composed after spending a year exploring how artists, like authors, make deliberate decisions to represent and communicate meaning. We demonstrated how in their compositions the first graders blurred traditional definitions of writing and art. They did not merely write words and draw pictures; they compose meanings by writing pictures and drawing stories. The children's picturebooks reveal that multimodal composing in writing and art offers numerous opportunities for critical, multidimensional thinking.

## Setting the Context

The school the children attended was located in a metropolitan area on the east coast; 25 percent of the students received free/reduced-price lunch. The twenty-seven first graders included thirteen European Americans, five African Americans, four Asian/Pacific Islanders, and five Hispanics. Seven of the children received English as a Second Language support and three received special education services.

We met regularly as a team to plan instructional experiences. Jenna and Michelle, the two first grade teachers, were required to use Houghton Mifflin (2001) materials for reading instruction, which they supplemented with children's literature. They knew the curricular standards/skills they needed to address and sometimes substituted picturebooks for a curricular lesson and other times scheduled time to read them in addition.

## Learning to Compose in Art

Our focus on how artists represent meaning occurred in the context of two text sets of global literature and we highlighted specific art concepts in each set. For the Identity Text Set, focused on children exploring their intercultural identities, we discussed how artists use color to represent feelings/emotions and line to represent movement. For the Taking Action Text Set, focused on ways to take action to make the world a better place, we examined how artists use contrast in color, pattern, shape, and line to express meaning.

Our usual procedure was to read the picturebook on a document camera and then invite the children to respond orally. Through these discussions, the children constructed rich meanings together, building on each other's insights and connections. As the discussions and responses progressed, we went back to closely examine two or three illustrations and talk with the children about why the artist made the particular decisions he/she did to represent story meanings. Following these discussions, we invited the children to explore and connect to aspects of the story using that particular art concept.

For example, *A Child's Garden: A Story of Hope* (Foreman, 2009; Taking Action Text Set) is the story of a boy living in rubble walled by a barbed wire fence. The boy finds a green sprout and takes action by watering and caring for it. The plant grows, hides the fence, and provides hope for renewed life.

Foreman uses contrast to emphasize the mood and emotion of the story. The beginning art is monochromatic (gray) to stress the devastation and lack of life and hope. Color is visible only in the tiny sprout that gradually grows and overtakes the gray, offering hope for the future.

The action the boy takes in the story is as simple as nurturing the small vine and bringing beauty to his broken world, but the first graders found deeper meanings as they considered the contrasts in the art. For example, when the green vine signifying life flourished, Saida commented, "Now it's getting happier because it's more colorful." After examining the contrast in color on the front and back endpages (red background with white barbed wire cutting across horizontally), Aashi thought that Foreman used red, "maybe to show hope."

After discussing the meanings in the writing and art, the decisions Foreman made, and how the writing and art worked together, the students explored using contrast to convey their own important ideas. While some students focused on taking action, others concentrated only on using contrast. Karen, for example, contrasted herself, drawn using colors, at ballet with other ballerinas drawn in pencil. In her writing she explained, "In my picture I am doing ballet. The part of my picture that is dark [is] the ballerinas around me. The part of my picture that is colored is me. The ballerinas that are dark are dark because they are not doing as well as I am. I am colored because I am doing the best at ballet."

## Creating Their Picturebooks

In May, after numerous reading, writing, and art experiences, the children began creating their own picturebooks about how they might take action in the world. We limited the stories to four pages to keep them manageable for the children (and us). In their classrooms, Jenna and Michelle spent several days brainstorming and exploring possible "taking action" ideas with the children. To help their students plan, they created a storyboard that included: Characters, Before (problem), Taking Action (to solve the problem), and Result (what happened). Using their storyboards, the children drafted their stories on paper that included a box in which they also made a quick draft sketch of the art for that page.

The children then wrote, revised, and edited their stories, and parents typed and bound them into books. Before beginning the art for the books, Jenna and Michelle reviewed with the children what they had learned about art and artists' decisions over the year. The children then took several days to independently create the art in their books. When they completed their books, Prisca and Ray interviewed (audiotaped and transcribed) each child. The children first read their books, then page-by-page explained their art and why they made the decisions they did related to color, line, etc.

## Analyzing the Picturebooks

We analyzed the children's picturebooks to understand their thinking and how they used the cueing systems [i.e. semantic (meaning); graphophonic (letters/ sounds; EA); syntactic (grammar; PD)] to represent their meanings multimodally. We coded the written text for sentence complexity by examining clauses within sentences for whether they were dependent or independent. We coded each sentence as: (a) simple (one independent clause); (b) compound (two independent clauses joined together); (c) complex (one independent clause and one or more dependent clauses); and, (d) compound/complex (two or more complex sentences joined together).

We analyzed the art alongside the interview transcripts to ensure we focused solely on the children's thinking. This page-by-page analysis (including the cover and endpapers) involved reading the child's page, reading the transcript for that page, and coding the children's comments on how/why they used particular colors/lines, etc. We only analyzed what the children actually said and did not include things we noticed during the analysis that the children had not discussed. We created codes (Strauss & Corbin, 1998) as we needed them and went back through previously coded books/transcripts and revised the codings to include any new codes. We also coded the written text and art for each page together for whether what was stated in each written clause was also represented in the art [i.e. *both writing and art* (BWA)] or was information given only in the clause [*writing only* (WO)] or only the art [and referred to in the interview transcript; *art only* (AO)].

## Multimodal Picturebooks: Writing Pictures, Drawing Stories

The children's picturebooks were amazing! Their stories focused on taking action in such ways as building bird houses, donating clothes to those who need them, conserving water, and saving electricity. Several also addressed protecting the environment by picking up trash, not cutting down trees, and not driving to cut down on pollution. While the extent to which individual children composed meaning in art varied across the pages of their books, all of the children created multimodal picturebooks by weaving together meanings in writing and art.

## Written Meanings

Most (72 percent) of the children's writing was in simple sentences (one clause). All but one child, however, also incorporated compound, complex, and/or compound/complex sentences into their written text. Half of the meanings the children stated in written clauses they also represented in their art and half of the clausal meanings were in the written text alone. Meanings stated only in the written text provided additional information that advanced the story and was sometimes difficult to visualize. For example, on one page of his book titled *The Bird Poem*, Joseph, an English language learner, drew a bird in a nest, thinking about an egg, and another bird eyeing a fish in the water. His written text stated, "Some birds don't have a home to live to make new eggs. Sometimes their wings get tired, so they can't fly far away to another country." Joseph's written text provided information (i.e. "wings get tired") not available in his art.

## Artistic Meanings: Realistic Details

All of the children extended the meanings of their stories through art beyond simply depicting what they explicitly stated in their written text. One way they all did this was by adding realistic details to the art not stated in the written text.

### Setting Details

Many details not mentioned in the written text that the children embedded in their art were in the setting. These included houses, the sun, trees, or animals, but sometimes extended to other information. Georgia's book was titled *Friendship*. The first page of her written text stated, "One day Hana and Shantal were hanging out. It was 6:30. Four hours later they went home. It was a nice day." Georgia's art, however, provided other details, including a mailbox, sun, tree, and cloud, cats Hana and Shantal were walking, and a drawing of a girl (only shown on this page) who is sad because her ball was stuck in the tree.

### Details That Support/Advance the Story

Some children also provided information in their art that related to and supported the story line or moved the story forward. Mateo's book *My Family and Me*, for example, told how his family worked to pick up trash in their neighborhood. Mateo, an English language learner, used the sun on each page to indicate the environmental changes happening in the story. The sun went from being mad and hot, drawn in red with diagonal eyebrows, on the first page when there was trash, to gradually getting happier on each page. The sun on Mateo's final page had a big smile and brighter colors since the trash was gone.

### Speech Bubbles

Many children also added details through speech bubbles. Monica's book *Don't Make the Animals Scared* focused on the importance of not cutting down trees because animals need them. Monica's first page showed Monica and Carolyn with wheelbarrows getting ready to plant trees and someone cutting them down with a chainsaw (see Figure 9.2). Monica stated in her speech bubble, "Let's plant some trees," and Carolyn responded, "That's a great idea!"

## Artistic Meanings: Symbolic Representation

The children also extended their meanings beyond what was stated in the written text in other ways. All but two children chose a color, line, or shape to represent something in their art symbolically. These decisions most often related to ways the children chose to show movement in their art and how they symbolically emphasized emotions.

### Movement

Artists have various techniques, such as through the use of repeated lines or shapes, for providing readers with the sensation of movement on two-dimensional pages. Eighteen children used these techniques to indicate either the physical movement of a character or object.

Monica represented movement by drawing a pattern of short parallel lines on both sides of the blade of the chainsaw "because chainsaws move around when they are turned on" (see Figure 9.2). She also drew lines around her body and feet to indicate, "I'm walking to plant trees." Monica also used the artists' technique of only drawing part of a person/object at the very edge of a page to give the sense of movement. In talking about Carolyn's wheelbarrow in her picture Monica said, "I put the wheelbarrow off the page because they were walking. It's going to continue on."

Robbie was one of the children who used repeated shapes to indicate movement (see Figure 9.3).

In his book *Too Messy!* Robbie told how his cousin helped him clean his messy room. On the first page, Robbie drew himself and his cousin in three places: the bottom of the stairs, the top of the stairs (with a line connecting those), and in his room inside the house. He explained, "It's not two Robbie's. That's me and my cousin. I drew a line to show that we were going up the stairs. You can't see the lines for us to go to my room." On one page, then, he represented himself and his cousin moving from the sidewalk, to the top of the stairs, and into his room.

### Emotion

Artists also use a variety of techniques to indicate emotions in a story. One familiar means is in the use of lines and shapes on faces. A big smile with large eyes and raised eyebrows, for example, indicates happiness. Artists sometimes use color too

**FIGURE 9.2** The first page of Monica's book.

My cousin came over to play. He wanted to go in my room. We went up the stairs. We went in my room. It was too messy.

**FIGURE 9.3**  The first page of Robbie's book.

to represent emotions. Warm colors (red, yellow, orange) are often used to indicate something good, happiness, or anger and cool colors (blue, green, purple) to indicate something bad or sad. Sixteen of the children represented emotions in their stories through their use of color.

In his book *Bob the Bad Bully*, Brian used color in a variety of ways throughout his book to highlight emotions in the story. The story tells of how Brian and Drew defended their classmate Davis when he was being bullied by a fifth grader. On the first page of his book, Brian drew himself and Drew in the center of the page and the fifth grader and Davis on the far right. The background of the picture is colored gray. When asked about his choice of color, Brian responded, "[The background is gray] because everything was doom and not nice and bad... [The lines in the background are diagonal] to show where the good stuff is happening and all the bad stuff," indicating the direction of his gray lines aimed at the fifth grader and Davis. On the second page Brian drew himself and Drew talking to the fifth grader. Brian's speech bubble said, "He didn't," and Drew's said, "hurt you so why hurt him." The bully responded, "Ok." Brian's and Drew's speech bubbles were outlined in red. Brian explained, "I put red around these and not [the bully's] because I'm showing you pay attention to these speech bubbles instead of that one ... It's contrast."

Some children selected clothing colors for their characters to indicate emotions. Towards the end of her book Monica dressed her characters in "warm colors, yellow mixed with orange, because they're good characters planting things." Others used color in different ways. In *The Perfect Planet*, Lauren, a child with special needs, gave one of her characters a blue, cool-colored eye, "because he doesn't like smelling all the trash and cigarettes." On a later page where the characters are cleaning up the trash, Lauren explained that, "Mrs Blossom is red and orange because she's happy that everyone is cleaning up … [This boy] with the blue face is not happy. He's really sad because the cleaning up is getting boring."

Some children combined color and line to represent emotion in their stories. Dane's book *The Day My Friend Got Hit* related how he witnessed his friend being struck by a car. On one page, Dane colored his face yellow because "[I'm] surprised … My kneepads and my elbow pads and my helmet are off … My face is big and my mouth is wide open. I have big eyes … My arms and legs are moving because of those two lines … The three triangles above my head show that I'm shocked." Through his use of color and line, Dane strongly represented his response to his friend's accident.

## Peritextual Elements

Published picturebooks include peritextual elements that contribute to their overall aesthetic quality and coherence, help readers predict and confirm the plot, characters, etc., and enrich readers' overall understanding of the book (Sipe, 2001). These elements include any physical features other than the author's words, such as the endpages, title page, front/back covers, dust jacket, and dedication page. Most of the children (22) added some of these elements to enhance their picture-books.

Endpages, located inside the front and back covers, are the first and last parts of the interior of picturebooks that readers see and transition readers from the out-side world into the story and back again. The children made deliberate and thoughtful decisions in designing the endpages of their books. Some children drew the same art for their front and back endpages, highlighting some part of their story. Karen, for example, drew trees and flowers "because it goes with what the characters planted in the book." Other children made their front and back endpapers different. Josie, a child with special needs, had two main characters, Francis and Gloria, in her book *House Cleaning* and drew Francis on her front endpaper and Gloria on her back.

In addition to the title, author, illustrator, and publisher information, title pages often have art that introduces and welcomes readers to the story. Eleven children included art on their title page, usually to foreshadow what was to come. Dane colored an ambulance, a car, and a fire truck headed to the accident. Darin's book, *The Boy Who Would Not Stop Teasing Yet*, told how Darin defended his friend who was being continually teased by a boy. On his title page, Darin intro-duced the boy by having only his head peek around the corner of the page at the reader. Darin explained, "I drew myself and a tree and showed the boy [on the edge] because he's going to be coming next in the story."

## Closing Thoughts and Insights

As these examples reveal, the first graders' picturebooks were sophisticated, complex multimodal texts. Composing in writing and art challenged the children to be creative and critical thinkers and problem-solvers. In written language, the children told their stories/meanings linearly, left-to-right, page-to-page, through their choices in wordings. In art they represented their meanings multidimensionally at various places on the page and through different *elements of art* (EA) and *principles of design* (PD). Like other picturebook authors/artists, these first graders worked to seamlessly weave together their composing across both modes to create meanings that were "a richer experience than just the simple sum of their parts" (Nodelman, 1988, p. 199).

The children reclaimed writing as a multimodal process of composing meaning. While writing and art were both essential to the children's picturebooks, we live in a very verbocentric world in which written language is privileged as *the* form of communication. Schools and society politically and financially support language/linguistics (reading and writing), while art and other modes are often considered frills. While the children's written stories were good, it was composing in art, thinking, and symbolically representing their meanings through the EA and PD that enhanced the details and added depth to their stories. They knew they weren't "done" when they finished writing. They eagerly looked to art as a wide horizon of possibilities for thinking and embedding meaning more deeply. We agree with Eisner (1982) and Greene (1988), strong proponents of expanding the acceptance and use of different modes, that rather than a competition between modes, each needs to be valued for the contributions it brings to meaning making.

Our intent here is not to minimize the value and importance of written language/linguistics. We recognize, as schools and society do, the vital role written language plays in communication. We argue that positioning written language above art and other modes narrows and constrains the thinking and composing young children do, and blinds adults to considering and appreciating the full spectrum of children's imaginative and inventive resourcefulness. Reclaiming multimodal composing, so children are "bilingual" and "biliterate" in art and written language, as these first graders were becoming, greatly expands and deepens the resources children draw on and challenges them to think and create in broader multidimensional ways that they cannot do with written language alone. This is true for all children, including English language learners and those with special needs.

In his memoir *Drawing From Memory*, award-winning author/artist Alan Say (2011) describes how his passion for drawing and determination to become an artist led him to meet Noro Shinpei, a famous cartoonist in Japan, who became

Say's Sensei (teacher/mentor). Say quotes Shinpei as stating in their first meeting, "With Van Gogh, each brushstroke is like a word in a book. Painting is a kind of writing, and writing is a kind of painting – they are both about seeing" (p. 46). We concur and hope others encourage children to write pictures and draw stories.

## Note

Our work was supported by a Literacy Communities grant from Worlds of Words (wowlit.org).

## References

Bader, B. (1976). *American picture books from Noah's ark to the beast within*. New York: Macmillan.

Bezemer, J., & Kress, G. (2008). Writing in multimodal texts: A social semiotic account of designs for learning. *Written Communication, 25*(2), 166–195.

Eisner, E. (1982). *Cognition and curriculum*. New York: Longman.

Foreman, M. (2009). *A child's garden: A story of hope*. Somerville, MA: Candlewick.

Goodman, K. S. (2003). Reading, writing, and written texts: A transactional sociopsycholinguistic view. In A. Flurkey, & J. Xu (Eds.), *On the revolution of reading: The selected writings of Kenneth S. Goodman* (pp. 3–45). Portsmouth, NH: Heinemann.

Greene, M. (1988). *The dialectic of freedom*. New York: Teachers College Press.

Houghton Mifflin. (2001). *Houghton Mifflin reading: A legacy of literacy*. Boston: Houghton Mifflin.

Kiefer, B. (1995). *The potential of picture books: From visual literacy to aesthetic understanding*. Englewood Cliffs, NJ: Merrill.

Nodelman, P. (1988). *Words about pictures: The narrative art of children's picture books*. Athens, GA: University of Georgia Press.

Piro, J. (2002). The picture of reading: Deriving meaning in literacy through image. *The Reading Teacher, 56*(2), 126–134.

Pumphrey, R. (1996). *Elements of art*. Upper Saddle River, NJ: Prentice Hall.

Say, A. (2011). *Drawing from memory*. New York: Scholastic.

Sipe, L. (2001). Picturebooks as aesthetic objects. *Literacy Teaching and Learning, 6*(1), 23–42.

Sipe, L. (2008). Young children's visual meaning making in response to picturebooks. In J. Flood, S.B. Heath, & D. Lapp (Eds.), *Handbook of research on teaching literacy through the communicative and visual arts, Volume II* (pp. 381–391). New York: Lawrence Erlbaum & Newark, DE: International Reading Association.

Strauss, A., & Corbin, J. (1998). *Basics of qualitative research: Techniques and procedures for developing grounded theory*. Thousand Oaks, CA: Sage.

# 9 Extension

## RECLAIMING MULTIMODAL RESPONSES IN FIFTH GRADE

*Renita Schmidt*

Like the four authors of this chapter, I also believe multimodal composing in writing and art offers a variety of opportunities for critical and multidimensional thinking. In my work with a group of fifth graders, students created artistic meanings (semantic system) in the ways they organized their writing (syntactic system) and in the graphic symbols (graphophonic system) they used that were very similar to the first graders' picturebooks. While the fifth grade students in the work highlighted here did not create picturebooks, they responded to literature using multimodal responses, and in these responses I saw the interweaving of communication systems – writing, images, spatial, and gestural – that deepened meaning making (Kress, 2010).

### The Setting

When many soldiers in our community were deployed to Afghanistan, Anne, a fifth grade teacher, wanted to introduce literature discussion to her students but also wanted to help them to learn more about Afghanistan. I agreed to help her by putting together a text set of materials about Afghanistan and by being a participant observer in her classroom on the days students were discussing *The Breadwinner* (Ellis, 2000). We used Daniels' (2002) ideas about literature discussion roles as the students began to read.

In *The Breadwinner*, an eleven-year-old Afghani girl named Parvana helps her father walk to the market each day to translate, read, and sell trinkets. The novel is set in the early 1990s during the first Gulf War, when Afghanistan has been at war for over 20 years. Parvana and her family (her parents, older sister, and two younger siblings) live in a small one-room apartment. Schools have closed, and although Parvana's parents are both educated and once were prominent citizens of Afghanistan, they struggle to survive in this war zone.

Soon after the story begins, uninvited Taliban soldiers enter Parvana's family apartment and take her father away to prison. The terror of living in conflict is immediately evident and issues of survival are palpable, as the students' written responses below demonstrate.

## Written Responses to *The Breadwinner*

Anne and I asked students to respond to the reading in a variety of ways. Their multimodal responses were filled with critical, multidimensional thinking that also offered the students opportunities to write for different purposes. We wanted their written responses to motivate discussion but also to build community and highlight how engaged students were with the text. Here I discuss three examples and analyze ways students showed meaning making in semiotic ways.

Some students used sticky notes to prepare for different roles as participants in the small group literature discussions. In gathering data for the study, I collected each child's sticky notes on one sheet of paper. Each sheet became a collage of valuable and unique meaning making.

Katie used sticky notes to note important information in the text, create drawings as representations, ask questions, and record affective comments she felt were relevant for inclusion in the discussion. She noted chapters, page numbers, and even the words "last paragraph" as tips for remembering what she wanted to read aloud to the group as Literary Luminary. Other times, Katie created small illustrations to capture her thinking about the main ideas in the book. She drew the dramatic part of the story when Parvana and Shauzia witnessed a public display of amputation while they were disguised as trayboys selling cigarettes and gum. She also included a small drawing of Parvana and her mother walking to the prison in search of her father. The prison was the largest figure in the drawing and it faced the reader with Parvana and her mother pictured from behind. Finally, Katie used the sticky notes to ask questions in her role as Discussion Director and sometimes these questions identified Katie's misunderstandings. Early in the story, she asked, "Who are the Taliban? p. 7," and then responded, "The government." This question provided Katie's teacher with valuable information about her confusion about the Taliban, and prompted her to include an important lesson about the Taliban to clear up misunderstandings about this radical military presence in Afghanistan.

Detailed drawing/writing was also important in students' response artifacts. Adam provided several detailed drawings he created as he made meaning during his reading of the text. In one sample he did not include the protagonist Parvana in his drawing, but labeled her place on the rug with the words "Letter Reader." The shot focus Adam chose for this drawing/writing was interesting because the detailed drawing of the trayboys faced the reader at a crucial point in the plot when Parvana disguised herself as a boy in order to make more money. The details in the drawing emphasized that Adam indeed considered, felt, and understood

The Bread Winner
chapter 11
Summerizer

First, Parvana went home.
Then mother found she was
digging ~~up~~ bones. Then the
whole family started to
arguing. Then mother agreed.
In a few weeks Parvana +
Shanzia got trays. They
sold cigarette's and gum.
Then they went into a
stadium. They thought it
was a soccer game but
they were cutting off
thevies arms. Then they
went home.

Key Points8
Trays
Cuting Arms off
Bone Digging

**FIGURE 9EXT.1** Adam's summary of one chapter from *The Breadwinner*

Parvana's feelings – her willingness to take risks for her family, the conflict she felt about disguising herself as a male, how she might have organized her stall in the market, and even the cost of particular items she offered for sale.

Finally, in Figure 9EXT.1, notice the interesting written organization Adam used in his summary of one chapter. Here, Adam's writing took on the feel of a social studies textbook with the headings and underlinings he added for emphasis in his own writing structure. While Adam certainly addressed the semantic elements of a meaningful summary in this figure, he also listed "Key Points" at the bottom of the page and underlined names of characters and important points within the summary. His playful attempt to emulate the social studies text was meant to teach the others in his discussion group about what was important in this chapter. As a student in a classroom that predominantly read a textbook during social studies instruction, Adam used the organizational structure of that text as a form of academic capital to support the information he created as a summary.

## Writing and Drawing as Tools for Understanding

Allowing intermediate-aged students to create written responses using multiple modes for a variety of purposes helped students realize that writing has different functions. In the multimodal examples offered here, students used writing to mark important places in the text, visualize the story world, and to summarize reading – all critical for life in a world that continues to become more and more complex. Too often, fifth graders are expected to only write for academic reasons, showing expertise about what they understand after reading. That kind of writing too often takes on a serious form that does not include drawings or notations like the samples exemplified in this chapter extension, thereby missing opportunities for rich meaning making.

Daniels' (2002) ideas about literature discussion provided a way for Anne to support her students in using multimodal responses as a way to prepare for and enrich literature discussions. As the students read, drew, wrote, and then talked their way into meaning making, they soon realized that art and written language work together as communication processes that support complex thinking about the world. These kinds of classroom writing events are pivotal in our work to reclaim writing.

## References

Daniels, H. (2002). *Literature circles: Voice and choice in book clubs and reading groups*. Portland, ME: Stenhouse.

Ellis, D. (2000). *The breadwinner*. Toronto: Groundwood Books.

Kress, G. (2010). *Multimodality: A social semiotic approach to contemporary communication*. London: Routledge.

# 10

# SING ME A SONG OF WRITING

## Transforming the Writing Curriculum With the Help of One Child's Determination

*Jane Baskwill*

In the current climate of control and increased accountability, writing classrooms have become increasingly formulaic as teachers look for shortcuts to compact instruction in order to meet outcomes. Time for writing is being squeezed out to make way for the multitude of curriculum areas needing more time in an overcrowded instructional day. Many teachers feel they no longer have time to allow students to linger with a piece of writing, to experiment, or to pursue genres of their interest to any extent. The writing curriculum is becoming a cover-it checklist of measurable skills.

As teachers find themselves bound by a rigid curriculum and high-stakes tests, they often look to self-contained boxes and books of formulaic programs to help them cover the greatest amount of skills in the most efficient way. Disappearing is the teacher-as-writer, spontaneously exploring and experimenting along with her students. Creativity in teaching is frowned upon; standardization is encouraged.

Nevertheless, there are small exchanges between children and teachers in every classroom that beg to be examined, considered and acted upon. This chapter shares how one "critical incident" (Baskwill, 1992, p. 15) – a child's desire to write a song – transformed the writing community in an English-speaking, rural, Grade 2 classroom, and affected the teacher and her view of what is possible within an outcomes-based curriculum. This transformational process resulted in the teacher reviewing what was pedagogically possible, re-visioning the writing classroom, and reclaiming the writing curriculum.

## The Context

REANNA: But I want to write a song!

The above comment by Reanna (a pseudonym), a Grade 2 student, was in response to the writing the class was asked to do following a mini-lesson introducing the way authors begin their stories. Clearly, Reanna had another idea that she wanted to pursue.

Writers know that when they have that unshakeable urge, the persistent idea that won't go away, that itch that has to be scratched, nothing short of acting on it will satisfy them. Reanna wanted to write a song, but her timing didn't coincide with the focus of the lesson. The more Karen, her teacher, tried to steer her away from her goal, the more insistent Reanna became. Both teacher and student were frustrated:

REANNA: But I want to write a song.
KAREN: Well, maybe you can do that at recess. Right now we are working on beginnings. You remember, we looked at all those wonderful picture books and read how authors begin their stories. We shared our favorites. Remember? (Reanna nodded that she remembered.) Well, now it's your turn. Think about how you want to begin your story and ...
REANNA: ... I already know how I want to begin.
KAREN: Well, okay, that's good. Tell me, how do you want to begin your story?
REANNA: I want to begin with a song. (Reanna folded her arms across her chest.)

Although later Karen and I both laughed at the exchange, I recognized that these are dilemmas many teachers face (see Pierce, Chapter 8): how to teach the curriculum and yet find room for individual interests; how to report on learning outcomes when the district rubric does not address what children want to write about; how to support a student when you, yourself, know little about the genre (i.e. songwriting).

The most pressing question for Karen was what to do about Reanna. She felt they were at an impasse. Other children in the class were also asking to write songs. She wondered if she should just give in and have a songwriting day. They could write songs in their writer's notebooks, perhaps satisfying Reanna and the others. Then she could get back to what she really *needed* to teach.

At this point, Karen didn't view songwriting as a distinct form for learning and representation, and she didn't see how she could weave it into her writing program. However, Karen was an excellent teacher and it bothered her that she was unable to reach her students, especially through writing. She took great pride in her writing workshop and the learning going on. It was at this point that Karen invited me into the classroom.

Before Karen made any adjustment to her classroom writing program, we began by mapping the influences she felt had made an impact on her practice. She made a list of authors who had influenced her thinking; among them Donald Graves, Jerome Harste, Carolyn Burke, Ralph Fletcher, Joanne Portalupi, and William Zinsser. She listed teachers she had and teachers she worked with that she considered her mentors. She listed workshop leaders and conference speakers.

Karen spoke with passion about what she learned at various points in her career and how her writing program had evolved. When she returned to school for her Master's, her definition of literacy changed to include multiple literacies. It was at this point in our discussion that Karen realized her practice had slowly been moving away from her beliefs about teaching and learning. She was allowing her writing program to become more formulaic. She spoke about the Department of Education roll-outs of professional books for teachers and admitted that some were less child-centered and more skills-centered or procedure-focused. She also admitted that in an overcrowded schedule, books and modules that focused on particular skills or provided ready-to-use materials, especially in writing, made it easier for her to keep in step with the district's plan and fit everything in. She realized that instead of putting each child at the center of her instruction she had allowed her curriculum to be co-opted. She was relying more on teaching techniques, strategies, and curriculum outcomes rather than having her teaching practice be informed by the needs of the learner.

## The Songwriter's Notebook

One of the mainstays of Karen's writing program was the writer's notebook. In fact, Karen was a student of the writer's notebook and even kept one herself. In the early days of her teaching, she shared her own notebook writing with her students. She realized she wasn't doing much of this of late. Instead, she opted to use the examples in the prepackaged program. She was afraid that, if she deviated from these examples (which she felt were much more polished than hers), she wouldn't get the results she hoped for and the district demanded.

Karen's use of the writer's notebook with her students became a practice space. Once a concept or skill was taught, students tried it out in their notebooks. This resulted in the notebook becoming an assigned space, rather than an exploratory one. It lost focus and momentum and became just another school ritual. In my experience, many students and teachers have lost sight of what Ralph Fletcher says the writer's notebook is: a unique space in which to "live like a writer ... wherever you are, at any time of day" (Fletcher, 1996, p.3). Most notebooks never leave the classroom.

I like to think about the writer's notebook as something organic, a container that expands and contracts as needed, like Hermione's magic purse (Rowling, 2007). This metaphor makes me think of the multitudinous shapes and sizes writing takes and its ever-changing nature, along with the infinite number of writing ideas a notebook can hold.

Karen and I decided that revisiting the notebook was a good place to start. We gave each student a blank notebook and renamed it the *Songwriter's Notebook*. By having a designated space in which to create, reflect, and try on the songwriter's role, we moved songwriting from the margins and on to the page. It was no longer relegated to the noncurricular times of the day (i.e. recess, free time). We honored its status as an official way of knowing.

We had students divide their notebooks into three sections. The first was *Songs I Want to Write*. In this section students generated ideas they thought they might like to turn into a song, along with where the idea came from. We weren't sure if this was too difficult for Grade 2 students, but we thought it might get students thinking about collaboration. They also collected melodies they might use in the future (i.e. familiar tunes from childhood or pop songs).

The second section was *Songs-in-Progress*. Here students did their actual writing of the lyrics of their songs and for some, their own melodies. We provided music composition paper for gluing into their notebooks for this purpose.

The third section we called *Music-Full Thinking*. This was the place for reflection on the process of songwriting. We wanted to try to gain an understanding of what students like Reanna were thinking as they engaged in the songwriting process. We invited students to think like songwriters (Leland & Harste, 1994) and to capture that thinking in their notebooks.

## Music as Learning

Reanna was engaged from the moment we distributed the songwriter's notebooks. She carefully and deliberately decorated the page that signaled the start of each section. Instead of staring at a blank page, as she had been doing of late when asked to write, Karen noticed Reanna plunged right into the writing with a sense of purpose and a renewed enthusiasm.

One of her early songs was called *Treasures*, about all of the things that can be found when on a beach walk:

> *Treasures*
>
> When you walk along the shore,
> There are places to explore
> There are treasures to be found
> In the water and on the ground.
>
> Rocks and shells and other things,
> Purses, sponges, silver rings.
> Driftwood, seaweed, tidepools, too.
> Lots of treasure for me and you.

A growing body of research suggests that the musical arts are key components of cognitive processing and they can impact positively on the brain and other human systems. Brewer (1995) argues that there are three areas in which music can be effectively integrated into the classroom: (1) learning information; (2) attention, attitude and atmosphere; and (3) personal expression. When music is integrated into the education experience of children, it enhances their creative, emotional, social, and cognitive development (Bamberger, 1991; Brewer, 1995; Jensen, 2000).

The creation of musical compositions offers a pathway to the expression of personal feelings and beliefs, while also developing a student's musical intelligence (Bamberger, 1991; Gardner, 1983) through the development of the understanding of form, pitch, and rhythm. Writing songs allows students to express what they know and feel about a topic or issue (Bjorkvold, 1992) in a way that narrative may not. Reanna seemed to find a compelling vehicle through which to create, think, and compose.

## The Songwriting Workshop

Karen continued her mini-lessons during the songwriting workshops. We listed topics and skills that she taught during other genres that also applied to songwriting. Karen reflected on some of her favorites:

> I didn't realize how easy it would be to have my mini-lessons do double duty. When we talk about having great beginnings to pull the listener in, it also holds true for the reader. Poetry, fiction, non-fiction, and songwriting, have to hook the reader/listener from the opening line … Another … is the one on "wonder words" [Baskwill, 2010, p. 142] because of the direct connection to reading. As students look for words that they wonder about in their reading, I remind them to consider words their listeners/performers would want to know more about or are so wonderful someone else would want to remember them or use in their writing … And of course there's the notebook one that comes from Ralph Fletcher … It's perfect for poetry and songwriting. He says that it is important for writers to learn to "write small" [Fletcher, 1996, p.22], to notice the little things, the details. That's what songs are after all, small moments or stories!

After Karen's mini-lesson on writing small, we started to get a better picture of how Reanna envisioned her songwriting process when she wrote:

> When Mrs G. taught us about thinking about something small to write about and then told us we should stretch it out using the details, I thought about my song. I thought it was just like when you first learn to play the piano. You play each note. Then when you get good at that you add the chords. My small moment is just like the note and everything else comes along after. My small moment song is called Don't Get Your Feet Wet!

*Don't Get Your Feet Wet!*

Don't get your feet wet!
Don't get your feet wet!
Splish! Splash! Splish! Splash!

Here comes a new wave!
Here comes a new wave!
Get back! Get back!
You'll get soaking wet!
You'll get soaking wet!
Oh, no! Oh, no!
Don't get your feet wet!

Karen's classroom took on the look and feel of a songwriting workshop. Music found its way into all parts of the curriculum. Students wrote songs about math computations, social studies topics, and science themes. Karen put some of their work on the bulletin board. She filled the class library with picture books, fiction and nonfiction, related to music. She brought in a variety of sheet music and it wasn't long before children brought in items of their own: homemade instruments, songs written by parents and relatives, and books to add to the collection.

We created a learning station and provided notes and musical composition paper, along with several digital recorders. With the help of the music teacher, we borrowed some instruments, including xylophones, keyboards, and recorders. In order to handle the noise, Karen brought in a refrigerator packing box to serve as a sound studio. Students signed up to use the instruments inside the box, which helped to muffle the noise. We also introduced several computer programs that allowed students to create melodies on a keyboard and save them. This they could do anytime, as we provided them with headsets. However, it was not uncommon to hear melodies-in-progress as students sang their songs into the digital recorders or into the computer!

Throughout, we asked the students to choose their best songs and put them in a songwriter's portfolio. They could use a word processor or hand-write them, copying them from their notebooks. The students helped decide what the criteria should be for choosing songs. Reanna's list contained:

1. You like the song.
2. It is your best work or something new you tried.
3. It sounds good.
4. It makes sense.

Once a class list was agreed upon, they made portfolios out of legal-sized file folders, decorated with each student's name. A key decision the students made was to only include songs that they had conferenced on with their peers or with their teacher.

Reanna told me how the conferencing helped her with one of the songs she had chosen for her portfolio:

I was having some trouble with this one (The Tide Comes In). I already had the tune. I was going to use the Worm Song ... but I couldn't get enough words … um … and so when Jake and Nora (students) conferenced me they told me what about following the pattern I made at the beginning and do the same thing sort of each time. It was a great idea. I did that and it worked.

*The Tide Comes In*

The tide comes in,
The tide goes out,
All day long,
In and out!

The waves crash high,
The waves crash low,
All day long,
High and low!

The wind blows North,
The wind blows South,
All day long,
North and South!

The tide comes in,
The tide goes out,
All day long,
In and out!

## Music in a Collaborative Community

We wanted to provide an opportunity for students to share their writing as a community of songwriters and so we renamed the peer conference part of Karen's writers' workshop as the *Songwriter's Circle*. We invited several local songwriters into the classroom to share their songs and talk about their writing. We employed the Fishbowl strategy so students could "listen in" on the discussion the songwriters had about their songs, their process, and any connections they made among their writings. The songwriters sat in the center and the class sat surrounding them (Schlick Noe, & Johnson, 1999).

Prior to the session, Karen and I spoke with each of the songwriters and explained what we were trying to do. Each songwriter sang their song and then talked about it. Some focused on where their idea came from, others on some of the struggles they encountered with the words or the lyrics, and some talked about what they hoped would come across through their songs. We encouraged the songwriters to ask each other questions and to make comments, demonstrating a process we hoped the students would draw from during their writing conferences. We asked the students to listen carefully to the discussion and to the questions the songwriters asked each other. We had them listen to the connections the songwriters made with each other's work and what they had to say about the meaning in their songs.

Later, we asked the students to relate the songwriter's Fishbowl session to their own songwriting in their songwriter's notebook. Reanna wrote:

> I know just what Carla and Dan (two of the songwriters) were talking about when they said they worked hard to get the meaning of the song in the feeling of the song. I am writing a song about seagulls and I want the song to be kind of like you were flying. Like a seagull. Like you are in the air, flying.

> *Seagulls*

> Seagulls fly,
> In the sky.
> How I wish I was a bird.

> I would fly,
> Right on by,
> Not saying a word.

Reanna understood that in songwriting, as with any other genre, meaning is at the center. Karen realized that meaning making was not a focus on the Grade 2 writing rubric and that it ought to be. She agreed with Reanna that songwriting, too, is all about meaning.

The *Songwriter's Circle* also proved to be an excellent vehicle by which students could share their finished work. In addition to having our songwriters talk about their process with each other, we eventually encouraged connections and questions from the "audience." After a few of these, some students invited another student to sing or accompany them, depending on what they felt would work best for their song.

We also noticed that students were collaborating in other ways; not only on songs, but, in the case of two students in particular, they wanted to use Reanna's songs in a musical performance. They saw the intertextuality (Short, 1992) of Reanna's work and envisioned something beyond the songwriting experience.

## Seeing Beyond the Songwriting Workshop

In science, the class had been studying water and the environment. Prior to beginning songwriting, the class went on a beach walk. Ardra and Lee were able to connect Reanna's songs with their class experience and began writing a play that incorporated the songs as an integral part of the structure of the performance. Although Ardra and Lee were not writing songs per se, we noticed they were still thinking like songwriters when they consulted with Reanna during a songwriting workshop and commissioned a new song for their show:

ARDRA:  We need a song for this part (points to her writing in her notebook).

LEE:  Yeah, we need a garbage song. This is the part where we see all the garbage. Remember?

REANNA:  Oh, yeah, I remember. It was gross!

ARDRA:  Will you write us one?

REANNA:  I can try. Okay if I borrow a tune?

Ardra and Lee knew exactly where they needed a song and what it should be about. By linking it to a shared experience, they helped Reanna understand what they wanted. Reanna quickly had something in mind, if not words then a melody she thought would work. Reanna ultimately wrote *Clean the Ocean*, sung to the tune of *London Bridge*:

*Clean the Ocean*

Clean the ocean,
Clean the sea, clean the sea, clean the sea,
Clean the ocean, clean the sea,
Won't you come and help me?

Pick up garbage
That you find, that you find, that you find,
Pick up garbage that you find,
Won't you come and help me?

I can't do it all alone,
All alone, all alone,
I can't do it all alone,
Won't you come and help me?

As Ardra and Lee crafted their play, there were other songs they asked Reanna to write. In addition to her original four, Reanna wrote four more songs. When they were ready, the threesome shared their work during a *Songwriter's Circle*. Ardra and Lee talked about their connections to Reanna's first song, *Treasures*, and how this got them thinking about their beach walk. They talked about working with Reanna and how they worked out the order of the songs. Reanna talked about how she turned Ardra's and Lee's ideas into songs. Later, Reanna wrote about their collaboration in her notebook, describing a process in which each contributor's piece or part dissolved into one seamless piece:

It was awesome to work together talking about the story and the songs and how they fit together. I feel as if the whole thing is ours. I wrote the songs and Ardra and Lee wrote the story, but the whole thing together is all of ours, because we worked so hard together to get it just how we wanted it.

> We started out separate, but now you can't tell. If you didn't know I wrote
> the songs and they wrote the story you wouldn't be able to guess I bet.

Ardra and Lee read their narrative and Reanna sang each song at the appropriate point. When they were finished, the class applauded. Someone suggested they perform it for the parents. That was all the class needed to move the project forward. With Karen's help, the class made plans to take their show to the stage; *A Beach Walk by the Bay, a Musical* was born.

There was a lot to be organized. Committees were struck and jobs assigned. Advertisements were written for the morning announcements, notices went home, rehearsals, props and costumes decided upon, scenery designed and made, publicity and programs written. An evening performance of *A Beach Walk by the Bay, a Musical* was held for parents and friends. Reanna, Ardra, and Lee prepared a short introduction and they talked about the evolution of their collaborative effort. The performance was a great success and Karen received a lot of positive feedback from parents. Beyond the expected appreciative comments, Karen was pleased and surprised to learn that the parents recognized how much learning had taken place overall and the amount of work that had gone into the writing. There were also references to how much their children talked about their songwriting experience. What started as a way to placate one student had turned into a learning experience for students, parents, and teacher.

## Concluding Thoughts

Looking back, Karen was amazed at all the authentic writing opportunities there were throughout and the degree of engagement on the part of the students. She reclaimed her writing program as more than a set of discrete outcomes to be taught. She saw that her writing program could be the lynchpin that holds the curriculum together and allows her students to make connections to their own experience and interests. She also came to see songwriting as another way for students to show what they know about a topic or issue.

Reanna's plea, "But I want to write a song" took on new meaning for Karen. It was the "critical incident" that had "significance or meaning beyond the event itself" (Baskwill, 1992, p.15). It became the catalyst for reflection on the specific encounter (the here and now), but it also caused Karen to reflect upon her beliefs and practices, especially with respect to the writing program, the teacher she felt she had become and the teacher she wanted to be. These small moments, when viewed through the critical incident lens, allow teachers to peel back the layers of their assumptions regarding teaching and learning, and support them in reclaiming a professional teaching identity. Karen wrote in her notebook:

> I thought everything was going so smoothly with my writing program. I
> was organized and could march my students from one genre to the next,

checking off outcomes with ease. My teaching was getting sooo easy – especially my planning. And my administrator kept praising my teaching. I loved showing off my students' writing. I didn't recognize that they were all a bit formulaic. If you read one, you read them all!

In the beginning I found that Reanna was more of an annoyance than a blessing. She was getting in the way of my streamlined writing program. But Reanna was persistent and she wore me down. Thank goodness! She brought me back to a place I knew once – that of the reflective practitioner – someone who doesn't just use someone else's ideas because it's convenient. Instead, the reflective practitioner examines each idea, each tool, each professional resource, each writing event in light of her own practice and the needs of her students. Thank you, Reanna, for helping me rediscover and re-vision the writing workshop as a space that embraces multiple literacies as ways of knowing. And Reanna, now I want to write a song!

## Author's Note

A special thank you to Karen and Reanna for allowing me to share their journey.

## References

Bamberger, J. (1991). *The mind behind the musical ear: How children develop musical intelligence.* Boston, MA: Harvard University Press.

Baskwill, J. (1992). *Finding common ground: Building a dialogic community.* (Unpublished master's thesis), Mount Saint Vincent University, California.

Bjorkvold, J. (1992). *The muse within: Creativity and communication, song and play from childhood through maturity.* New York: Harper Collins.

Brewer, C. (1995). *Music and learning: Integrating music in the classroom.* Retrieved from http://www.newhorizons.org/strategies/art/brewer.htm

Fletcher, R. (1996). *A writer's notebook: Unlocking the writer within you.* New York: Avon Books.

Gardner, H. (1983). *Frames of mind: The theory of multiple intelligences.* New York: Harper and Row.

Jensen, E. (2000). *Music with the brain in mind.* Thousand Oaks, CA: Cornet Press.

Leland, C., & Harste, J. (1994). Multiple ways of knowing: Curriculum in a new key. *Language Arts, 71*(5), 337–345.

Rowling, J. K. (2007). *Harry Potter and the deathly hallows.* New York: Scholastic.

Schlick Noe, K., & Johnson, N. (1999). *Getting started with literature circles.* Norwood, MA: Christopher-Gordon.

Short, K. G. (1992). Researching intertextuality within collaborative classroom learning environments. *Linguistics and Education, 4,* 313–333.

# 10 Extension

## TRUSTING STUDENTS' VISIONS FOR A PARTICIPATORY VIDEO PROJECT

*Lenny Sanchez*

The art of composing is complex, and as Karen rediscovered from her songwriting venture, never predictable. I remember early on in my teaching career attending my first workshop by Isoke Nia, during which she delivered a moving tribute to her grandmother. She then turned her attention to the audience and requested we think about the stories that grounded our spirits and made us real. I learned an important lesson: Writing requires that we dig into, reflect on, and understand ourselves.

Unfortunately, this principle was not always easy for me to maintain in the classroom. Many times I, like Karen, became swayed by the excuses of an encumbered schedule filled with state and district mandates. I gripped even tighter onto my visions for the curriculum and classroom community. My tenacity may have resulted in a loss of student-driven choices as I preserved my own visions for classroom learning. Writing may not have been as responsive to students' ambitions as it needed to be.

Baskwill's story of Karen and her second grade champion, Reanna, offers an important reminder to remain attentive to students' ideas and concerns (in spite of our best intentions) so that students' opinions really *do* matter in the classroom. In this extension, I share how a class of third graders helped reclaim the writing curriculum during a final week of a school year by including their desire to produce participatory videos based upon multi-month inquiries in which they were engaged. Reflecting on this week-long adjustment, I came to appreciate how the students possessed an incredible (and insightful) understanding of how video compositions enabled them to dig in, reflect on, and understand their work more deeply.

## A Request for Time

A few years ago I joined a third grade classroom as the students conducted several school- and community-based projects during the year. Project topics ranged from publicizing assistance needs for displaced residents to exploring school safety problems to investigating the effects of white flight on the community. Although our conversations started in October, it was March before the class-wide inquiries gained full momentum. During this time, students generated questionnaires, photographs, interviews, posters, and flyers as they documented and researched family, peer, and other community members' experiences related to their particular issues.

At the end of that school year, the students decided they wanted to produce videos as a way to voice their concerns and generate awareness about their selected topics. They wished to shoot extemporaneous skits and documentary-like recordings of their researched locales and compose photomovies to capture short project summaries. They hoped they could share these videos with classes and community groups in order to receive additional support for their work. By the time the students first began making their films, the last few days of school were approaching, making it difficult to find time to accommodate these wishes. End-of-year assessments, school- and grade-level programs and celebrations, and other curricular goals already filled the seams of the days. The classroom teacher, Ms Harris, and I were concerned with how to honor the students' request given the week's time constraints.

In this moment of panic, I reminded myself how Ms Harris and I had organized these projects throughout the year. We faced numerous interruptions each week, yet found ways to sustain the inquiries by conceiving them as interdisciplinary endeavors informed by our reading, writing, and social studies conversations. We remained flexible in rearranging the daily schedule to accommodate ongoing group work and, when possible, invited students to work at home, over lunch periods, and after school. We characterized the projects as in-process learning engagements that extended over time rather than curriculum studies that conformed to the starts and stops of school days and weeks. Students understood their work would not be evaluated based on the merit of polished pieces alone, but on the development of their ideas, the seriousness of their work, and the impact of the work on the community. Consistent with Freire's (1970) idea that literacy and life are not separate, the third graders' reading, writing, and collaborations were a way of knowing and a way to name their world.

By stitching together the minutes available in the remaining days of school, Ms Harris and I sacrificed curricular goals such as final book discussions and semester reviews in order for students to work towards their goal of producing movies. Some students worked over lunch, others obtained parental permission to stay after school, and several volunteered their recess time. The third graders demonstrated that inquiry is an orchestration of many dimensions of learning all at once

(Berghoff, Egawa, Harste, & Hoonan, 2000) through their desire to use several types of texts (e.g. drawings, photos, surveys, notes, acting, interviews, letters, observations, scripts, books, websites, videos) to better explore their questions.

## The Park Fixers: Movie Making and Sharing

The Park Fixers, a self-titled group, was one of four inquiry groups in the classroom. They spent the last several months researching the deteriorated conditions of a neighborhood park by gathering written survey feedback on people's perspectives of the park, taking photo documentation of the equipment, investigating park structures online, and constructing blueprints for a new park. The students imagined a film might pique additional curiosity about their project, so on the third to last day of school they met for an hour to discuss how to use the video camera. The Park Fixers decided to record video clips of people cleaning the park, depictions of how to recycle the trash, and interviews of school members describing their visions for the park. The group also hoped to integrate props such as posters and signs into their films.

During the next day and a half, the group reconvened several times. In addition to filming skits and capturing documentary-like footage, the Park Fixers created a photomovie to summarize their months of work. They spent a lunch period reviewing and selecting previously taken photos, such as the team posing with their notebooks and members hanging up posters in the hallways to request help from others, researching information on the computer, and writing notes on the class chalkboard. The pictures also depicted playground equipment issues like torn swings, broken basketball hoops, a burnt walking bridge, and a graffiti-covered slide.

The Park Fixers met after school in the computer lab to produce a video with their selected photos, using audio-recorded narrations as the movie's background. They also explored sound beat websites and crafted raps to include with their movie. The following lyrics were kept in the final version:

> I am a park fixer/I am a park fixer/Fixing a park,
> For everybody in this school,
> We need some supplies/Plus some tools,
> I love my park/And so do you,
> That's right!

This video was shared the next day, the last day of school, during class presentations. The Park Fixers, along with their counterparts, presented their newly constructed digital movies with other artifacts they collected. The Park Fixer's photomovie generated a good deal of friendly laughter as classmates joked about Malik's beatboxing and teased the group about a photo taken on the monkey bars where each group member hung upside down creating a silly face. Beyond the laughs, the Park Fixers revealed important lessons they learned through this experience, and I understood more deeply how relevant the video-making project was to the students. The movies communicated each group member's genuine concerns for fixing the park as they personally identified themselves as a "park fixer" who claims, "I love my park" (as announced in the rap). The videos further showcased the group's problem-posing and problem-solving interests through their inclusion of dialogue excerpts, interviews, and sharing of park blueprints. Additionally, the movies opened up an opportunity for others to think critically. Classmates raised compelling questions about: what the Park Fixers didn't have time to do, if they invited neighborhood members to safeguard the playground, whether or not Channel 9 News should broadcast a story about the park, and what they would do if people weren't interested in taking care of a new park. Through the discussion, the classmates rose to the Park Fixers' challenge of listening to their story and giving it meaningful attention.

## Closing

Even though many roadblocks exist to students and teachers finding time in a school day to exercise their visions for what they want to learn, opportunities burst forth through unexpected requests to write songs, such as in Karen's room, or in sudden pleas to explore video making as in Ms Harris' room. Listening to students' visions for composing is an essential part of reclaiming the writing curriculum. By trusting in our students, we are more able to invest in opportunities that really *do* matter in the classroom.

## References

Berghoff, B., Egawa, K., Harste, J., & Hoonan, B. (2000). *Beyond reading and writing: Inquiry, curriculum, and multiple ways of knowing*. Urbana, IL: National Council of Teachers of English.

Freire, P. (1970). *The pedagogy of the oppressed*. New York: Continuum.

# PILLAR IV
# Language

# 11

# USING MULTIPLE LANGUAGES TO WRITE WITH PASSION AND PURPOSE

*Katie Van Sluys*

Focusing specifically on knowledge and values associated with multilingual writers and writing, this chapter examines how what young authors and their teachers value shapes the roles multiple languages play in thinking and expression in elementary classrooms. I use classroom vignettes to animate the passion and intentionality with which young writers have learned to make use of *all* of their linguistic resources as they meet the many purposes of writing as well as their visions for themselves and the world.

## Visions for Writing, Writers, and Writing Instruction

School programs and practices "impact who students become and the lives they lead ... it's only when we have identified a particular worldview or vision for the world's people that we can set about planning a curriculum that will turn this vision into reality" (Wilson, 2006, p. xiii). School practices grow from goals and visions for students, so the steps we as educators take to bring visions to life in classrooms, and what our students see as possibilities for themselves as people, and more specifically as writers, matter. It is well worth the time to pause and consider our visions for writers and the possibilities for continued *re*visioning of what we know and do with young writers. Such work is at the heart of reclaiming writing.

The connections among beliefs, theoretical orientations, and visions for what it means to write, become a writer, and teach writing have long been part of research and pedagogical conversations (Fang, 1996; McCarthey & Ro, 2011). Our visions grow from professional knowledge, experiences, and larger contexts (which include our schools, states, policies, etc.). To teach with intention means engaging in a process of studying contextual conditions, our students, and our instructional decisions to see how they measure up to our best and most current thinking. Clarifying our beliefs and reflecting on our practices is not enough; kids need to be in on thinking about what we do and why we do it.

To create shared visions, teachers with whom I collaborated engaged themselves and young people in regular thinking about why writers write, what writers create, and how and when they may choose to compose. They discussed writing in progress, engaged learners in on-going self-reflection, and shared publications while inviting writers to articulate insights gained en route (Van Sluys, 2011). This chapter focuses on multilingual writers, the decisions they made, and how their decisions reflected the visions and values of their teachers and learning contexts.

## Multilingual Writers

As educators have studied how writers live, compose, and communicate their thinking, some attention has been paid to the unique needs of writers new to English. Working with learners new to English, Fu (2003) and Franklin (1989) offer counter narratives to erroneous beliefs that oral fluency or grammatical knowledge in English must precede expression of ideas and thinking. This research challenges notions that students will be "confused" between languages, but emphasis remains on the temporary use of multiple languages. For example, writers new to English are often encouraged to draft in their first language and then translate to English, or they are encouraged to use native language words as placeholders in their writing so as not to disrupt thought processes (Buly, 2011). While potentially helpful strategies, these are only the tip of the iceberg when it comes to the many reasons writers may use distinct languages as they compose. Furthermore, what often emerges is the value of writing in one language, English. Other research related to multilingual writers learning English examines links between "errors" and linguistic knowledge in L1. Emphasis is placed on more complex understanding of the thinking that informs such "errors" so that they can be eradicated. For example, if we understand writers' uses of grammatical rules from L1 in their use of English, we can use this insight to teach writers about English language conventions. While such insight may indeed be helpful and adding conventional English to one's linguistic repertoire powerful, writing exclusively in one language is far from real practices alive in the world today. Published works showcase ways writers select just the right language(s) to share tales of lived experiences, use diverse language(s) to make characters come to life, play with the sound within and across languages, and more. If kids are encouraged to draw from their reading lives to help shape their writing lives, it only seems right to invite young writers to use their knowledge of multiple languages as writing resources, not just as stepping stones to exclusive use of English. Activity within this chapter's vignettes not only reclaim genuine, rich writing practices – it reclaims research on multilingual writers repositioning what, why, and how multiple languages can and ought to be used.

## Multiple Languages as Tools for Writing

The teachers and young writers featured in this chapter spend their days in one of four public school classrooms. Children in the classrooms ranged from first to sixth grade, and they brought to school distinct family lives, linguistic histories, experiences of school, and more. Their teachers also came to teaching with unique experiences: two of the four teachers were bilingual and fairly new to teaching during my time in their classrooms; another more experienced teacher had extensive Spanish language knowledge but was still working to see herself as fluent; and one teacher was well versed in teaching and monolingual. While distinct in ages, histories, and experiences, the teachers shared some common visions and values when it came to working with young writers. They saw writers as knowledgeable people who selected and used appropriate tools for the job. Teachers valued the use of first languages not only as a transitional tool in becoming English-dominant writers but also as tools to communicate, connect with audience, create desired effects, and develop as knowledgeable and recognized multilingual human beings. A notebook entry by Mia, a second grade writer, captures how teachers and students saw membership and activity in these classrooms. Mia wrote:

> In class we are always reading about other people's history and heritage. My parents were born in Thailand and I would love for my classmates to learn about my culture. How can I share it with them? A[nswer]: It is excellent to celebrate your identity! Express your desire to your teacher and ask for some class time to show everyone photos, and …

Teachers' visions were shared with learners in their care and visible through the texts, talk, and reflections of young writers like Mia, as well as those featured in the vignettes that follow. The snapshots from these classrooms draw from students' daily writing work (in other words, featured examples are not published or necessarily final products). While reading, remember that students' actions are intimately tied to their visions and decisions as well as the visions of those in their company (i.e. teachers, family members, friends, and so on) and that their stories offer possibilities for reclaiming language as a powerful writing tool.

## Connecting With Audience

In January, second graders in a bilingual classroom welcomed Ms Alvarez and new writing practices in their classroom. One of the first things their new teacher did was deliver a clean composition book to each child. Art supplies, scissors, and glue were spread on the front table as students took time to personalize the covers of their new notebooks as a way to share a bit about each writer in the room. This cutting, creating, and conversing was followed by many invitations to write.

Over time students made the transition from school days filled with journal prompts and copying sentences to edit from the board to making decisions and exploring new possibilities for what it means to be a writer. They grew to love their notebooks. Some reported on what they read in newspapers; others started drafting chapter books inspired by the early chapter books they were beginning to read. Some reflected on their days, and others wrote notes of apology to their teacher after a rough day with a substitute teacher. What they wrote varied; *how* they wrote also shifted according to need. These multilingual writers were learning to use their linguistic knowledge and intentional decisions to fill their notebooks and accomplish real goals reflective of shared visions they and their teacher were constructing.

Consider Carlos. As an energetic young learner who had lived most of his life speaking Spanish, he felt it was risky to write in English. He often wrote in Spanish – the language he knew best. When talk of pets began to permeate classroom life, he wanted his collection of creatures to be known. And, not all of his classmates spoke and/or could read Spanish. So, he wrote in English.

> I heve a pet and hes name is Memo he it's hes food and I have a ader turtle and they it's to much They are getting fat and a ker so much about my turtle and they are getting so big and strog.
>
> *I have a pet and his name is Memo. He eats his food and I have another turtle and they eat too much. They are getting fat and I care so much about my turtle and they are getting so big and strong.*

While Carlos's writing approximated English language conventions and indeed reflected evidence of how his first language knowledge was being brought into his writing in L2 (i.e. his use of the letter "i" to spell *eats* as the sound of the "i" in Spanish makes the "e" sound), this writing represents a time when Carlos decided to shift from the security of his first language to English so that he could reach out to friends, contribute to a collective interest in pets, and become part of the group of pet-owning classmates. His choices here were more than linguistic, they were tied to Carlos's growing vision of himself as writer and person. Claiming English as a communicative tool in his writing toolbox led Carlos to choose English (even if emergent in nature) to forge relationships, invite potential relationships, and connect with others through writing.

Carlos's classmate Dolores's writing notebook also reflected understandings of language choice, audience, and relationships. Upon receiving her writers' notebook, she and other classmates began filling the pages with the daily schedule, hearts, Hello Kitty stickers, paragraphs about their lives, lists of things they loved, facts about people and the like. Dolores consistently composed in close proximity and in the company of other girls, frequently sharing and comparing their work. When it came to writing, Dolores preferred English though she frequently spoke Spanish and often chose to read books in Spanish. In early May, when Mother's

Day drew near, a page in Dolores's notebook reflected a shift in decision making and perhaps an expanding vision of what writing was about and for. Dolores began drafting potential notes and poems for her mother. Given her audience, she drafted in Spanish.

| | |
|---|---|
| Te amo mama. | *I love you mama.* |
| Te amo tanto que quiero | *I love you so much I want* |
| Hacer como tu. Tu eres | *to be like you. You are* |
| Como una rosa y | *like a rose and* |
| mariposa. | *a butterfly.* |
| Te voy a dar un regalo para | *I am going to give you a present for* |
| eldía de los madres! | *Mother's day!* |
| | |
| Querida mama te vas a sorpren | *Dear Mom, you will be surprised* |
| der con lo que te voy a dar | *with what I am going to give* |
| en el día de las madres. | *to you on/for Mother's Day.* |
| Te quiero muchísimo. | *I love you very much.* |
| El Día De Las Madres. | *Mother's Day.* |
| Para; Tere De: Dolores | *For: Tere From: Dolores* |
| Gracias Mama. | *Thank you Mama.* |

Like Carlos, this young writer knew her audience and that, in order to harness the power/potential for writing to connect people, she needed to write in a way that would connect her and her intended audience.

## Using Language of the Experience

Across the city, Elisabeth actively used both Spanish and English when composing, but she explained her choices differently. In mid-fall of Elisabeth's first grade year, students were asked by their teacher to write about things that really happened in their lives. Using paper with lines and open space, the kids were encouraged to use pictures and words to share their lived experiences with others. Elisabeth went straight to work. She wrote about a time when her family went to see an *X-Men* movie. She decided to share this family moment in Spanish.

As members of a bilingual first grade, everyone in her classroom had varying degrees of experience in both Spanish and English, including her teacher. For Elisabeth, choosing to write in Spanish was not a decision anchored in audience; it was more personal. When talking about her writing, she simply explained, "It happened en español." She went on to clarify that the movie was in English, but the experience with her family was in Spanish; and therefore it only seemed logical to this bright, decisive writer that one should tell about a given experience in the language in which it occurred (see Figure 11.1).

**FIGURE 11.1**  Composing in the language of lived experience. [Yo y mi papa y mama van al cine para ver una pelicula de X-men.] [*Me and my dad and my mom went to the movies to see an X-men movie.*]

## Writing to Process, Think, Remember, and Reflect

A sixth grader and new immigrant from Algeria, Sara was introduced to writing notebooks in the first week of school. Being new to an English-dominant learning environment, this young Arabic and French speaker was not immediately clear on what students were doing and why. Her teacher was the one who first wrote in her notebook. She wrote a note in English that explained, to Sara's father, that writers' notebooks were places for writers to write what was on their minds in the ways writers felt most comfortable. While the contents and purpose of writing seemed clear to Sara all along, in the early days of the year, her teacher and I had to work collaboratively with Sara's father to understand the contents of her writing. Sara's writing compared life in her American schools to years of schooling in Algeria, noting physical differences, languages, and expectations for teachers and students. She wrote about her new surroundings: the fish tank, new classmates, playground life, and poetry she had read. She also wrote about class discussions and lessons, recording her understandings from talk about maps and cardinal directions.

Visual cues provided others with initial insight into Sara's visions and decisions. Interactions with family members experienced in Sara's first language and in the process of learning English themselves added insight into her thinking. And over time, Sara's skills in English developed. Her growing comfort with English enabled monolingual English speakers to better understand Sara's intentions, thought processes, visions, and decisions, as Sara often walked readers through her notebook using her emergent English and written Arabic thinking to share

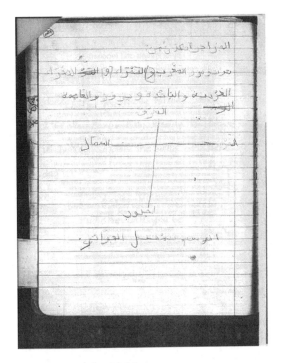

**FIGURE 11.2**   Writing as a tool for thinking.

insight into the words on the page (see Figure 11.2). Writing in Arabic, for Sara, was a way to remember, synthesize, and reflect on experiences (new, old, and projected). As Sara herself reflected in an end-of-year interview with me, "In the beginning I was quiet, I wrote down what they were talking [about], now I talk." We know writing is a tool for thinking; we need to value thinking across languages.

## Making Characters *Real*

Early in her third grade year, Celia was becoming more confident in her new school. For Celia and her classmates, everything was new – their teacher, the recently constructed building, the furniture, the books in the library, their principals, their lockers, etc. This new beginning for Celia and her multiage (eight to eleven years old) classmates meant they began the year with a diverse range of schooling experiences and diverse visions for what it meant to write and become writers as this community of young people had been assembled from many distinct school sites. With each day, they gained new insights as their teacher invited their lives and languages into the classroom. Celia, along with her classmates, grew in her confidence and intentionality when it came to writing. For Celia this meant writing regularly, sharing quietly, and always having more to say about what she'd written, why she'd written it, as well as how she'd crafted her thinking in print. She shared her thinking with me, her teachers, and classmates in conferences, table talk, and sharing time discussions. One day she decided to write about getting ready for a recent trip with her dad. Celia wrote the entry with ease and decided to use short snippets of dialogue in her piece.

> One day me and my "dad" went to a trip. We gete package to get ready to go triping but a had 40 dolors and the core of my dad dosant have ani more gaseline so we went to grabe more and I give my 10 dolors and now I gabe 30 dolors and Dad set gracias Hija por pres tarme and I sad you welcome dad and we get to there end that's.
>
> the end

> *One day me and my dad were going on a trip. We got packed and ready to go on the trip but I had 40 dollars. The car of my dad doesn't have any more gasoline so went to grab more and I give my 10 dollars and now I gave 30 dollars and Dad said gracias hija por prestarme* [thank you daughter for lend this to me] *and I said you're welcome dad and we got to there and that's the end.*

In a conference with me, Celia made visible the thinking behind the words on the page. She explained her reasoning for highlighting her decision to infuse Spanish into her English-dominant entry, noting that, "it's because my dad speaks just Spanish." As the conference continued, Celia thought aloud and eventually reasoned that characters, or real people, talk in stories just like they talk and sound in real life – which meant her father's words should be in Spanish, and her reply in English as these ways with words reflected typical interactional patterns in her family. In this case, Celia's notebook entry and conference helped her articulate an important line of thinking about dialogue as a tool for conveying character traits; this insight carried potential for shaping future writing decisions.

## Playing With Languages

The year passed quickly in Celia's third and fourth grade classroom. It was marked by many opportunities to write, to study other writers' work, and to have a go with new genres, tools, and practices. These third and fourth grade writers and their teacher engaged in the intentional study of fiction and personal narratives, they wrote alongside scientific and mathematical inquiries and learned about nonfiction, and they made initial forays into essay reading and writing. As a regular visitor to this classroom, I admired the intensity of the students' engagement. Each week when I visited, I could often sneak in unnoticed as kids went about their work writing, conferring with tablemates, and thinking with their teacher. Their conversations were serious. Their work was real.

To further envision life in this classroom, picture a mid-year table conference with a group of young essay writers, one of which was writing about the challenges of being an older sibling. While steeped in personal experience, through talk with teachers and friends, writers began to see that the support for one boy's argument was anchored in his personal experiences. However, writers at the table were convinced others shared his experiences, especially when it came to being frequently awakened in the night by younger siblings with whom they shared a bedroom. Seeking proof for their suspicion, two boys set out to collect data by surveying classmates. With clipboard in hand, they tallied the number of classmates with younger siblings and then asked about their experiences with sleepless nights. During sharing time, the boys put their data sheet on the document camera and explained how and why they had conducted a survey. As a class, they talked about how the data could be used as a tool for convincing readers of the genuine challenges and hardships associated with being an older sibling. Equipped with proof, the boys talked about their plans to use the data in their essay writing the next day and they did. Whether they were writing about the nuances of caring for a Chihuahua, family members in the armed forces, safety concerns in their neighborhoods, the earthquake in Haiti, inventing fictional characters, or conducting surveys to strengthen an essay argument, they moved about the room with clear missions and were willing to put their day's work on display on the document camera and talk to classmates about their decisions and progress. And as the end of the school year approached, poetry became popular.

The teacher introduced students to a few anthologies of poetry, including several with collections that included CD or mp3 audio recordings of poets reading their work. However, what transpired grew from the children's interests and intentions. As might be expected because of the visions of themselves that these writers had cultivated all year long, they began crafting poems in their notebooks. Not cinquains, haikus, and acrostics but poems where poets had control over rhythms, rhyme, sound, and language – poems that imitated the play with language they were hearing and seeing from poets like Nikki Grimes, Gary Soto, Kanye West, and others (Giovanni & Vergel de Dios, 2008). And soon, poems began to creep out of notebooks onto pieces of paper – some "polished," others "rough," some construction paper "framed," others on scraps that writers had composed beyond the classroom setting, using any accessible writing material. The kids decided the poetry needed a place.

While May is often a time of taking down and packing up for schools following traditional calendars, poetry was just starting up. Kids inquired where their poetry could go and asked the teacher about a bulletin board near the classroom door. Their teacher agreed the social studies display could be taken down, and they could create what they called their poetry museum. Each time they lined up to leave the classroom, they read a little. They noted new additions. They talked about contributions and often asked the poets to read their works aloud or talk about their pieces. Kids repeatedly asked Enrique to read his poem about Chocolate. It was a rather quick creation; the first stanza was in English, the second in Spanish, the third in English (see Figure 11.3).

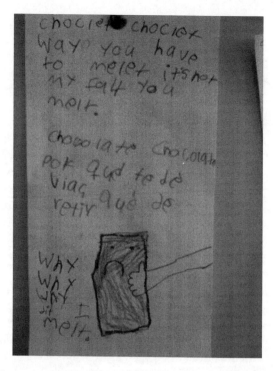

**FIGURE 11.3** Playing with languages to create rhythm and sound. [Chocolate, chocolate/Why do you have/To melt. It's not/My fault you melt./Chocolate, Chocolate/Por que te de-bías/que de-retir/Why/Why/Why/Did I/Melt.]

The more they read this poem, the more they talked about the sound of language. While the second stanza is very much an echo of the first in terms of content, the children often joined in and chanted the second stanza while moving their bodies with its rhythm and sound as the poet led the performance. Children talked with their teacher and each other about this poet's work and concluded that, in this case, the *sound* of Spanish, the rhythms of the syllables, is what made the poem memorable and entertaining. For these writers, the syllabic rhythm of Spanish became another tool they could consider using as they composed.

## Learning From These Writers' Decisions

Visions for multilingual writers in these classrooms led these educators to facilitate inquiry into and reflection on the nature and potentials for languages as writing tools. Through discovery, reflection, conferences, and intentional teaching, children learned how, why, and when writers might decide to use particular language(s) within writing tasks. They (re)claimed the languages in their lives as important tools for writing. For Carlos and Dolores, this meant making decisions based on imagined or growing relationships with the intended audience. In Carlos's case, he might not have been linguistically comfortable composing in English but was motivated by potential relationships that could follow. Dolores deviated from her regular practice of composing in English to write a message in the language of her lifelong relationship with her mother – Spanish. Elisabeth, the youngest of the writers featured, offered a simple, yet clear line of thinking regarding why writers choose particular languages. Writers sometimes decide to write in the language in which an experience occurred because writing is about composing, not translating. At first glance, Sara's moves may appear to be the opposite of Elisabeth's decisions, but Sara's choice is informed by a different line of thinking. Sara used Arabic because while she was still an emergent learner when it came to expressive English language, she was an experienced learner steeped in knowledge about the world and life. For Sara, deciding to use English would have limited what she could say about her learning and participation in class conversation and thinking (even if her participation was seemingly silent). Enrique and Celia demonstrated choices available to writers when it came to crafting their work to create just the right sounds, characters, and meanings. Their decisions reflected visions for writing where writing meant creating believable characters and using all resources to meet the purpose of a piece – be that to make readers laugh, cry, change their minds, understand others, and so on.

Writing is more than putting words on the page or screen. Print/text is what we see, but beneath the surface lies diverse processes, thinking, decisions, people, lives, identities and visions for writing, writers, and the world. Each step taken, each move made, reflects thinking and decision making on the part of the writer – thinking that is at times tacit or implicit and at other times more explicit or known. Decisions about when or why to write, what to write, and how are all decisions shaped by visions and understandings held by writers. It is our job, as educators, to help young writers see the range of possibilities and repertoire of tools, including multiple languages, to become writers who compose with intention and are able to achieve their own developing visions for themselves and the world.

## References

Buly, M. R. (2011). *English language learners in literacy workshops*. Urbana, IL: National Council of Teachers of English.

Fang, Z. (1996). A review of research on teacher beliefs and practices. *Educational Research*, *38*(1), 47–65.

Franklin, E. (1989). Encouraging and understanding the visual and written works of second language children. In P. Riggs, & V. G. Allen (Eds.), *When they don't all speak English: Integrating ESL students into the regular classroom* (pp. 77–95). Urbana, IL: National Council of Teachers of English.

Fu, D. (2003). *An island of English: Teaching ESL in Chinatown*. Portsmouth, NH: Heinemann.

Giovanni, N., & Vergel de Dios, A. (2008). *Hip hop speaks to children: A celebration of poetry with a beat*. Naperville, IL: Sourcebooks.

McCarthey, S. J., & Ro, Y. S. (2011). Approaches to writing instruction. *Pedagogies: An International Journal, 6*(4), 273–295.

Van Sluys, K. (2011). *Becoming writers in elementary classrooms: Visions and decisions.* Urbana, IL: National Council of Teachers of English.

Wilson, L. (2006). *Writing to live: How to teach writing in today's world.* Portsmouth, NH: Heinemann.

# 11 Extension

## TRANSLANGUAGING

## A Language Space for Multilinguals

*Susana Ibarra Johnson and Richard J. Meyer*

Van Sluys' research brings to light the importance of encouraging students to write with passion and purpose by reclaiming a vision that invites into the classroom multilingual students' rich and varied linguistic resources. In this extension, readers will meet Tracy as she integrates translanguaging into her classroom as a way of honoring the linguistic richness of her students.

García and Kleifgen (2010) explain the term translanguaging (Williams, as cited in Baker, 2001) as a hybrid language practice that is part of a sense-making process. Translanguaging invites multilingual students to use their full linguistic repertoires as resources for learning and serves as an identity marker of students who have innovative ways of understanding, being, and communicating. For example, code switching is a form of translanguaging in which a language user weaves in more than one language during an interaction, just as Van Sluys presented.

Tracy is a fifth grade dual-language teacher who created a translanguaging vision and space in which reading, writing, listening, and speaking overlapped as mutually informative processes. Tracy relied on her students' multiple languages to generate discussions about texts and also understandings of languages and cultures. Tracy's motivation for such discussions about texts (whether written by the students or others) was to provide a space for all students to read and subsequently write interesting pieces that drew upon their linguistic and cultural experiences. In this extension, we show the children involved in reading like writers as they made sense of an author's choice of words, enlightened by their multilingual lives. The literacy activity took the students through a study of the language and cultural elements presented in the story of *Lluvia de plata* [Silver Rain], by Sara Poot Herrera (2001). Tracy explained that, "Lluvia de plata fue una de las lecturas más interesantes para mis alumnos/as porque muchos de ellos son de Chihuahua." [*Lluvia de plata* was one of the most interesting readings for my students because many of them are from Chihuahua.] Her text selection reflected her dedication to the use of languages and texts that resonated with her students as a point of origin for studying and writing other texts.

Tracy began literature study one day by collaboratively reviewing with the class their reading of *Lluvia de plata*, a story about Mariana, a young lady that visits the Tarahumara region in Chihuahua, Mexico, and experiences a cultural and language transformation. The strategy Tracy utilized was *Cuentame algo* [Tell me a story], which began with a review of the setting of the story. Tracy created an illustrated backdrop (on a long, wide strip of paper) of *la Barranca del Cobre* [Copper Canyon] with the moon overlooking *la sierra Tarahumara* [the Tarahumara mountains], inspired by several scenes from the text. Tracy and the students relived the story with picture cards and text of the main events that the students generated the previous day. The students placed the illustrations and text onto the illustrated backdrop.

Tracy's purposes for reviewing the story with this strategy were to encourage peer interaction and discussion about the text, to study the use of language, and to consider literary elements they would use in their own writing, such as characters, setting, time, etc. As Tracy read aloud sections of *Lluvia de plata*, the students listened actively and often raised their hands or boisterously questioned or commented about the story. The excerpt below shows an exchange between Tracy and several students related to a certain scene in the story in which the students find a *phonetic* cognate expression, *si te cansas* [if you get tired], and discuss the meaning. Typically a cognate is a word that is easily identified between languages because the words are similar in look, sound, and meaning; examples include (Spanish words are in italics): *electricidad*/electricity, *ciencia*/science, and *planta*/plant. In the translanguage context of her classroom, Tracy's students discovered *phonetic* cognates, words with similar pronunciation (sounding quite alike) between Spanish and English, but with different spellings and meanings. The students related to these expressions both linguistically and culturally.

ALUMNO: *Esta parte que lee me gusta porque los trabajadores que construyeron el ferrocarril le llamaban al tren que venía de Kansas a Chihuahua 'si te cansas.' Yo creo que no sabían cómo decir Kansas entonces para recordar cómo decirlo solamente mencionaba 'si te cansas.'* [*Todos comenzaron a reírse.*]

TRACY: *¿Por qué encuentran esto chistoso?*

ALUMNO: *En mi casa nosotros usamos este tipo de palabras...*

OTROS ALUMNOS: *Si es cierto a oído algo así también en mi casa*

TRACY: *¡Muy interesante!*

[STUDENT: The part I read I liked because the workers that built the railroad would call the train coming from Kansas to Chihuahua 'if you get tired' (*si te cansa*). I think they did not know how to say Kansas so then in order to remember how to say it they would mention 'if you get tired.' (Everybody begins to laugh.)

TRACY: Why do you find this funny?

STUDENT: In my house we use these kinds of words...

OTHER STUDENTS: Yes this is true. I have heard something like this at home too.

TRACY: Very interesting!]

This example demonstrated how the language used in the story by the railroad workers had cultural and linguistic connections with the students. Tracy asked the class why they found this funny. The sense-making process of translanguaging was well articulated by one student in Tracy's classroom when he explained how the railroad workers adapted the word Kansas [/kæzðs/] to a Spanish word that was similar in pronunciation, *cansas* [/kanzás/]. Several students responded that using one language to remember the sounds of words in the other is something they heard at home. The Spanish word *gel* [pronounced "hel" in Spanish, as in hair gel] is used to remember how to pronounce the word "help." The Spanish word *flor* [flower] is used to help recall the pronunciation of the English word "floor." Many Spanish *chistes* [jokes] use these phonetic cognate words/expressions to connect Spanish and English words in a humorous way. The play-on-word jokes or *chistes* that emerge from these phonetic cognates are entertaining; however, to find words that create a *chiste* takes much linguistic and cultural knowledge – across languages and cultures. The students found the translanguage moment amusing, yet the humorous moment reflected the complexity of their understanding of language use across contexts and languages. That complexity was invited into Tracy's classroom as a strength and asset upon which her students could draw.

After this literacy activity, Susana asked Tracy if she had planned for this interesting language connection. Tracy replied, "No es algo que yo planea pero seleccione el cuento Lluvia de plata porque sabía que muchos de los estudiantes son de Chihuahua e iban a tener una conexión." [It is not something I planned but I selected *Lluvia de plata* because I knew that many of my students were from Chihuahua and they could make a connection.] This translanguaging strategy that Tracy's students came upon was due to her willingness to create a language space where multilingual students could hear and see themselves in the text and feel safe enough to experiment with, take risks in, be tentative about, and explore languages. The teachers in Van Sluys's chapter also invited their students to engage in this way as a vehicle for becoming proficient language users.

Creating a translanguaging vision demands that teachers generate and support language spaces that provide opportunities for multilingual students to use their translanguaging strategies in various educational contexts (including spontaneous settings, such as Tracy's classroom, or structured settings, as a regular part of writing workshop). The multilingual students in Van Sluys's research demonstrated that they could write with passion and purpose if given the opportunity. Creating such hybridized writing opportunities in which shared visions of the possibilities for writing are composed collectively by students and teachers is at the heart of reclaiming writing. Reclaiming a vision that uses multilingual students' linguistic resources will move us from the deficit view of *asi no se dice* [this is not how you say it] to a more positive *asi se dice* [this is how you say it] view, where both children and teachers offer a variety of ways to express ideas. This positive outlook could provide multilingual children a space in which they can draw upon their growing knowledge of the functions, intentions, and power of written languages.

## References

Baker, C. (2001). *Foundations of bilingual education and bilingualism* (3rd ed.). Clevedon, UK: Multilingual Matters.

García, O., & Kleifgen, J. A. (2010). *Educating emergent bilinguals: Policies, programs, and practices for English language learners.* New York: Teachers College Press.

Herrera, S. P. (2001). *Lluvia de plata.* New York: McGraw-Hill School Division.

# 12

# INTENTIONAL MOVES TO BUILD COMMUNITY IN WRITERS' WORKSHOP

*Amy Seely Flint and Sanjuana Rodriguez*

*My grandpa has a mother goat at his house. The mother goat had two little goats and the little goats could not walk because they were babies. If you tried to get close to the little goats, the mother goat is going to try to hit you with her head. One of the little goats became my friend. One day my grandpa got a knife and he cut the mother goat. The baby goats were sad because we ate the mother goat. The good thing was that my grandpa said that I could play with the bones. He also said that now I would be able to feed the baby goats.*

When Antonio, a first grader, finished sharing this story, I (Sanjuana) did not know how to react. Another teacher in the classroom looked at me with a horrified look on her face. I responded with one question, "What happened to the mother goat?" The six year-old replied that his family had eaten the goat. I was unsure of what to say next, so I asked the other students if they had any questions about the goats. Many hands went up and the conversation continued focused around Antonio's love for the baby goats and how excited he was to be able to play with the bones.

Antonio's story offers a way to delve deeply into the complexities and processes young children engage in to become literate beings in a multifaceted and global world. We share this story as an example of how a teacher can reclaim writing by listening to students' stories and celebrating when students write about their lives and experiences. As Antonio shared the oral version of a story he was preparing to put on paper during the first week of school, it became evident that through language (oral and written), these first graders drew upon diverse cultural and language resources, values, and networks of relationships to navigate their understandings of local communities and the world.

According to survey results from a nationwide sampling of primary grade teachers (Cutler & Graham, 2008), the majority of teachers offer a process approach (Calkins, 1994; Graves, 1983) with traditional skills. Teachers report implementing common structures of writers' workshop, such as conferencing, revising, and author shares while also emphasizing spelling, conventions, and grammar. The most common assignments include story writing, drawing a picture and writing something to go with it, writing letters, journal writing, completing worksheets, composing a personal narratives, responding to material read, and writing poems. Opportunities for taking a critical and personal perspective to the world are often missing (Kamler, 2001). Children writing about their worries, their concerns for others, and familial experiences that are unique to a particular culture are less noticeable. To address this absence and challenge the belief that writing in primary grades is mostly representational and often about personal likes (e.g. "I like ___." "I like ___." ) and retellings of classroom events ("We went ___." "We saw ___."), we highlight the work of Sanjuana Rodriguez and her first grade students, many of whom are English language learners. Moreover, we make the argument that, through an ethic of care, we are able to reclaim writing for the purposes of working "for a better world" (Bomer & Bomer, 2001).

## Writing in Sanjuana's Classroom

Sanjuana teaches in a small school district in a town dominated by carpet mills and factories in the southeastern part of the United States. Sanjuana's students often mirror the school's demographics; in this particular year, she had nineteen culturally and linguistically diverse students, seventeen of whom received ESOL services. Sanjuana's intentional moves and decisions supported children in creating a vision of writing as an avenue for change, agency, and voice. We address the consistent and protected time in the school day to write; how dialogue and sharing are essential to the process; and how everyone was viewed as a writer with something important to say. These intentional moves contributed to creating a community of writers that embraced empathy, care, and support for each other.

### Writing Every Day

Process writing researchers and educators (such as Lucy Calkins, Ralph Fletcher, and Donald Graves) talk about how important it is for children to write on a regular and consistent basis. Much like any activity, we become better at the craft when we have opportunities to engage with it every day. While this may seem simple enough, the writing curriculum is regularly shortchanged or cancelled when there are scheduling disruptions, when teachers lack confidence in their abilities to teach writing or when they do not have an understanding of what good writing looks like (National Commission on Teaching Writing in America's Schools and Colleges, 2003). These factors often lead to children having fewer opportunities to fully engage in the process (Cutler & Graham, 2008; Graham, Harris, Fink-Chorzempa, & MacArthur, 2003).

Yet, Sanjuana's first grade classroom was different. Sanjuana understood how important it was for her students to be engaged in the writing curriculum on a daily basis. She embraced the recommendations from the National Commission on Writing (2003) to double the writing time in classrooms. Sanjuana's excitement and enthusiasm for writing was extended to her students. In a reflection about writing instruction in her classroom, Sanjuana wrote:

> Despite my attempt to hide my elation, one of my favorite times of the day is when we are ending the writing workshop time. Not because writing is my least favorite part of the day, but because every day one or many of my first grade students grumbles and complains about having to end their writing time. Students plead for just one more minute to finish a piece or a page of a book. Many times, students beg me to take pieces home so that they can finish them. Early in the year, the hour set aside for writing workshop did not seem sufficient. Students saw me working before school in my classroom and asked if they could write instead of sitting in the hallway. While other teachers' students sat outside talking or playing games, my first graders were busy writing and talking about their writing before the school day even began.

The excitement that both Sanjuana and her students shared about writing was contagious as students sought opportunities to write in the cracks of the schedule – before the official school day, on the playground, and at home. The wealth of writing engagements and opportunities encouraged these children to take risks, try on new identities as writers, and discover the communicative power of writing.

## A Dialogic Classroom

Classroom literacy events and practices occur in socially situated and negotiated contexts (Barton & Hamilton, 2000; Greeno, 1998). Learning in these contexts is not characterized by knowledge acquisition or outcomes, but rather is viewed as a process of social engagement and participation (Greeno, 1997, 1998; Lave & Wenger, 1991; Pella, 2011). Children learn to formulate their inner thoughts and ideas, communicate them to others, and reflect on their learning through language (Vygotsky, 1978). For children for whom English is a second language, purposeful and authentic oral language around the writing process plays a central role in writing growth and development. As exemplified in the opening vignette, Sanjuana encouraged storytelling as an avenue for moving into more formal writing experiences. Talk permeated the writing process as children drafted and revised their pieces. Sanjuana explained:

> One of my essential beliefs about literacy learning is that oral language supports and promotes writing in the classroom. This belief comes into play when the writing workshop year begins with celebrations about students' oral stories …Oral storytelling not only lets students know that their stories are valued, but helps to build the classroom community. As a teacher, this is a time to get to know students' interests, families, and personalities. Stories are told about pets, trips to Wal-Mart, the park, and many other ideas that are seemingly commonplace. What I have come to understand, however, is that these stories about ordinary events are intimately tied to family, community, and students' sense of self. While one student tells his/her story, the rest of the class listens in and thinks about things they wonder about that they could ask. I jot notes from the students' stories and also ask questions. My goal is for students to feel safe telling their own stories and sharing how they feel with the class. Not only does the practice of oral storytelling build community, but it sets the stage for meaningful conversations about writing.

The classroom community grew as the children listened carefully for the intent of their classmates' drafts and responded in authentic ways, noting the emotions and feelings of the piece. Students' experiences were validated as they shared personal stories. The oral sharing of stories provided a foundation of safety and trust that enabled these ELL students to take risks in writing about their experiences, rather than stay with the safe "I like…" frames.

## All Students Were Writers and Storytellers

One belief apparent in Sanjuana's classrooms was the idea that all children in her classroom were writers with important ideas to communicate. Responding to each child as a writer was consistent with the idea that writing conferences are opportunities to understand the writer's intentions (Anderson, 2000; Ray, 2001). The writing conference, then, was a space where children's identities and voices became visible. In her reflection journal, Sanjuana commented:

> One of my personal goals is to respond to students' writing first as a human and then as a teacher. I assume from the very beginning that they are already writers with important contributions to make. I make connections to other authors by telling students that writers such as David Shannon wrote about things that happened in his own life. Although at first it is difficult for students to come to grips with the fact that they are writers, this is an identity that they come to embrace. They are able to share their stories about their lives that will later be drawn or written about. They begin to write for authentic reasons as we construct charts and books that we will revisit all

year. For this very same reason, I have to not give my students sentence starters such as "I like ____" or "This is my____."

Through the writing workshop and the multitude of writing engagements, students were able to construct and share their personal and social identities. These decisions of identity were based on the community, the available discourses, and personal histories (Flint & Capello, 2003).

## Creating a Community of Writers

The choices and decisions Sanjuana and her students made as they created a community of writers suggested that they understood how writing transformed their own sense of self and others. Through the varied writing events (e.g. journal writing, stories, notes, letters, and personal narratives), students made their identities visible and showed who they wanted to be in the world. As Dyson and Freedman (1991) write, "writing can be an avenue for individual expression and at the same time it can serve to construct or proclaim the individual author's membership in a social group" (p. 754).

## Taking Care of Others

Alongside the notion that learning and teaching are socially mediated events, an ethic of care responds to the inferred and expressed needs of those in the classroom. Noddings (1984) asserts that caring is an essential quality of meaningful teaching. Her definition of caring focuses beyond simple warmth and empathy; she describes care as active engagement with the learner that is responsive, motivational, and collaborative. When teachers and students engage in this relational zone, there exists a range of opportunities for intellectual growth and personal transformation (Goldstein, 1999).

As noted earlier, students in Sanjuana's class began the day by writing. While waiting in the hallway for the "official" school day to begin, students wrote stories, as well as notes or cards for classmates and others outside the class. They often wrote get-well cards for those who were sick. Sanjuana also received hundreds of cards from students ranging in topics such as "I missed you" on days when she had district meetings to "Do you love me?" cards with invitations to choose "yes" or "no." The writing and sharing of notes and cards became a private activity; they were not public documents for everyone to see. Sanjuana recounted one such experience:

> As I was getting ready for the day Alondra walked in and gave me a note. I immediately noticed drawings of different colored ice cream followed by a note asking for permission to purchase ice cream for another student. Students in first grade were able to bring money each Friday to purchase ice cream after lunch. In the mornings, students gave me the money … and

I would record who had brought money. This was in the middle of the year and students were used to this routine. I did not keep up with who did or did not bring money because this was something that they were able to purchase in addition to their lunch. What I did not know was that students in the class were aware of who did or did not bring in money to purchase ice cream. Alondra had noticed that one of her classmates had not brought in the 50¢ needed the entire year. At home, Alondra wrote me a note asking if she could give me ice cream money for herself and for another student in the class. She handed me the letter and went to her seat without speaking. After I read the note, I called Alondra over and she told me her mom had given her a dollar and told her it was okay to share with the other student. Alondra proudly watched as I wrote her name and her friend's name on the list of students who were purchasing ice cream that day. Then, she called over the other student to look at the list. As I reflect back on that school year, Alondra began a trend in the class. Students began to bring in ice cream money for two and purchase ice cream for those that had not brought money. Through her writing, Alondra demonstrated how young students use writing in a classroom community to take care of each other.

Alondra's written request invited others to consider who else may need additional support or help. Families in this community were greatly impacted by the failing economy with many facing unemployment or significant cutbacks in hours worked. For Alondra and her classmates, taking care of others signified an important step towards building a critical writing curriculum.

## Worries

Sanjuana's deliberate pedagogical decisions led to a community of writers who shared personal worries and concerns. Students regularly sought opportunities to share concerns ranging from personal interactions and friendships, to family issues and academic growth. Often students shared such experiences in whole group conversations, but there was also space in the writing curriculum to express and examine these ideas. Sanjuana regularly conferenced with students about their writing; she also read over and responded to the writing in the students' journals and notebooks on a weekly basis. This personal communication enabled students to see that their writing mattered and that their teacher evoked an ethic of care as she authentically responded.

Sometimes the children's concerns were not ones that we, as adults, worry about. Natalia exerted agency and worked to position her personal life as important, thus dealing with a very real first grade concern. Sanjuana commented:

Our class had been focusing on writing informational books on different topics. We had set a goal for everyone to publish one book to share at an authors' celebration. The authors' celebration spotlights each young author and is a time for parents, former teachers, and other students to listen and provide comments for the author on sticky notes. With the excitement of this day approaching, one student in the class worried that everyone would forget about her birthday. Natalia had expressed this concern to me and to her classmates verbally, but she wanted to make sure that we did not forget with the excitement of the publishing party. The week before the event Natalia wrote about her concerns. After she finished writing, she posted her writing outside of our room. Students in our class were able to choose what piece of writing they wanted displayed outside our room. During the authors' celebration, guests saw the pieces of informational writing that were displayed on the students' desks and outside. By writing about her concern, Natalia made sure that her worries about whether anyone would remember her birthday would be known in our community. She even went a step further by posting her writing so that everyone would see that two special events were happening in our community – the publishing party and her birthday.

Exposing vulnerability through writing is typically not a part of a writing curriculum in the early grades. Disrupting the more commonplace writing topics and assignments enabled Natalia to take a risk and share a part of herself. The thoughtful decisions that Sanjuana enacted in her classroom allowed her and her students the opportunity to reclaim writing as a powerful tool that could be used for different purposes. Through such opportunities, Natalia positioned herself and constructed an identity that invited response from others. Sanjuana's pedagogical decisions supported writers' choices in what to write and what to display, contributing to the ongoing development of a community of writers.

## Expressions

For these first graders, writing became a vehicle for expressing emotions and feelings. Sanjuana recounts how José constructed his piece to share his understandings of missing an important class event (see Figure 12.1).

The Friday before Valentine's Day as I was looking through the students' writing folders after school, I came across a book that one of the students had created. José was a student in class who had been having behavior issues at school. His behavior was getting in the way of his learning and I had talked to him several times that week about consequences if his behavior continued to disrupt the learning in our class. I mentioned he would not be able to participate in the class party and several other steps that would be taken if his behavior did not improve. The day continued and José

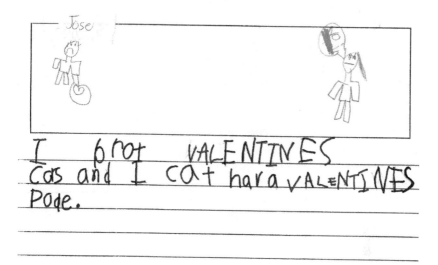

**FIGURE 12.1** Excerpt from José's book [I brought Valentine's cards and I can't have a Valentine's party.].

became quiet and worked diligently. As I conferenced with students about their writing, I noticed that he sat at his table during writing workshop and wrote the entire time, only getting up when he needed more paper. This was unusual for José; most days he used writing time as a time to talk and write, but he often struggled to finish a piece. When I saw his writing after school, I immediately knew what he had been thinking all day. José had taken some of the things that I had said to him that week and had written a book about them.

José's illustrations showed him with a sad face throughout the book. The Valentine's Day party was something that mattered to him. José's writing on that day made me realize how writing had become an important part of our class culture and how José had used writing to express his feelings. I called José's parents, shared with them what he had written, and asked them to assure him that he would participate in the class party.

The perspectives José raised in his writing reflect how important it was for him to be a part of the class celebration. Being excluded from this event was more than José had bargained for and through his writing he was able to express his emotions and feelings. Such feelings are not a part of the hurried curricular space that occupies many classrooms. Sanjuana's attention to her students' writing revealed that her students used writing to process and understand events, as well as to share feelings that may not otherwise be verbalized.

## Reclaiming Writing as a Caring Act

Sanjuana and her first graders constructed a community of practice that promoted an important, dialogic space for learning to be writers in an interconnected world. Sanjuana made pedagogical decisions and created structures that shaped the writing events in her classroom. Her intentional moves to incorporate writing every day, to support talk and storytelling in the process of writing, and to see all students as writers meant her students participated in meaningful ways. Handley, Sturdy, Fincham, and Clark (2006) explain that "participation entails a sense of belonging (or a desire to belong), mutual understanding and a 'progression' along a trajectory towards full participation which – indirectly – defines the community which is the target of 'belonging'" (p. 649).

The dialogic nature of the writing time enabled Sanjuana and her ELL students to draw upon their cultural and linguistic resources, understandings of the world, and networks of relationships. They used their social and cultural knowledge and discursive practices to form personal and collective identities of what it meant to be a writer and citizen in this classroom. They were "supported in entering new kinds of textual conversations, new sorts of dialogues with the world" (Nystrand, 2006, p. 152). The emphasis on oral storytelling and conferencing during writing time provided opportunities to use language as a tool to help students organize their thinking and as a scaffold into more sophisticated writing.

When writing went beyond a formulaic script and a limited view of what children can write about, and the students recognized what it meant to care for each other, the result was powerful. Sanjuana and her students made visible their worries and challenges, and used oral language and writing to connect to and support each other. An ethic of care transcended beyond one individual (Sanjuana) to another (a student); a community that embraced an ethic of care emerged.

Sanjuana's reflections and the students' compositions we highlighted in this chapter describe the kinds of possibilities that occurred for children when their everyday voices and experiences were welcomed in the classroom. Antonio's goat story, Alondra's request to help a classmate, Natalia's invitation to the publishing party, and José's immediate concerns of being left out suggest that these first grade students were learning to write as democratic citizens within an ethic of care. By reclaiming writing and writing instruction as more than prompts, grammar exercises, or a list of traits, the children learned to collaborate with others and to compose for the purposes of creating a community of care, compassion, and empathy.

## References

Anderson, C. (2000). *How's it going?: A practical guide to conferring with student writers.* Portsmouth, NH: Heinemann.

Barton, D., & Hamilton, M. (2000). Literacy practices. In D. Barton, M. Hamilton, & R. Ivanic (Eds.), *Situated literacies* (pp. 7–17). New York: Routledge.

Bomer, R., & Bomer, K. (2001). *For a better world: Reading and writing for social action.* Portsmouth, NH: Heinemman.

Calkins, L. M. (1994). *The art of teaching writing* (2nd ed.). Portsmouth, NH: Heinemann.

Cutler, L., & Graham, S. (2008). Primary grade writing instruction: A national survey. *Journal of Educational Psychology, 100,* 907–919.

Dyson, A. H., & Freedman, S. W. (1991). Writing. In J. Flood, J. Jensen, D. Lapp, & J. Squire (Eds.), *Handbook of research on teaching the English language arts* (pp. 754–775). New York: Macmillan.

Flint, A. S., & Capello, M. (2003). Negotiating voice and identity in classroom writing events. In C. Fairbanks, J. Worthy, B. Maloch, J. Hoffman, & D. Schallert (Eds.), *52nd Yearbook of the National Reading Conference* (pp. 181–193). Chicago, IL: National Reading Conference.

Goldstein, L. (1999). The relational zone: The role of caring relationships in the co-construction of mind. *American Educational Research Journal, 36*(3), 647–673.

Graham, S., Harris, K. R., Fink-Chorzempa, B., & MacArthur, C. (2003). Primary grade teachers' instructional adaptations for struggling writers: A national survey. *Journal of Educational Psychology, 95,* 279–292.

Graves, D. H. (1983). *Writing: Teachers and children at work.* Portsmouth, NH: Heinemann.

Greeno, J. (1997). On claims that answer the wrong questions. *Educational Researcher, 26*(1), 5–17.

Greeno, J. G. (1998). The situativity of knowing, learning, and research. *American Pyschologist, 53*(1), 5–26.

Handley, K., Sturdy, A., Fincham, R., & Clark, T. (2006). Within and beyond communities of practice: Making sense of learning through participation, identity and practice. *Journal of Management Studies, 43*(3), 641–653.

Kamler, B. (2001). *Relocating the personal: A critical writing pedagogy.* New York: SUNY Press.

Lave, J., & Wenger, E. (1991). *Situated learning: Legitimate peripheral participation.* New York: Cambridge University Press

National Commission on Teaching Writing in America's Schools and Colleges. (2003). *The neglected 'R': The need for a writing revolution.* New York: College Board.

Noddings, N. (1984). *Caring: A feminine approach to ethics and moral education.* Berkeley, CA: University of California Press.

Nystrand, M. (2006). Response to David Orson's "Oral discourse in a world of literacy." *Research in the Teaching of English, 41*(2), 160–163.

Pella, S. (2011). A situative perspective on developing writing pedagogy in a teacher professional learning community. *Teacher Education Quarterly, 38*(1), 107–125.

Ray, K. W. (2001). *The writing workshop: Working through the hard parts (and they're all hard parts).* Urbana, IL: National Council of Teachers of English.

Vygotsky, L. (1978). *Mind in society: The development of higher psychological processes.* Cambridge, MA: Harvard University Press.

# 12 Extension

## UNCOVERING CHILDREN'S EXPOSITORY WRITING WITHIN HOME AND COMMUNITY LIVES

*Charlene Klassen Endrizzi*

Purposeful yet normally untapped literacy demonstrations are present within students' homes. My class of pre-service teachers, Title I teachers, and I became aware of hundreds of written interactions occurring in kindergarten through fourth grade homes once we intentionally set out to uncover each family's nurturing role.

Through conversations at an evening family literacy gathering at New Springfield Elementary, Kelly (the mother of third grader Dino) encountered a new perspective: teachers praising and valuing families' efforts to support young writers' desire to communicate. Two weeks later, I received a letter from a Kelly describing a written conversation with her son. Kelly's letter resonates with Flint and Rodriguez's efforts to value children's home literacy lives.

> Dear Dr. Charlene Klassen Endrizzi and preservice teachers,
>     Thank you for coming and speaking with families about their role as learning partners. I now see that Dino not only learns from his teachers at school, but from me at home also…
>     The best writing experience that Dino and I have [recently] had was when I was upset with him for misbehaving. I went into my room, closed the door, and told him I would come out when he decided to behave. I was in there a couple of minutes when a note was slipped under my door. It said, "Mom, can I come in?" I wrote back, "Not until you're ready to be good!" So he wrote back, "Can Biscuit come in?" (dog) We continued to write back and forth, putting the notes under the door … I thought it was great because we were able to communicate (without yelling) …
>     Kelly (Dino 3rd grade)

Family–teacher interactions like these can be seen as acts of reclamation, when educators obtain useful demonstrations from overlooked experiences. In an educational era heavily focused on standards, teachers might overlook hidden literacies that occur naturally in children's lives outside the classroom (Rowsell, 2007; Voss, 1996). Rich, intentional writing experiences like Kelly and Dino's permeate home lives yet many remain unknown and underutilized by teachers unless we set out to discover them. Given that only 25 percent of a child's waking hours each year encompass time at school, family literacy nights can focus on uncovering writing engagements that occur quietly and naturally in the 75 percent of children's lives usually hidden from teachers' limited perspective. Our intention was to think about how Dino's current teacher could use revelations from Kelly to help shape and mold the writing curriculum in his classroom beyond a focus on covering standards-based topics identified by the Pennsylvania Department of Education.

## Family Literacy Gatherings Within Two Communities

Dino's elementary school served as the site for one of two family literacy gatherings held over two years. Both schools were situated in the rust belt of rural Pennsylvania and offered school-wide Title I programs. Frackville had a $29,000 median income and struggled to meet state testing benchmarks, and 36 percent of New Springfield families were considered low-income. Diversity prevalent in Dino's school was socioeconomic while Frackville families reflected both socio-economic and ethnic variation (70 percent African American and 30 percent White). Federal mandates require a portion of Title I funds to involve family–school partnerships, so on-going collaborations with both school administrators and several of the Title I teachers, planned family interactions focused on unmasking home literacy practices.

In addition, my recent work with undergraduates indicated they were uncertain about working with families. Therefore, family literacy gatherings offered pre- and in-service teachers an opportunity to deepen their understanding of the whole child through interactions with their first learning partners (Klassen Endrizzi, 2008). Pre-service teachers joined families to informally explore home writing experiences for the initial thirty minutes. Then children were organized into grade level groups for interactive read-alouds with quality children's literature. Some of the pre-service teachers remained with the families and classroom teachers for a conversation I facilitated.

I opened the parent–teacher brainstorming period of our evening by explaining the teachers' intention to value their children's first learning partners – families. I focused our collaborative, small group brainstorming around two questions:

1. How do you as family members write with your children away from school?
2. How do your children see you writing away from school?

Teachers feverishly recorded onto large chart paper a plethora of writing experiences relayed by family members. Later, as small groups reported back to the whole group, I was taken aback by the sheer diversity of purposeful, functional writing.

## Discoveries Across Communities

Ken Goodman's four functions of literacy (Goodman, Watson, & Burke, 1996) helped pre-service teachers and me make sense of the multiplicity of family members' intentions to communicate. We saw that each distinct writing function (environmental, recreational, occupational and informational) enabled family members to express ideas and needs for specific audiences and purposes. What follows is a fraction of the writing evidence offered by over one hundred families.

Initially we hunted for differences between communities. Frackville families offered unique evidence of writing letters to President Obama that celebrated recent national elections. We considered these to serve a recreational function in the context in which they were described. Religious texts also appeared to permeate African American community lives through several ministers' occupational writing. Financial matters rose to the forefront with Frackville families' informational writing, in part from significant unemployment levels.

Yet these differences became minor when considering commonalities. Families from both communities used environmental texts to organize shopping trips, family calendars, and children's chores. Recreational texts built connections with family and friends through cards, text messaging, and digital game systems. Occupational texts supported the workplace for farmers or small business owners (New Springfield) and health care professionals or teacher aides (Frackville). Informational texts organized financial matters for family budgets as well as for community sports and fund-raising endeavors. Rural White and African American families used an array of written texts to navigate their home and community lives.

## Utilizing Untapped Literacy Demonstrations

Looking across the four functions of literacy, we realized that expository texts dominated families' writing events outside of school. This discovery aligns with the preponderance of nonfiction texts in adults' lives. Life and workplace events necessitate intentional writing yet many teachers using a writers' workshop approach remain focused on exploring story writing (Purcell-Gates, Duke, & Martineau, 2007). Understanding Frackville and New Springfield families' rich writing lives beyond school reminded us of the need to significantly increase children's expository writing engagements.

This inquiry into real-life literacy suggests that teachers search for ways of knowing in each child's literate home in order to build a sense of connectedness across family and school literacy communities and to reveal elements potentially missing within their writing curriculum. "Our society asks that schools teach children to be literate, but values only certain literacies and remains uncertain of how to develop others, leading to the irony that our diverse society does not know how to value and celebrate diversity" (Voss, 1996, p. 188).

As our class considered avenues for reclaiming these families' writing experiences outside of school, Brett, a pre-service teacher, wrote in his written reflection about the work with families. "[Frackville] families experience an abundance of writing ... This removes many myths about people who live on the poverty line." As pre-service teachers personally connected with families, they uncovered common literacy ground. Another pre-service teacher, Andrea, wrote about the usefulness of uncovering connections between teachers' and children's home literate lives. "I learned that [Frackville] families are really no different than my family. The parents had a real concern regarding their children's learning at home, [demonstrated] by exposing them to such things as cards, grocery lists, Sunday school lessons, money orders." I believe that as teachers recognize the need to uncover an abundance of life-centered writing experiences similar to Dino's, family demonstrations can lead us down curricular avenues for reclaiming and utilizing each family's distinct literacy resources.

## References

Goodman, Y. M., Watson, D. J., & Burke, C. L. (1996). *Reading strategies: Focus on comprehension* (2nd ed.). Katonah, NY: Richard C Owen.

Klassen Endrizzi, C. (2008). *Becoming teammates: Teachers and families as literacy partners.* Urbana, IL: National Council of Teachers of English.

Purcell-Gates, V., Duke, N. K. & Martineau, J. A. (2007). Learning to read and write genre-specific text: Roles of authentic experience and explicit teaching. *Reading Research Quarterly, 42*(1), 8–15.

Rowsell, J. (2007). *Family literacy experiences: Creating reading and writing opportunities that support classroom learning.* Markham, Ontario: Pembroke.

Voss, M. (1996). *Hidden literacies: Children learning at home and school.* Portsmouth, NH: Heinemann.

# 13

## "LEARNING HOW TO MEAN"

### Writing and Gardening in Two Urban Schools

*Patricia Paugh, Mary Moran, and Geoff Rose*

> Language is a potential: it is what the speaker can do … hence the description of language as a "meaning potential" (Halliday, 1978, pp. 27–28)

In this chapter, readers meet two urban teachers who believe that for learning to be meaningful it must connect to "doing something." These two teachers created classroom gardens on mostly asphalt schoolyards. While gardening, their students simultaneously explored academic language. In their instruction, the teachers encouraged students' active learning while also pushing them beyond their comfort zones as academic writers. The featured classrooms were in two urban US schools directly dealing with high-stakes testing pressures and their district's growing political investment in *Race to the Top* era restructuring (United States Department of Education, 2009). Both teachers, co-authors of this chapter, retained a moral imperative that building literacy proficiency only happens when curriculum "matters" to students. Their writing instruction reclaimed what Halliday (1978) describes above as the "meaning potential" in language. Basically they expected that children invest in school literacy because that literacy holds meaning for their lives. This commitment involved helping their students see the relationship between academic skills and social purpose. However, under pressure to improve test scores, writing in their schools was often limited to practicing with test-like prompts, leaving little room for students' own choices and purposes.

Both teachers wanted to provide student writers with "choice and voice" while also counteracting negative messages fostered in schools that were publicly displayed as "failing." Gardening offered an opportunity for students to participate in positive community building, and provided a context for language and content learning. Geoff worked with fourth and fifth graders to plan and create a school garden as part of a unit on science literacy. Mary created a school garden with her third grade students. She also engaged them in a local urban farming project where gardens cultivated on vacant lots supported a community farmers' market.

## Theory Can Be Practical: Connecting Meaning With Academic Success

Michael Halliday's (1975) theory relating language and meaning is known as Systemic Functional Linguistics (SFL) and posits that all language works within a context. That is, no text holds meaning outside of use. SFL theory supports teaching about how language works (Macken-Horarik, Love, & Unsworth, 2011) in classrooms where literacy is considered a social practice not simply a set of skills to be learned. Keeping language visible in all aspects of the curriculum supports a sense in children that learning language is really "learning how to mean" (Halliday, 1975). Mary and Geoff enhanced their already student-centered writing instruction using this theory so that students simultaneously learned language, while learning about language, and learning through language (see Knapp & Watkins, 2005).

In order to begin teaching student writers how texts "worked," both teachers reclaimed two related ideas: (1) the language arts are a set of integrated processes that include speaking, listening, reading and writing, and (2) content and literacy learning are interdependent. In a district where curriculum was targeted toward demonstration of skill proficiency (i.e. test performance), reading, writing, and science were taught separately. The garden projects provided the contexts for integration. For example, Geoff and his colleagues chose the poem, *The Rose that Grew from Concrete*, by Tupac Shakur (1999) to introduce the gardening unit. While this poem was not intended to teach an audience how to garden, its author, a hip-hop artist, provided a metaphor about a plant growing where none expected it to thrive, a powerful message for the fourth and fifth graders battling negative perceptions about their "failing" school.

Before writing, both teachers engaged their students as text analysts to unpack how authors choose language to achieve specific goals. Two related aspects of SFL theory, *genre* and *register*, provided linguistic information through which they were able to focus this process and offered students a range of language choices they would use as writers. The first aspect is *genre*. In SFL theory, genres are defined as expected patterns of language recognized within a cultural context and serving a specific social function or purpose (Derewianka & Jones, 2010). The genre features of written texts differ depending on their intended purpose. In order to succeed in school, students need to use a range of language forms and features found in academic culture. These include: *story genres* such as narratives and recounts; *information genres* such as procedures, descriptive reports, and explanations; and *persuasive genres* that include arguments and essays (Derewianka, 1990). Both teachers assembled sets of multigenre texts about gardening and plant growth for group read-aloud/discussions and also made them available for independent exploration prior to writing. As they initiated their unit, Geoff realized that the focus of the school writing curriculum was exclusively a single genre, the personal narrative, because this was the format of the fourth grade state writing prompt and consequently the type of writing emphasized on the district practice prompts. Therefore, they purposefully included informational as well as narratives in the sets of texts they assembled.

For example, Geoff engaged his class in creating posters about the language features of both fictional narratives and informational books. His first round of questions was very general: "Is it fiction or non-fiction?"; "What do you notice about the language?"; "What plant vocabulary do you notice?"; "How do other features, such as illustrations, diagrams, or charts help you understand ideas about plant growth?" Students broke into pairs and created posters to address the questions. One poster about the nonfiction book *Plant Life Cycles* (Delta Education, 2010) contained items such as "Genre = Non-fiction" and "The book has paragraphs, subtitles, diagrams and graphs." Several facts about plants were shared such as, "The seed has three main parts: the embryo, stored food and a seed coat." Also the poster reproduced a diagram of a bean seed with labels including vocabulary such as "embryo," "seed food," and "seed coat." Comparing language features across different text genres introduced students to text features beyond those found in personal narratives.

The next entry point for text analysis was the SFL construct of *register*. Register is the deeper structure of a text that is specific to the situations in which it is used. Register helped the classes to dig deeper and consider how three dimensions or layers of language, *field*, *tenor*, and *mode*, are used by an author to achieve her purpose (Derewianka & Jones, 2010). The *field* can be addressed by considering the question: "Who is doing what to whom under what circumstances?" Geoff and Mary used this question to direct students' discovery of how the grammar of a text worked. For example, Geoff engaged his students in a comparison of the informational text mentioned above, *Plant Life Cycles*, with a fictional narrative, *The Ugly Vegetables* (Lin, 1999) about a Vietnamese American family garden. He asked students to offer "what they noticed" about the differences in these two picture books and charted students' responses. In the narrative, the students noticed that drawings were used rather than "real life pictures" found in the informational book. They also noticed that "characters with names" and "dialogue" were distinct to the fictional narrative while "scientific words and details" were found in the latter. When Simran (all student names are pseudonyms) asked, "Why isn't the [informational language] in the past tense?" Geoff recorded her observation and prompted students to explore how past tense allowed the author to show "what happened" in the narrative, contrasted with the informational book where the author used present tense to deliver factual information that is timeless (Paugh, Abbate-Vaughn, & Rose, 2012). In this way, Geoff was teaching verbs and verb tense but directing students to the idea of how each functioned differently to achieve a desired purpose.

A second function of register is *tenor* or how the exchange of information in a text reflects a relationship between the author and the reader (Derewianka & Jones, 2010). Mary frequently asked students to notice the language on seed packets used in planting, comparing tenor differences within a single text (Paugh & Moran, 2013). An example is a student's annotation of a sunflower packet based on a class discussion (see Figure 13.1).

She wrote that the author offered a "sales pitch" based on an excerpt that begins, "This stunning variety produces outstanding ... blossoms." Mary's students considered how tenor was communicated through the use of descriptive adjectives. The adjectives "invited" readers to imagine how sunflowers would look in the garden. In contrast, more direct language was found lower on the page, where command verbs "directed" the reader about how to plant and nurture the seeds. Students noticed how language affected the tenor; first the author posed as a friend inviting the reader to buy. Later, the author was an expert teaching the reader how to plant.

A third aspect of SFL text register is *mode*. Mode involves asking, "Does the author organize the language in the text so it is cohesive and coherent? How does the text 'hang together'?" (Paugh & Moran, 2013, p. 255). For example, in a set of instructions (a procedure), the organization includes a goal, a set of materials, and a sequence of steps to be followed, which may also include supportive diagrams or illustrations. Another type of multimodal text is a website that includes digital channels such as animation, video and/or sound in addition to print (Macken-Horarik, Love, & Unsworth, 2011). The seed packet used print and diagrams to communicate with the reader.

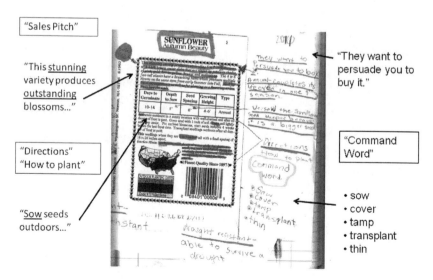

**FIGURE 13.1** Seed packet annotation.

## Exploration as an Entry Point for Meaningful Writing

Mary and Geoff provided both choice and direction as the students planned writing projects for the garden units. The teachers invited students to play with language (Williams, 2000). That is, students had social spaces to first explore and try out specific plant-related language with their peers before attempting more formal, academic writing. Geoff's classroom offered a rich environment for students' language exploration as they researched what they were learning in the garden. He reserved the school's laptop cart to enable access to both print and digital texts. He noted, "for a very visual generation, it was helpful for them to start with a picture that they found online and then use the picture to communicate their ideas" (Paugh, Abbate-Vaughn, & Rose, 2012, p. 123). Students were charged with creating group presentations about plant growth for an audience of peers. They chose from a list: "PowerPoint presentation, non-fiction book, realistic fiction book, labeled diagram with 'how to' descriptions, picture strip (like a cartoon) with pictures and captions, or a descriptive summary with paragraphs." The assignment sheet included the prompt, "HOW??? ... It is up to YOU!!! Your choices might include the following or if you have another creative idea, write up a plan, and persuade your teacher why it is good!" (Paugh, Abbate-Vaughn, & Rose, 2012, p. 119). Several children took this to heart, proposing to design two- and three-dimensional posters, while most worked in teams creating PowerPoint slides. Visiting the classroom, Pat noticed students gathered around laptops. Eva and Skyla shared their slide show, "How a Seed Grows into a Plant," compiled from Internet searches as well as observational activities Geoff organized for the garden. The slides included: several diagrams (e.g. parts of a plant, the cycles of photosynthesis, and germination with definitions of both processes), a vocabulary list, a sequence of steps explaining "how a plant grows," and finally keeping their personal touch visible, an elaborately decorated "authors'" slide which included a graphic of a rose with a heart. The girls' attention to academic language, in the form of connector words used to build sequence, emerged in this excerpt from their conversation with Pat as they pointed out the sequence of steps in their "how a plant grows" slide:

> SKYLA: [advancing the slide] We have how a plant grows ...
> PAT: Oh, so is this sort of how they grow?
> EVA: [pointing] ... and it is sort of a step by step ...
> PAT: ... and you know I'm really impressed you used step by step words ...
> SKYLA: [pointing] ... first, then, after, so ...
> PAT: ... yes, those are really important so when I read that it helps me go in order ...

Presenting to peers challenged them to communicate both organizational and technical vocabulary in meaningful ways. Students had the space in these projects to explore organizational language, such as the connector words above, and technical language. Javier and Marco's slide show entitled, "Flower Project: How a Plant Grows," contained examples that included technical words such as "germinate" and "nutrients" (italics added; original spelling):

> You don't just put a seed in a hole of soil … there is a time to put [in the seed in the spring or the summer].
>
> When the seed starts to grow it is starting to *germinate* when it begins its life cycle.
>
> Also the plant needs lots of good things like orange carcass and apple skin … also it needs worms, cows, elephant, bears and horse poop for *nutrients* so the plant can grow.

Through these peer activities, students created social bridges between everyday language and more academic forms of writing.

Mary's students were required to compose a dated notebook entry after gardening and farming activities. However, she did not dictate any forms for these entries. As a result, the notebooks reflected a range of language choices. Some students created lists of new vocabulary they found interesting. Several focused their observations on a single plant over time, measuring its height and counting the number of leaves, while others shared new information learned at the urban farming sessions, such as how to build a compost bin or harvest a carrot correctly. Jay provided a weather report ("it is sunny and the temperature is 80 degrees … it looks like a good day to go swimming"), leading into "rules" for weeding/picking the carrot and followed by a recount ("we picked carrots") with an illustration (see Figure 13.2).

Halina shared what she learned about pollination:

> Pollination is very important. It leads to the creation of new seeds that grow up into new plants. Pollination is the transfer of pollen from the stamen to the stigma. When bees, butterflys [sic] and others visit the flower they are looking for the sweet nectar made at the base of the pedals [sic]. They accidently rub against the pollen on the stamen and move it to the stigma.

In addition, Halina taped samples of a flower, stem, and leaf directly onto the page. Jama's entry featured playful anime-like drawings that accompanied her reports on farming activities. Like Eva's and Skyla's heart graphic, Jama's figures created a personal "signature" to claim ownership of her learning.

## Meaningful Choices as Entry Points for Academic Writing

Language exploration created spaces where students developed independence by asking and answering their own questions. Elements of SFL theory provided a

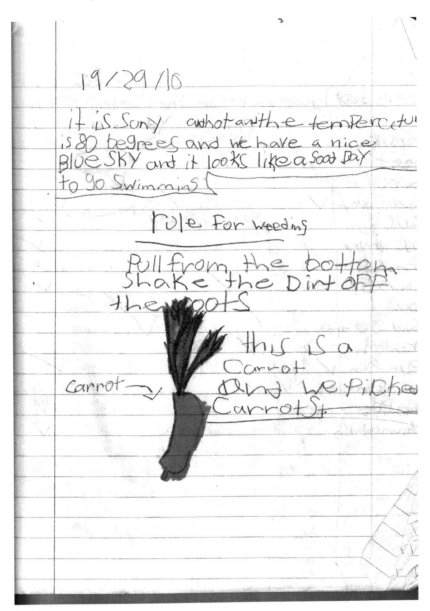

FIGURE 13.2 Jay's notebook page.

bridge that helped them craft with more academic language. Focusing on *genre*, Geoff and Mary encouraged students to first consider purposes for writing and then they offered instruction in language forms that helped achieve these. For example, Mary asked students, "What final project could we create using our gardening reading, research, experience, and notes?" Some expressed a desire to share their excitement about gardening with upcoming third graders. Others wanted to teach how to plant seeds or create compost bins. From this feedback Mary chose to explicitly teach two genres: *recount* ("write about what interesting events happened during the gardening project") and *procedure* (instructions/directions on "how to do" some gardening). Mary invited students to "pick a purpose." Then, based on the classroom discussions about specific *register* features to fit the genre, the class collaboratively developed writing rubrics. For example, Mary asked students, "If you are going write a recount of what happened, what would readers need to know first?" She guided students through discussion of a flow of meaning beginning with an orientation, followed by a sequence of events, and a concluding statement. The class also brainstormed "action verbs" and time sequence "signal" connectors that help an author recount a "doing" experience such as gardening. Below is a transcription of a class-developed rubric for writing a recount charted by the class (SFL register features were added for this chapter):

> Rubric for writing a recount
> A *recount* is writing to describe and tell about your experiences. [Tenor]
> Orientation that tells about: who, what, when, why, and how are included. [Field/Mode]
> Important events are in chronological order and supporting information and details are provided. [Mode]
> A recount ends with a concluding statement. Wrap it up. Let your readers know how you felt about this experience. [Tenor/Mode]
> *Action Verbs*: dig, water, germinate, planted, blooming, sprout, absorb, grow, cycle, dying. [Field]
> *Signal words*: first, next, then, when, afterwards, later, after, lastly, suddenly, beginning, middle, end, night, finish, morning, evening, before, secondly, third, day, afternoon, earlier. [Field]

Geoff also offered students a choice for a more formal writing project. His students decided on writing either a set of instructions (a procedure) about planting or a report on what they had learned about plant growth. Both teachers developed writing rubrics for procedural, recount and/or report writing in dialogue with their students.

For Mary and Geoff, SFL provided linguistic knowledge for guiding students toward effectively communicating the "purpose" in a situation. Grasping SFL as a theory was initially a challenge as both had little experience with introducing deeper levels of grammar into their student-centered writing workshops. They were used to more generalized writing rubrics, such as the Six Trait plus one rubric (Fang & Wang, 2011) to guide their instruction and feedback. The teachers found that embedding ideas from the SFL framework into classroom discussions provided specific criteria that enriched the generalized writing guidelines already in place. At one point Mary laughingly exclaimed, "Oh, it's a theory!"

The gist of her comment was that a theory of language encouraged her to reclaim her own professional voice as the designer of her writing instruction, as opposed to the rigid prescriptions or test-centric writing prompts that dominated the curriculum in the school environment.

## What Did Students Learn?

Mary found that negotiating rubrics around purpose retained students' ownership and voice while also expanding their repertoires of language choices. As an example, Mario's recount, with his original spelling and punctuation preserved, is transcribed below:

> Story of Our Lettuce by Mario
> I'm going to teel you how fun it was planting the lettuce.
> On April 26, 2011 my class and I read the package to the lettuce. It took my class 15 or 20 min to read it because we had to figer out what every thing means. Then on April 27, 2011 my class and I planted the lettuce seeds it was fun. First we made two rows out of string in the bed. Next each person made 1 hole to put their seeds in. The seeds take 10 to 14 days to germinate but ours took 5 days. I was surprised about that. That day we put the 400 pounds of top soil from Mrs. Moran's car, then my class and I spreaded the top soil around after we got the watering bukets and watered the seeds. Today it is June 7th and this is an update on our lettuce. They look like they came right out of the store. When I see them they make me want to eat them. It was really fun planting lettuce. I was thinking that it will be hard but it was easy. I hope you have fun when you plant lettuce and I hope you enjoyed my story.

Mario used the class's rubric to include features of a recount to tell what happened when the class planted lettuce. He developed his account through a series of events. He used past tense and built the time sequence using dates as well as connectors such as "then," "one day," and "after that." At the same time, his natural voice is clearly present. For example, "The seeds take 10 to 14 days to germinate but ours took 5 days. I was surprised at that." His language fits his intention to attract the reader to the pleasure of the gardening project through his unique perspective.

At the end of Geoff's unit, he and Pat evaluated students' growth as informational writers. Pre- and post-experience prompts asked, "How does a plant grow?" Certain patterns emerged in the class. For example, focusing on field, the use of *generalized participants* (rather than specifically named familiar persons or things) and the use *of technical vocabulary* showed more than a point gain on a three-point rubric. In terms of field and mode, *logical organization, consistent use of tense*, and *choice of relational and active (vs. thinking or feeling) verbs* showed an average gain of approximately a half point. What this indicates is that writers, who previously had written only personal narratives at school, could distinguish between personal and informational writing. This addresses an important expansion of language choices for Geoff's students. For example, in her pre-experience writing sample Eva wrote, "A plant grows by having soil and then adding your seed." We compared this with a sentence from her post-experience writing which illustrates a general pattern among the students, "While a plant is growing the roots go down to get nutrients and the stem shoots up to catch sunlight." Eva's example provides a sense of how students on the whole became more aware of consistent use of person (first to third for factual writing), and began to include more technical nouns and verbs, more technical uses of everyday language (nutrients, stem, shoots, sunlight) and more compact information so distant readers can understand the message (use of prepositional phrases to elaborate on actions of roots and stems).

## Conclusion

In their urban district, Mary and Geoff faced daunting challenges teaching in an environment where high-stakes testing defined the instructional practices their school community. They explored Halliday's SFL theory to support explicit teaching of the academic language necessary for school success while retaining a commitment to development of student voice and agency. Their experiences show that academic accountability can be addressed without sacrificing responsive, student-centered instruction. As Derewianka and Jones (2010) explain, when "teachers make aspects of the text explicit to students, the criteria for success can be shared" (p. 13). Through their instruction, Geoff and Mary provide insights for teachers who wish to reclaim their own agency as knowledgeable and professional decision-makers while achieving the same for their students.

## References

Delta Education LLC (2010). *Plant life cycles*. Retrieved from: http://www.deltaeducation. com/downloads/teacher_guide/1278152_DSCR_TG_PlantCycles.pdf

Derewianka, B. (1990). *Exploring how texts work*. Newtown, Australia: Primary English Teaching Association.

Derewianka, B., & Jones, P. (2010). From traditional grammar to functional grammar: Bridging the divide. *NALDIC Quarterly, 8*(1), 6–17.

Fang, Z., & Wang, Z. (2011). Beyond rubrics: Using functional language analysis to evaluate student writing. *Australian Journal of Language and Literacy, 34*(2), 147–165.

Halliday, M. A. K. (1975). *Learning how to mean: Explorations in the development of language*. London, UK: Edward Arnold.

Halliday, M. A. K. (1978). *Language as social semiotic: The social interpretation of language and meaning*. Baltimore: University Park Press.

Knapp, P., & Watkins, M. (2005). *Genre, text, grammar: Technologies for teaching and assessing writing*. Sydney: University of New South Wales Press.

Lin, G. (1999). *The ugly vegetables*. Cambridge, MA: Charlesbridge.

Macken-Horarik, M., Love, K., & Unsworth, L. (2011). A grammatics 'good enough' for school English in the 21st century: Four challenges in realizing the potential. *Australian Journal of Language and Literacy*, *34*(1), 9–23.

Paugh, P., Abbate-Vaughn, J., & Rose, G. (2012). Flexible, reciprocal and on-site research: Developing praxis that productively challenges all participants in a US urban school community. In T. Kress, C. Malott, & B. Porfilio (Eds.), *Challenging status quo retrenchment: New directions in qualitative research* (pp. 105–127). Charlotte, NC: Information Age Publishing.

Paugh, P., & Moran, M. (2013). Growing language awareness in the classroom garden. *Language Arts*, *90*(4), 253–267.

Shakur, T. (1999). *The rose that grew from concrete*. New York: Simon and Schuster.

United States Department of Education (2009). *Race to the top executive summary*. Washington, DC: US Department of Education.

Williams, G. (2000). Children's literature, children, and uses of language description. In L. Unsworth (Ed.), *Researching language in schools and communities* (pp. 111–129). London: Continuum.

# 13 Extension

## "SO MY GRANDPA KNOWS WHAT WAY TO DRIVE THE TRACTOR"

### Children Engage Rural Ways of Knowing

*Lori Norton-Meier*

### A Beautiful Day for Investigating

> This is a great day to be a scientist! Two weeks of thinking and building stuff! We finally get to go outside and TEST the weather like REAL weather people! What's that saying? One small step for second grade, one big jump for all people (Anthony, eight years old; all names are pseudonyms).

In the previous chapter, Paugh, Moran, and Rose illuminated learning how to mean in two urban classrooms. Anthony, quoted above, lives in a rural poverty area of the Midwest United States. In this classroom vignette, we will see how the notion of "place" impacts the way students engage with language, writing, and thinking.

Ms Ellingson's nineteen second grade students were abuzz as they prepared their weather experiments. For the last two weeks they worked diligently to create anemometers – a tool to measure the wind. They knew all about "thermometers" and wondered if they could create a similar instrument to measure the wind. During their weather unit, they focused on the conceptual idea, "Weather impacts the way we live our daily lives." Through discussions, the students decided it would help if they knew how strong the wind was – for knowing how to dress, if they could play ball outside, or if the wind would whistle through the windows during reading time. Each student created a design on paper and used consumables (paper plates, cups, yarn, pencils, foam, straws and other art supplies) to create something for measuring wind. Finally, the students were ready to go outside to gather data with their own anemometers.

## Where's the Wind?

The children emerged from the school and quickly set up their wind devices on the large area of green grass. When the children were ready, the teacher declared, "Okay, I have the timer set ... one minute begins ... now!"

Nothing.

Silence.

No movement.

"What's going on?" Ashlyn asked, "Where's the wind?"

"Maybe we need to go over there, over by the cement (pointing). I think the grass is blocking the wind!" Jeremiah wondered. The other second graders agreed so they moved to the cement. Once again, they waited. Watch. Nothing.

Amanda exclaimed, "All that work for this? Where is the WIND?"

And with that, little Elijah exclaimed, "HOLD IT!"

He stuck his finger in his mouth, licked it, and pointed it high in the air. "Yep, I feel it, the wind is there! It's coming!" The others followed his lead and did the same thing agreeing that there was wind.

Ms Ellingson appeared discouraged. She called the students over asking questions, "Elijah, tell us what you are doing ... why does licking your finger and poking it in the air tell us that there is wind out here today?"

"Well, when you do that, if there is wind, you feel a little tickle on the wet part of your finger ... that tickle is WIND."

Ms Ellingson rubbed her forehead. "And, how do you know that?"

"Well, that's what my grandpa does so he knows what way to drive the tractor!"

"And you think that is important?"

"YEAH, because if he drives it the wrong way in the wind, the dirt blows away or right back in his face. That is not good farming."

Showing frustration, Ms Ellingson said, "So, are you telling me that instead of spending the last two weeks creating these anemometers all we needed to do was lick our fingers and stick them in the air?"

Elijah tilted his head to one side, "Well, that would be silly to measure the weather with just your finger. My finger tells me there is wind out here and where it is coming from but I don't know how hard it is coming so we still need an anemometer for that."

Jeremiah added, "Yep, and think how much smarter Eli's grandpa will be about farming if he knows more about the wind."

Sarah said, "Yeah, I think we better find a way to tell the farmers about our wind anemometers so they will know there is something to use other than just a tickle on your finger."

Elijah interjected, "We have to learn how to measure the wind or my grandpa won't know what way to drive the tractor! We need to get back to work RIGHT NOW!"

With that, the students went back to their investigating and when they returned to the classroom, decided to make a brochure to market their anemometer wind tools to the farmers.

## Engaging Rural Ways of Knowing

I can't begin to tell you how frustrated I was by this whole anemometer fiasco today! All I could see playing out before my eyes was our small rural Podunk Midwest farm town "redneck" mentality playing out before my eyes. I want them to think like <u>scientists</u>. I want them to question what they know and think in different ways to solve problems. And guess what, THEY DID JUST THAT! They reminded me today that THEY control learning. I had this beautiful lesson all laid out in my head. There it is … it was in MY head, not theirs. It was not the way they needed to negotiate and make sense of the old way of thinking – like a rural farm kid – and new ways – like a scientist. In my frustration, they ignored me and kept on talking together putting together rural know-how and the science … and the thinking was truly great. What if I would have shut that all down by yelling, "licking your finger is NOT science." I am not certain who learned more today – them or me. (Ms Ellingson; email reflection after the lesson, emphasis in the original).

Ms Ellingson participated in a three-year professional development research study working with twenty-eight early elementary (K-3 grade) teachers to integrate science inquiry and literacy practices. The anemometer vignette represented a pivotal language moment in this classroom described through the learning cycle processes of perceiving, ideating, and presenting (Goodman, 2003). The children began by *perceiving* there was an issue or a problem leading to the creation of a concept map about weather and developing a question board. This led to the important question they asked about how to measure the wind and *ideating* by making plans for their own wind tool, drawing out plans on paper, trying it out, and redesigning their tool. After interviewing a meteorologist, they learned that an anemometer is the name for a tool to measure wind. In the final stage, they *presented* their learning in the form of a brochure informing farmers of a new tool they had available to help know what way to drive their tractors.

Interestingly, this perceive–ideate–present learning cycle also applied to Ms Ellingson in this vignette. She perceived a problem or issue with her planned lesson – her students were coming at their anemometer experience from what she perceived as a "wrong direction." She ideated by exploring their thinking through questioning and, finally, in her email presented a critical review of her own thinking – originally that rural ways of knowing would be a detriment to her students and actually realizing that they were essential to their process of "learning how to mean" (Halliday, 1975), giving them time to negotiate their rural funds of knowledge (González, Moll, & Amanti, 2005) with new scientific understanding.

## New Questions

In developing understanding related to the role of place-conscious learning in writing classrooms (Brooke, 2003), several important questions emerge. First, how are conceptualizations of rural ways of knowing influenced by popular culture and what is constructed by "redneck" thinking? It is imperative that we recognize these stereotypes are damaging and affect the way we engage students. Second, why is it that rural spaces are not researched in the way we approach urban spaces, particularly the effect of rural spaces on language and writing? Finally, Ms Ellingson draws our attention to a key question: Are rural ways of knowing so embedded in the teacher's way of knowing that it is not recognized and thus, not taken up in classrooms? To reclaim writing, we recognize being from different places and ways of knowing (as in Rose and Moran's urban classrooms and Ms Ellingson's rural second grade classroom) actually adds a richness and complexity to our thinking that could lead to the creative problem-solving necessary to approach the challenges of the future.

## References

Brooke, R. (2003). *Rural voices: Place-conscious education and the teaching of writing*. New York: Teacher College Press.

González, N., Moll, L. C., & Amanti, C. (Eds.). (2005). *Funds of knowledge: Theorizing practices in households, communities, and classrooms*. Mahwah, NJ: Lawrence Erlbaum.

Goodman, Y. M. (2003). *Valuing language study: Inquiry into language for elementary and middle schools*. Urbana, IL: National Council of Teachers of English.

Halliday, M. A. K. (1975). *Learning how to mean: Explorations in the development of language*. London,: Edward Arnold.

# PILLAR V
# Sociocultural Contexts

# 14

# PRODUCING CULTURAL IMAGINARIES IN THE PLAYSHOP

*Karen Wohlwend and Carmen Liliana Medina*

In this chapter, we consider play and drama as more than pleasurable pastimes or enrichment activities but as core literacies for critical cultural production that enable children to explore who they are expected to be in a global world. Using this lens, we examine how play enables children to engage in *cultural imaginaries* in the multiple spaces they encounter at home, at school, on television, in the mall, on the Internet, on the phone, or across international communities. We use the term *cultural imaginaries* (Medina & Wohlwend, 2014) to describe collective visions of idealized communities, constructed through shared imagination rather than located in a specific physical geographical location (Anderson, 1991; Appardurai, 1996). Within these imaginaries, we write and play ways of being through the stories we tell, the films we watch, and the books we read, but also, through the media we play and the products we use. For example, media imaginaries circulate scripts for fantasy worlds in animated films or for melodramas in television programs that are distributed globally and replayed locally among children who enact and embody those worlds. But cultural imaginaries are not limited to media portrayals of fictional scripts; they include our idealized models of real places, whether schools, neighborhoods, communities, or countries. In our literacy research in early childhood and elementary classrooms, we found children playing in transnational imaginaries, trying out cultural repertoires handed down across generations and continents as they pretended to be in distant places where children had never lived but that they knew through family stories, picture books, photo albums and television texts.

Here we look specifically at the ways children collaborate to imagine together in pretend play in a kindergarten classroom in Iowa and in dramatic productions in elementary classrooms in Puerto Rico. Karen studied how play and writing developed among children who have transnational connections to China and

Iowa while they "played school." In Puerto Rico, Carmen studied children's dramatizations of telenovelas, a Latino television genre that features melodramatic series, sometimes compared to soap operas. In our research at these sites, we teamed with teachers who worked intentionally to bring in children's cultural repertoires and literacy resources through play and dramatization. In both places, we found play and dramatic performances provided ways of improvising scripts and performing identities that have rich potential for reclaiming writing.

Resituating play in relation to writing opens possibilities to expand writing workshops beyond a focus on honing an author's craft or producing individual child-made books; rather, it focuses on collective cultural production through what we call a *playshop*. Playshop is a curricular approach that recognizes play as a literacy that produces cultural texts and a tactic for reimagining cultural contexts (Wohlwend, 2011). By making drama and pretend play central to literacy instruction, playshops encourage children to imagine familiar cultural spaces into the classroom and make diverse literacy practices available for enactment. This approach moves beyond allowing popular media into school as a way of providing interesting topics. Playshop is a more fluid model that moves within and across spaces and imaginaries, moves that require children to negotiate and to improvise ways of belonging in these worlds. Further, in the playshop, all literacies merge together: neither reading, writing, designing, nor playing is privileged over the other. This is not play in the service of writing but assemblages of literacies in moment-to-moment interactions.

In many classrooms, writing is individualistic, with each writer held accountable and expected to fit into mainstream norms for writing measured by rubrics of traits on standardized assessments. In contrast, playshop builds upon dramatic play and performance that require on-going co-operation among players who work together to create and maintain a pretend situation (Corsaro, 2003; Sawyer, 2003). During pretense, all the players contribute to the emerging script with ideas openly under construction as children work together to keep the play going. Their collaborative imaginings rewrite the meanings of a chair that becomes a throne, a pencil that becomes a sword, a classmate who becomes a queen, and so on. Such rewriting facility can produce a contested and transformative space, dense with opportunities for children to improvise and productively use power. In this chapter we ask: "How do children use play and performance in playshops to reclaim writing and themselves as writers in and out of cultural imaginaries?"

## "My China": Playing School in a Transnational Imaginary

In this section, Karen shares classroom excerpts from children's pretend play in a kindergarten in a K-6 public school in Iowa. Anna, an experienced teacher, provided a play-based literacy curriculum and worked to establish an atmosphere of mutual respect and learner independence. She intended to provide an "accepting, peaceful" atmosphere where children could actively participate and feel "comfortable and safe." In a typical morning meeting, Anna welcomed the class, explained her planned activities, and adjusted the day's agenda displayed on a large pocket chart to include activities that children suggested. These plans structured the day into segments: shared reading of big books and poetry charts followed by three consecutive 45-minute activity periods that mingled play and children's self-directed reading, writing, and drawing.

This playshop supported a transnational imaginary, "My China," for a Chinese international child who wrote in English and Chinese as she played school. Min was one of three girls in this class who had transnational histories with China and the United States with important similarities and variations in their relationships to these spaces. All three girls attended the same extracurricular Chinese language school on Saturdays and were learning to letter pictograph characters. The girls spoke English at school, and said they could speak Chinese, although they rarely demonstrated this. At school, the girls imagined "My China," a shared transnational imaginary that drew in their parents' and grandparents' desires to transmit Chinese values and their own experiences in Chinese school. This shared imagining created an affinity group, a regular play group of children who share a common play interest.

Individual desires, family histories, and cultural resources created important differences in the ways that each girl interacted with "My China" as a transnational imaginary. Michelle and Lily are Chinese–American students whose mothers had grown up in China. Lily was born in the United States and Michelle was born in China. Both girls' parents and grandparents stressed their desire to honor and transmit Chinese culture through cooking, language, literacy, and arts. Anna regularly invited parents to school to share their funds of knowledge (González, Moll, & Amanti, 2005) and for one week, Michelle's mother came to class several days to teach papermaking to the kindergartners. Michelle's mother characterized papermaking as a Chinese invention and tradition and helped the children to create their own sheets of personalized art paper. At school, Michelle and Min often drew, wrote, colored, or made Japanese origami crafts.

Min is the daughter of two international graduate students who plan to return to China in a few years. For Min, the Chinese language extracurricular school that all three girls attended was a link to her future classmates and imagined school in China. Min's parents were concerned about Min's preparation for Chinese schooling. Min approached school with a seriousness that stood out in this playful kindergarten. During play periods when other children pounded playdough or played house, Min pulled Chinese books or worksheets from her backpack. In this reversal of homework, Min used classroom play periods to get a head start on her Chinese lessons. When Anna noticed Min's skill in Chinese calligraphy and Japanese origami, she set up a play center where Min could teach other children. These art-based literacy activities eventually enabled Min to join a boys-only play group who focused on paper-airplane folding. Min's writing and drawing provided a space to strengthen her personal connection and to share the cultural imaginary "My China."

One day, Min used markers to draw two red houses with roofs that curved upward at the eaves. She used pencil to write Chinese characters along the bottom margins and drew flowers and overlapping five-pointed stars around the houses. When Anna came by, she knelt next to Min momentarily and asked about the drawing. Min dictated "houses in China" and Anna recorded it as a caption (see the left side, Figure 14.1).

On another page, Min drew with crayons to make a serpentine blue river running from the top to the bottom of the page. One the riverbanks, she drew green grass with barely visible Chinese characters running vertically in green crayon. On the right bank, she penciled in a Chinese character. On the river a stick figure sailed a small boat at the top; in the middle, two triangles (looking like a small lamp) sat in the center of the river, and near the bottom, a large fish, a jellyfish, and another form that looked like a bubble letter backward R (see right side, Figure 14.1).

After Anna moved on to the next table, another child (who had her own transnational history with Sudan) looked over at Min's open journal and commented, "China, let me tell ya, let me tell ya, you know why I don't love China because – I don't know, I don't have a, I don't have *their* China." The children continued to talk about places as if they were personally owned. Min answered, "Well, I love my China." She pointed to places in the river that ran down the center of the page. "There and there and there. I'm going to make rain."

Anna worried that Min was filling her journal with Chinese writing and completing her homework during play periods; Min also could not be persuaded to share her work during sharing sessions in front of the class. Anna's concerns reflected her awareness of Min's vulnerability within the school culture, shaped by federal accountability policies with a deficit orientation to English Language Learners. Although Min's interest in repetitive practice of Chinese characters seemed to align with a skills mastery discourse and its focus on practice of discrete literacy tasks, testing, and measurable academic achievement, school district policies were based upon assumptions of monolingual (English) language and literacy skills. Additionally, in Anna's playful classroom, Min's preference for completing pages in her Chinese workbook as seatwork rather than engaging in group play activities sparked further concerns. A widespread play ethos (Smith, 1988; Sutton-Smith, 1997) in early childhood education (Roskos & Christie, 2001) constructs paper and pencil worksheet activities as "developmentally inappropriate" (Bredekamp, 1987). Paradoxically in Min's case, this developmental discourse also supports children's right to choose and direct their own play. When layered onto a classroom ethic of tolerance, inclusion, and respect for families' diverse cultural values, Min's choice to work alone and to seemingly eschew play with other children posed a complex problem for Anna: how to bring Min into the play activity of the peer culture while respecting her authorial intent to set and meet her own writing goals? Further, Min's desire to work on Chinese penmanship exercises aligned with her parents' goals for her and drew in important cultural resources.

**FIGURE 14.1** Min's "Houses in China" and "My China".

However, Anna's literacy curriculum was a playshop where play helped children reclaim writing. Using a culturally responsive approach integral to playshop, Anna used pretend play to integrate Min's desire to complete her Chinese homework and her family's value of a print-oriented model of literacy focused on correct copying. With this goal in mind, she offered Min an opportunity to play teacher, "to teach Chinese numbers to the other kids" and Min responded immediately by telling Anna all about her Chinese language lessons. Anna often collaborated with children to imagine a play school space within the classroom, and now she set up a table as a play center with a student acting as the pretend teacher. Other children could choose to join in the pretense to play students. This teaching strategy was learner-led and interest-driven, a good match with developmentally appropriate discourse. It also aligned with Anna's goals of partnering with parents and building on familial areas of expertise as a way to make children's cultural resources present and visible in the classroom. Accordingly, Anna announced during the next morning meeting that Min would be at a special play center during choice time to help children write numbers using Chinese characters. When Michelle heard the announcement, she cheered and held out her arms to embrace Min.

Michelle and Min were the first to sign up for this new center. Once at the table, Min drew practice grids on blank sheets of paper and demonstrated how to write each character stroke by stroke (see Figure 14.2). Michelle insisted that she already knew how to write the numbers because her grandmother had taught her. Min's "Chinese Writing" play center ran for several weeks and was so successful that Anna followed up a month later with another of Min's strengths: origami. She placed a how-to book and color copies of its pages in this play center and Michelle and Min worked on other independent origami projects regularly throughout the year, occasionally joined by their friend Lily. The girls' shared interest in paper folding strengthened their play group bond as well as their connection to China as an imagined participatory space. It offered classroom cultural capital when it became a valued design skill among members of another (all-male, all-White) affinity group that needed paper folding skills to make paper airplanes. Important to add, given the high-stakes testing environment, all the children in this fairly typical kindergarten met the school district benchmarks for writing and reading at the end of the school year. Additionally, due to the power of playshop to bring a cultural imaginary into the classroom, the children enacted inclusive ways of playing and ways of accessing and exploring transnational literacy resources and identities.

## Boys Playing *Barrio en la calle*: A Media Imaginary

*Barrio en la calle* [Barrio in the street] was a telenovela that was composed and performed by one group of third graders in an urban classroom in Puerto Rico. Telenovelas are melodramatic shows that in some ways resemble soap operas but with unique characteristics that respond more to Latino/a idiosyncrasies. They are

**FIGURE 14.2** Min's number practice sheets.

described as the most popular television genre among Latino/a viewers across Latin America and the United States (Joyce, 2008; McAnany & La Pastina, 1994) and are increasingly popular around the world (Werner, 2006).

Carmen and her colleague, María del Rocío Costa, from the University of Puerto Rico, Bayamón, worked with a local teacher in the development of a critical literacy inquiry curriculum grounded in students' out-of-school interests. The teacher, Maestra Vivian, worked hard to develop a critical and dynamic literature-based writers' workshop. Vivian's views of writing processes were grounded in her students' everyday experiences, including "playing" with genres within and beyond the school expectations.

In the project described here, students were invited to select from a wide repertoire of choices such as video games, television shows, movies, etc. to develop a critical literacy experience integrating dramatic inquiry, reading, writing, and media. When telenovelas were mentioned, one group of third graders decided almost unanimously to work on this kind of television show. In the dramatic inquiry that followed, the students analyzed, designed, and performed telenovelas. They brought rich knowledge of this genre and demonstrated an awareness of how the social words and interactions are constructed within the fictional worlds of telenovelas but also how these representations resemble (many times in very stereotypical ways) everyday lifestyles and issues that relate to power, gender, race, and the glorification of materialistic lifestyles. Their interpretations and representations became topics for discussions that frequently moved from the actual content of the televisions shows into everyday realties they live in their local communities.

In the devising and production of their telenovelas, the students brought multiple worlds that fit within the structures of telenovelas but also remade those in quite playful ways. Elements of irony, the creation of catchy titles, the mixing of genres, and the places they selected as settings were part of the elements that the students foregrounded as they authored and produced their work. The students did not limit their creative work to the worlds of the telenovelas as they knew them; they relocated and recontextualized their stories through the inclusion of a multiplicity of other semiotic resources and worlds. The telenovela *Barrio en la calle* was devised by a group of boys who were interested in hip-hop culture. In Puerto Rico, hip-hop is a popular global music genre and *reggeatón*, which mixes Puerto Rican, Caribbean, and hip-hop styles, has become nationally and internationally popular.

In the inquiries, the students devised their ideas, wrote scripts, and performed their telenovelas. At the point when they had finished the first drafts of their scripts, Carmen and Maria created a dramatic inquiry event by entering the room in the role of telenovela producers and asked each team's writers to present their telenovelas by explaining:

• Why should we (the producers) consider their telenovela for production?
• What makes an excellent telenovela?
• How might the audience respond to their work?

The students interacted with Carmen and Maria in role and shared the highest qualities of their telenovelas. The adults used the space to get familiar with the students' conceptualization of ideas in their production work and to suggest revisions.

One interesting interaction happened when the students presented *Barrio en la calle*. Carmen and Maria's initial thought when they heard the title was that the students' telenovela dealt with the theme of homelessness. Carmen and Maria were "lost in locations" and, because they immediately jumped to the conclusion that it was about homelessness, they had a difficult time following the students' proposed story line. In the students' frustration with Carmen and Maria they explained: "Porque no es un deambulante. Es que esta en la calle. Alguien que todo el tiempo esta en la calle y despues cuando va a acostarse va a la casa." [Because he is not a homeless person. It's that he is on the streets. Someone who spends all the time on the streets and when he goes to sleep goes to his home.] In this moment, the students borrowed from the spatial and cultural resources of hip-hop culture and re-presented it as new knowledge in their telenovela's design. The genre of telenovelas served as a space that brought the cultural imaginary of the street into the classroom and the possibility of the teacher and researchers to learn from the students.

A close look at the multiple versions of the students' telenovela makes visible the multiple layers of meaning making they negotiated. The initial version was written

**FIGURE 14.3** Original text for telenovela.

in a graffiti style, a transnational or globalized form of writing that has acquired popularity in Puerto Rico and is visible in the streets. The students' letter design in Figure 14.3 hints at and guides the reader to the notion of *la calle* [the street], signaling the urban hip-hop cultural imaginary that is at the core of their telenovela. Similar to the design of telenovela titles, the composition of the title provides the viewer an entire visual experience where shape and context references matter.

The interesting aspect, though, is that on the second draft of the telenovela, in Figure 14.4, the text is transformed more into a script that resembles the traditional representation of the genre of script writing. Whereas the first version was more situated in a stronger representation of *la calle*, the second revised version became a hybrid text that shows the students' negotiation of formats of the "street" and the classroom structures of writing.

In addition to the title and the graffiti style, the students chose characters to construct *la calle*. In the first draft they told a simple story about "The Game" and "T.I." who are friends. The Game falls in love with a girl and they get married. The Game stays alone for awhile and T.I. eventually dies. The Game eventually marries but he is not quite sure if he marries for money or love. The Game and T.I. are hip-hop artists whose artistic work speaks of their experiences living in urban centers. More

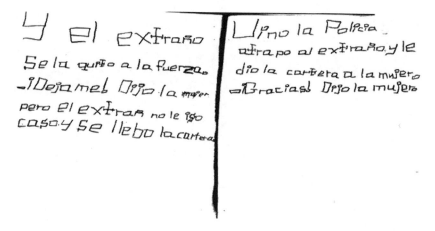

**FIGURE 14.4** Revised text for telenovela.

specifically T.I., who is a real music artist, producer, and author of the book *Power and Beauty: A Love Story of Life in the Streets* (T. I. & Ritz, 2011), centers his work as grounded in the streets. From a sociocultural perspective the students' telenovela story line showed their playfulness with the text, and they portrayed characters that are aligned to a larger urban hip-hop imaginary than was part of the composition with the graffiti writing. In their second draft, they wrote a more elaborate plot but they lost the characters T.I. and The Game. The main characters became *la joven/el joven* [the young woman/the young man] and *el esposo/la esposa* [the husband/the wife]. The story was also resituated as happening in San Juan where *la esposa* and *el esposo* go for a walk and get robbed, which made for another interesting perspective on relocalizations and the emergence of new cultural imaginaries.

In the first year of this project, playfulness focused on cultural production foregrounded the complex ways children lived in this world. Opening the classroom to an inquiry exploration of a television genre such as telenovelas created a space to make visible the overlapping ways children engaged in and with cultural production, and the playful ways they remixed and redefined the limits of any texts.

In the second year, Carmen and Maria deliberately created a new model of a literacy workshop that integrated the multiple worlds students navigate culturally. For example, instead of a writer's workshop Carmen and Maria constructed a possible vision for a playshop (for a detailed description of the second-year curricular process, see Medina, Costa & Soto, 2013,). The students brought action figures to the third grade classroom, played, and created texts with them. They were also invited to think beyond the classroom to a cultural imaginary and expanded ways of selecting topics. One interesting case that helped us reaffirm a space for youth and classroom culture was the hip-hop/*reggaetón* text created by Marcos entitled *El salon loco* [The crazy classroom], a story in which the *reggaetón* artists Jowell and Randy visit the classroom and sing their hit "Loco" [Crazy] about falling in love with a beautiful woman.

These perspectives allowed for the possibility for the teacher and university collaborators to learn from the students and to embrace the new hybrid worlds they presented. Furthermore, in their playful ways of constructing scripts and producing their telenovelas, hip-hop references, and hip-hop texts, the students created assemblages of literacies; writing in the classroom overlapped popular culture literacies and performance of particular lifestyles.

In a playshop perspective on cultural production and overlapping imaginaries, it becomes significant to pay attention to composition details across drafts, across literacies and across worlds. In the playshop, where composition works in relation to other forms of representation (writing, performance, embodied, visual images), it is significant to look at cultural and social production as a critical element of any authoring process.

## Conclusion

When we compared the two playshops, we saw several elements that are unique to this curricular approach. First, teachers and children negotiated the playshops, but their content came from children's cultural resources, whether writing Chinese letters or graffiti-inspired texts, playing school, or performing telenovelas. Second, playshops were imagined spaces but were also here-and-now exercises in collaboration and communication to produce shared scripts and sustain imagined contexts. Through playshops, children:

- accessed familiar cultural spaces to make diverse literacy resources available (e.g. popular drama, music, and art genres and scripts; multilingual writing forms);
- negotiated and improvised ways of belonging across multiple spaces (e.g. school and home);
- combined literacies to enact cultural imaginaries in ways that stretched classroom practices.

Today's schoolchildren need to be experts at collaborating, inventing, and producing texts together. The notion of cultural imaginaries, accessed through play and drama and actively and collaboratively invented, promises to be a powerful way to reclaim writing by forging new links between the classroom and worlds that originate in lived experiences, worlds that are populated by familiar characters and structured by deep attachments and connections among our individual and collective imaginations.

# References

Anderson, B. (1991). *Imagined communities: Reflections on the origin of nationalism* (2nd ed.). New York: Verso.

Appadurai, A. (1996). *Modernity at large: Cultural dimensions of globalization.* Minneapolis: University of Minnesota Press.

Bredekamp, S. (1987). *Developmentally appropriate practice in early childhood programs serving children from birth through age 8.* Washington, DC: National Association for the Education of Young Children.

Corsaro, W. A. (2003). *We're friends right? Inside kids' culture.* Washington, DC: Joseph Henry Press.

Costa, M. del R., Medina, C. L., & Soto, N. (2013). *Abrir la puerta: La escritura a travs de un lente diferente* [Opening the door: Writing through a different lens]. Cuaderno de Investigacin en la Educacin, University of Puerto Rico.

González, N., Moll, L., & Amanti, C. (2005). *Funds of knowledge.* Mahwah: Erlbaum.

Joyce, S. (2008). Telenovelas consumerism as empowerment. *Paper presented at the annual meeting of the NCA 94th Annual Convention*, November 23, 2008, San Diego, California.

McAnany, E., & La Pastina, A. C. (1994). Telenovelas audiences: A review and methodological critique of Latin American research. *Communication Research, 21*(6), 828–849.

Medina, C. L., & Wohlwend, K. E. (2014). *Literacy, play, and globalization: Critical and cultural performances in children's converging imaginaries.* New York: Routledge.

Roskos, K. A., & Christie, J. F. (2001). Examining the play–literacy interface: A critical review and future directions. *Journal of Early Childhood Literacy, 1*(1), 59–89.

Sawyer, R. K. (2003). Levels of analysis in pretend play discourse: Metacommunication in conversational routines. In D. E. Lytle (Ed.), *Play and educational theory and practice* (pp. 137–157). Westport, CT: Praeger.

Smith, P. K. (1988). Children's play and its role in early development: A reevaluation of the "Play Ethos." In A. D. Pellegrini (Ed.), *Psychological bases for early education* (pp. 207–226). Chichester, UK: Wiley.

Sutton-Smith, B. (1997). *The ambiguity of play.* Cambridge, MA: Harvard University Press.

T. I. & Ritz, D. (2011). *Power and beauty: A love story of life on the street.* New York: William Morrow.

Werner, J. F. (2006). How women are using television to domesticate globalization: A case study on the reception and consumption of telenovelas in Senegal. *Visual Anthropology, 19*, 443–472.

Wohlwend, K. E. (2011). *Playing their way into literacies: Reading, writing, and belonging in the early childhood classroom.* New York: Teachers College Press.

# 14 Extension

## THE GIRLS GO TO THE '70S AND THE '80S

## Self-Produced Videos and Play

*Chuck Jurich and Richard J. Meyer*

Wohlwend and Medina use the term *cultural imaginaries* to explain the ways in which writers work collectively to imagine, play at, and compose stories as they invent themselves and the spaces in which those stories may unfold. Chuck has sponsored an after-school video club for fourth and fifth graders for the past five years. In this unique and safe playshop environment, students played, experimented with roles and positions, and watched themselves perform on screen. We'll describe two student-made videos that depict the children's interpretations of life in the 1970s and the 1980s and analyze how they collaboratively experimented with representation, identity, and temporality in invented digital spaces.

In the video club, students made a wide variety of videos, from large productions involving an extensive cast and crew ("official" videos) to small, often one-shot clips made by an individual or a pair of students ("unofficial" videos). Large productions were done using a three-stage process (pre-production, production, and post-production) similar to how major motion pictures are made. In all of the downtime, students made a great number of unofficial videos – short, spontaneous, collaborative pieces for seemingly no other audience than themselves. Like the adults in the preceding chapter, the adults in the video club were considered "producers" who provided assistance in getting official videos completed. Unofficial videos were clearly "self-produced," as adults played no role in their making. They were marked by improvisation and a focus on humor and/or action. Unofficial videos had limited value, we thought, because they wouldn't be shown at the premier night. They weren't real but instead "play," which we respected as educators, but had not yet come to appreciate as an expression of the children's cultural resources. Students made no attempt to control background noises, sets were imagined or completely ignored, and editing was nonexistent. Regardless, these videos were very common and the students loved to make and watch them.

Framing unofficial videos as forums for cultural imaginaries within the play-shop legitimizes them. Through the use of props, language, camera filters and effects, and acting, the students presented and created idealized models of moments in time. An old telephone initiated the creation of a call-in show; a wig turned a young boy into an old man and his voice changed accordingly. A pair of glasses transformed the children into nerds, old ladies, or cool kids. In each case, the students collectively constructed the cultural context.

## Two Girls in the 1970s and 1980s

Sylvia and Rachel (pseudonyms) were close friends in the video club who often collaborated on both official and unofficial productions. They produced a number of videos, including a talk show, a newscast, a commercial, and more. Their ideas tended to initiate from props, which they transformed into cultural artifacts, and video effects that were built into the software. In these two companion pieces, the authors created what it was like in the 1970s and then the 1980s. Considering that they were both born after the year 2000, their imagining of these other eras was drawn from a variety of sources including (but not limited to) books, images, radio, TV, film, parents, and people who lived through these times.

In both videos, the girls sat in front of the computer, looked into the camera, and talked to each other. Sylvia took the leading role, introducing where they were: "So it's the 70s now, it's 1978 and I can't believe it ..." Rachel acted as her audience and sidekick, echoing what Sylvia said and interjecting funny comments in character. They talked about the "really good cupcakes" they just had, their "flat ironed" hair, how "new" the computers looked, and how the end of the world is supposed to happen in the year 2000.

They visually constructed the 1970s by tinting the image in sepia, which gave the video a vintage tone. They both parted their long hair down the middle with their foreheads prominently showing and Rachel wore oversized octagonal glasses. Despite other video club kids interacting behind them, an announcement on the intercom, and the decidedly modern computer lab, their attempt to pull off the 1970s worked because of the visual look and the lan-guage. Sylvia said, "We're here in video club and ... we're having *such a good time!*" They talked about the world like it was fun and fantastic with wonder in their voices.

The 1980s video is strikingly different, marked by an explosion of color, atti-tude, and style. To create the mood, they oversaturated the color and then slightly blurred the image, capturing the look of their understanding of video cameras from the 1980s. Compared to the subdued tone of the 1970s, the 1980s stood out strong. Hair was used as a particular signifier of the time period and they combed their hair over to one side covering one eye. They wore bright shirts that, with the color oversaturation, bordered on neon. It appeared as though they'd applied a bit of makeup to their cheeks and lips.

Unlike the first video, in the 1980s they used an additional prop, a "nerd" who they picked on and eventually kicked out of the scene. As a marker of changing styles, the nerd wore the octagonal glasses that Rachel wore in the 1970s. With a hint of Valley Girl dialect and tons of spunk, Sylvia introduced themselves: "Here we are in the '80s. It's, like, 1983 and *we're lovin' it!*" Rachel parrots, "Lovin' it!" and snarls right into the camera. They talk about "concerts," how "Tiffany" is their favorite singer, and then they sing "Head Over Heels" (Orzabal & Smith, 1985) by the band Tears for Fears, all the while playing with their hair. The 1970s was happy-go-lucky and mellow. In the 1980s, the students moved with speedy, jerky arm movements, and incessant hair flips. The children took a multimodal approach to reliably place themselves in the appropriate eras. They referenced popular culture (Dyson, 2003), such as singers and songs, as well as cultural indices ("flat ironing," slang and accents).

The two collaborators worked together to maintain the pretend situation until it inevitably fell apart. In the 1970s video, Rachel sensed a lull and actually said "cut," but Sylvia had an idea at that very moment and continued in character. Riding the new idea, Rachel went with it until that idea petered out. They concluded by asking "How does this thing work?" and the girls innocently poked at the computer, ending the recording gracefully. In the 1980s, the scenario ended more awkwardly. While playing with their hair, Sylvia noted out of character, "Look! You can see bald spots in my hair!" and Rachel replied in character, "That's horrible, you're already going bald." Another student off-screen overheard them and jutted in, "Who's going bald?" Rachel tried to save it by snottily retorting, "Who are you?" but by then other curious kids entered the screen and they stopped the recording.

## Making the Unofficial Official

One of the key elements of the unofficial videos is that the students nearly always used the cameras that were built into the computer. Those cameras offered ease of both use and monitoring. To make these unofficial videos, students clicked the record button; they could watch it immediately. Perhaps even more important is the instant feedback that they got by seeing themselves on the screen *as they were being recorded*. Prior to recording, the students rehearsed, gazing at themselves for long periods of time, making faces, posing, and trying on costumes, wigs, glasses, and hats. They were trying on identities and trying out cultural imaginaries, which they explored or discarded. These unofficial playshop spaces were where many ideas came into being, consistent with Wohlwend and Medina's ideas about how play can be understood for its literacy value. Rather than dismiss the unofficial, educators at all levels are encouraged to re-evaluate the potential of collaborative social dramatic performance in literacy development and as a vehicle for reclaiming writing.

# References

Dyson, A. H. (2003). *The brothers and sisters learn to write: Popular literacies in childhood and school cultures*. New York: Teachers College Press.

Orzabal, R., & Smith, C. (1985). Head over heels. On *Songs From the Big Chair* (CD). New York: Island/Mercury.

# 15

# DIGITAL MEDIA, CRITICAL LITERACY, AND THE EVERYDAY

## Exploring Writing in the Twenty-First Century

*Vivian Maria Vasquez, Peggy Albers, and Jerome C. Harste*

Texting, blogging, Facebooking, tweeting – today we are accessing the world of writing in ways never before imagined. Our opening image (Figure 15.1) characterizes one way of communicating that has become commonplace, texting. It is an exchange between adolescent students regarding a piece of writing they were doing together. Using software such as Google Docs, these students were even able to write synchronously from different places. Whereas once writing was confined to paper and pencil, in many of today's classrooms mini-tablets, iPads, and laptops have become commonplace and afford "anywhere" writing as represented by Figure 15.1. Some teachers today are concerned with hard drives, Wi-Fi connections, firewalls, and battery life, whereas before they were concerned with having enough writing supplies for their students. For many children today, digital technologies mediate between their everyday practices of living in a Web 2.0 world and schooled writing. We share examples of this later in this chapter where we take on the idea of "new writing" (Merchant, 2005, p.51) to describe the ways in which digital media have informed the writing practices of twenty-first-century children. While doing so we situate such writing within a critical literacy framework. We argue that in reclaiming writing, we reclaim that which is important to students – their everyday literacies and their right to use these as they tell stories, share learning, and collaborate with others through critical inquiry.

## A Brief History of Technologies and Schools

The teaching of writing has had a fairly conventional and well-documented history with initial emphases on writing legibly, spelling, and grammar. Emig's (1971) research in the composing processes of twelfth graders and Graves's (1983)

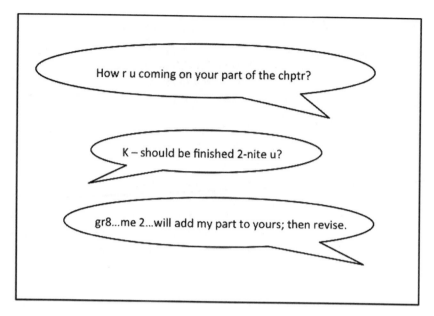

**FIGURE 15.1**  Texting between adolescent students about their writing.

work with a focus on process rather than product significantly altered the way writing was taught. The writing process took hold in many classes as an everyday practice, especially from the 1980s onwards. Teachers taught the writing process, supported assessment through on-going work in portfolios, and children learned about writing through mini-lessons, peer conferencing, and on-going revisions. Writing was often confined to classrooms, focused on written language (as opposed to broader definitions of composing, as in dance, art, etc.), and students used conventional tools like pencils, paper, and typewriters.

Fast forward. In their US Department of Education study, Gray, Thomas, and Lewis (2010) found that across all public school teachers, 97 percent had one or more computers in their classroom every day and 54 percent could bring computers into the classroom. Nearly all computers were connected to the Internet, with an average ratio of between five to six students per computer. Teachers reported that students sometimes or often used educational technology to learn or practice basic skills, prepare written texts, and conduct research. Unlike in the past, however, students were now using technology to create or use graphics or visual displays, correspond with others, contribute to blogs or wikis, develop and present multimedia presentations, and create art, music, movies, or webcasts that can be made accessible to a global audience.

We highlight the history of educational technology to further punctuate that the invention of new technologies has significantly informed new writing, resulting in making easier our older practices.

## Theorizing Digital Practices

As critical literacy scholars and teacher educators, one of our aims is to engage teachers in critical readings and viewings of the world. Now that our world is highly wired and connected and largely multimediated (Doering, Beach, & O'Brien, 2007), we place importance on teachers' awareness and understanding of reading and analyzing a range of multimodal texts in order to help their own students become critical writers of the world. We situate our thinking in theories of literacy as a set of social practices, especially those that have been shaped by digital technologies. Lankshear and Knobel (2006) argue that digital technologies do not just allow us to technologize our existing practice, they create spaces for us to move beyond where we are now to allow for greater participation, collaboration, and distribution of knowledge – to do things that were not possible with our previous level of technology. With increased participation in such practices, argues Janks (2010), must come a set of critical practices. Our identities shape and are shaped by what counts as knowledge, who constructs and who receives this knowledge, and how this knowledge is communicated. Communication is no longer confined to print-based literacy, but includes all representational modes (e.g. art, music, spatial, etc.), how they act on us, how we interact with them, and how they position us to take on identities we may wish (or not) to take on (Vasquez, Albers, & Harste, 2010). What this means is that we must create opportunities for teachers to:

- frame curriculum with digital technologies in mind, bridging the digital knowledge and experiences students bring to the classroom;
- study how modes operate in digitally composed and produced texts, and the messages conveyed;
- design composing engagements that encourage students to be critically aware of the messages conveyed in the digital choices they make;
- become critically aware of their own personal beliefs, and how these beliefs shape their communicative practices and the extent to which they include digital technologies; and
- encourage curricular engagements that have the potential to move students into social action in which their transformed beliefs are communicated to world-wide audiences using new literacies and various tools of technology.

## Digital Media, Critical Literacy and the Everyday

As educators and active participants in Web 2.0, we are instructionally positioned to ask, "How do we put in place a new set of technology-fused social practices to support more thoughtful and critically reflective students and teachers especially in light of digital technologies?" In this section, we talk about our own uses of digital technology and describe digital projects that we have designed. We believe that to best understand how to create spaces for the use of digital tools, one must, in some way, participate in the digital world as a content producer and/or user. For instance, in 2005, Vivian created CLIP (Critical Literacy in Practice), a series of podcasts that focus on critical literacy in different spaces and places as it is practiced in and outside of school (http://www.clippodcast.com) and across diverse settings. She started the online broadcast as a way to make accessible, to a broader audience, her work in critical literacy. The podcast is free and anyone who has access to the Internet can listen or subscribe to the show. Those with mp3 players can download the episodes onto their portable players to listen on the go. The episodes average 10–20 minutes long and primarily center on issues of social justice and equity. Each episode takes up some aspect of critical literacy.

The topic has a niche focus and yet Vivian's episodes have received thousands of downloads. What she discovered is that the show is used by a diverse audience of people who are attempting to find out about critical literacy, including parents, teachers, and university educators who have used various episodes as part of their reading lists in courses. Most recently, Vivian has initiated a critical literacy Twitter chat and the creation of a Pinterest site. Twitter is an online social networking service that enables its users to send and read text-based posts (tweets) of up to 140 characters. Twitter users who want to participate in a conversation about critical literacy simply add a hashtag (#) to the end of their tweets. Other Twitter users are then able to search for that hashtag, which allows them to see the thread of conversation focused on critical literacy (for further information go to http://criticalliteracychat.blogspot.com/). Pinterest is a virtual bulletin board that allows users to organize or pin different sites and images they find on the web. Vivian's Pinterest site (located at http://pinterest.com/criticallit/) includes a series of bulletin boards that focus on critical literacy. She created the site to make accessible to others a variety of resources that connect with her research and publications.

## Digital Media and Global Conversations

Three years ago, Peggy created an online series of free web seminars focused on literacy research called Global Conversations in Literacy Research (GCLR) (www.globalconversationinliteracy.wordpress.com) to engage global audiences in critical discussions regarding literacy practices and research. With the potential of Facebook to reach vast audiences, she has also created a GCLR page (http://www.facebook.com/pages/Global-Conversations-in-Literacy-Research/179326112144708). In combination, these digital tools have created spaces to engage in professional development with leaders in the field of education from around the globe for no cost, including: Brian Cambourne from Australia, Kate Pahl from the UK, and Jennifer Roswell from Canada. For the past 16 years, Peggy has also engaged in ceramics, conjoining literacy issues with art and has her own Etsy page on which she shows her clay pieces (http://www.etsy.com/shop/malbers2).

Clearly, digital media and technologies inform the very way we participate in the everyday world: social, professional, artistic, and more. Social networking has produced new spaces for interacting, where users can share ideas, activities, events, and interests (Janks & Vasquez, 2011). We have included some ways that digital technologies have intersected with our own lives because we believe this firsthand experience has helped us imagine how such technologies can intersect with the lives of students and teachers in school settings. Vasquez, Tate, and Harste (2013) note the importance of living a critically literate life as an important aspect of teaching from a critical literacy perspective. This critical perspective is also applicable to technology. Teachers who experience technology firsthand will more likely imagine what technology affords the work they do. From a critical literacy perspective, such literacy work should focus on agency and taking action. Critical literacy is not a spectator's sport and technology creates a space for us to participate in new ways. In the next section we will share one example of our work with teachers.

## Experiencing Technology Firsthand

In the summer of 2008, in a workshop setting that lasted five days, we worked with a group of ninety teachers to use visual discourse analysis (Albers, 2007) to better understand what it means to read everyday texts critically and then design, write, and produce counter-narrative texts. Having worked in the area of critical literacy for many years (Harste & Carey, 1999; Vasquez, 1998, 2000), we were very aware of the different interpretations of critical literacy in the world and that many of these interpretations treat critical literacy as a topic of study rather than as lived experiences. We wanted the teachers to "live" some strategies firsthand and experience what it means to use texts to impact others and to contribute to change.

In preparation for the workshop, we asked the teachers to look closely at their school and the community in which their school is located. We asked them to take digital photographs, record sound bites from the community or school, interview students, parents, and staff at the school, and gather other materials they thought might be useful for exploring issues of social significance to children, parents, families, and the community at large, as well as the systems of meaning that underpin them.

We started with the personal by having teachers identify a social issue such as race, class, or gender that was of importance to their school and the community in which it is located. They worked with their issue in a number of different ways including tweeting. Their work culminated in the production of a public service announcement (PSA). We defined PSAs as one-minute multimedia texts that present persuasive or informative messages about social issues of importance. We watched, discussed, and critiqued existing PSAs. This was an opportunity for teachers to use digital media as a format for communicating issues to a broader audience. Together with colleagues from their schools, they used the digital images that they collected, audio bites of children whom they interviewed, sound bites from the community, and material they had gathered prior to the start of the workshop to design and produce their announcements. They also went to sites like Flickr (http://www.flickr.com), one of the many free online photo-sharing tools available and where they could access and use copyright-free images. They then created PSAs using Windows Movie Maker, iMovie, or PowerPoint as platforms, integrating digital images, music, written text, and/or special effects such as transitions.

One of the announcements addressed pollution while another dealt with the inhumane treatment and slaughter of chickens. Through this experience, the teachers learned how new literacies create spaces for them to communicate across various platforms. Learning to use digital media to communicate and change perspectives was not easy and a great deal of time was spent working with groups on individual issues regarding technology, software, and hardware. Nevertheless, by the end, most of the teachers left excited about integrating this project and these technologies into their classrooms.

## Preschoolers Online

Vasquez and Felderman (2012) describe numerous ways in which technology is used by children between the ages of three to eight to do different kinds of life work. One incident they describe, which took place in a preschool classroom in Georgia, involved a group of four-year-old children who were frustrated with the trash accumulating in the river close to the school playground. The children used the Internet to research ways to clean up the problem. Their research generated other inquiries including water conservation. One of the things they learned is that much of the water used in their city was from toilet flushing, and there are ways to reduce the amount of water used when flushing. They explored various options online, with the help of their teacher, engaged in online communication with experts in the field, and found one solution that they themselves could produce and distribute. They recycled 12-oz plastic food containers (such as ready-made cake frosting containers), filled them with rocks, replaced the covers, and created instructions for putting the device in the water tank of a toilet to reduce the amount of water needed to flush. The devices were made available to the children's families and other community members. In their own way these young children contributed to a more sustainable community. Technology afforded them an opportunity to use the Internet as a source of information and communication to engage in critical literacy and "new writing" such as writing emails and conversing with experts online (Merchant, 2005, p.51).

## First Graders Use VoiceThread to do Social Action Work

In another classroom in South Carolina, first grade teacher Katie Stover also worked with young children on using technology as a text and tool for doing life work. She used children's literature as a springboard for engaging in critical discussions about social issues such as racism and bullying. She wondered whether VoiceThread, a collaborative multimedia site for hosting slide shows, might afford children an opportunity to make their work accessible to a broader audience (Vasquez & Felderman, 2012). According to the company website, "[a] VoiceThread is a collaborative, multimedia slide show that holds images, documents, and videos and allows people to navigate slides and leave comments in five ways – using voice (with a mic or telephone), text, audio file, or video (via a webcam)" (VoiceThread, 2012). When you share a VoiceThread with friends, family, colleagues, or anyone else you would like, they are able to record comments in audio, video, or text format directly on the image itself. The free version of VoiceThread allows you to do three minutes of phone commenting, three slide shows at a time with up to fifty slides each, and unlimited voice and text comments. (To set up an account, go to https://voicethread.com/ and click on the register or sign in link on the top right-hand corner of the homepage.)

One group of students from Katie's research used digital writing to inform a broader audience about one of the lost boys of Sudan. The project came into being because the family of one of the children was an adoptive family for Lubo, who recounted his history as a lost boy and his dream to build a school in his home village of Southern Sudan. Knowing someone personally who had gone through the kind of hardship he endured, and knowing that there are children who continue to experience such hardship, clearly impacted the first graders' desire to engage in fundraising. To bring awareness to their cause, the children created a series of ten VoiceThread slides. The slides consisted of both text and images with voiceover so that people viewing the slides could either read the text or listen to the narration. The children used VoiceThread as a tool for taking specific social action. They used technology to do work with social effects that contribute to changed conditions of living or being. The first five slides introduced the topic and offered definitions for the term "Lost Boy." The next two slides described Lubo, and the last three slides offered ways to help him. One of these slides also described how various donation amounts would fund school supplies, such as a literacy kit and art materials for one child ($35.00), or a cement block for the school structure ($20.00). In total, it would cost $200,000.00 to build a school that would accommodate 300 students. The children were able to raise enough funds to contribute eighty blocks towards building the school.

This work illustrates how one group of young writers capitalized on the advantages of using digital tools to advocate for social justice. Their efforts took several weeks of collaborative and critical literacy discussions, when students worked in collaborative writing groups to choose a topic of interest, write for an authentic purpose, and publish their writing for a wide audience using Voicethread.com. Public sharing meant the children reached a much wider audience, which resulted in raising more funds than if they had done the work without the use of technology. This type of writing helps children reclaim the essence of what writing is for, as presented in the introductory chapter by Meyer and Whitmore. The children wrote to have and express agency and have an effect upon the world.

## Investigating Gender Stereotypes With Third Graders

During physical education class one day, Christine Paul's third graders noticed that the basketball hoops the girls in the class were told to use by the PE teacher were significantly lower than those used by the boys. At the time of this observation, Christine's students had been looking closely at gender stereotypes and ways of responding to inequitable issues around them. The topic stemmed from their notice of gender stereotyping on the playground. In response to the hoop issue, some of the third graders decided to write letters to express their objections; one was written to the principal and another was written to each of the PE teachers. At the same time, they sent a survey to the other classes to see if other children felt there was a need to change the inequitable practice. Their actions were met with mixed reactions, and some adults categorized the issue as trivial, but in the end this gendered practice was disrupted and gender was no longer used to determine who could shoot at which hoops. In spite of having had their issue heard and resolved, the children recognized that the underlying stereotyping of what girls can and cannot do, and what boys can and cannot do, permeated other parts of school life. As a result, the group continued to explore gender issues as an ongoing inquiry.

Different groups of children chose to do different things. One group decided they wanted to design a public service announcement to raise people's awareness of stereotypes in different settings. From the start they realized that, in order to make their information accessible to the largest possible audience, the PSA needed to be a part of the school-based daily news shown on the closed-circuit televised announcement system. They began by studying PSAs with an eye for how to get a message across in a few minutes. They decided on a three-minute time frame. With that, they wrote their script. They debated about audience and what message to communicate. They wanted to be sure students would not only watch and listen, but that they would also remember the messages conveyed about stereotypes.

The next step was to explore their technology options. Christine shared with them a number of possibilities. One idea was to take digital photos and create a slide show. Another was to use iMovie to create and stitch together a series of video clips. The children decided to use iMovie and quickly learned the functions of the program. The final step was to create storyboards that involved playing with the text from the script. Once the storyboards were completed, rehearsals began.

Creating the video proved to be difficult and challenging. Producing the three-minute segment involved creating animation using Kid Pix Studio, doing live digital video clips, and recording voice overlays for the animation. Once these pieces were complete, the final task was to put all the bits together. The children enthusiastically took on the challenge because the project was one that had importance in their lives. In the end they were able to bring awareness of gender stereotyping and the need to disrupt gender inequities to the whole school.

## Writing: Then and Now

The world of composition is changing, yet some things have not changed. Writing is still a process. It may now involve several technologies, but writers still need a clear sense of what they wish to accomplish and what audiences they wish to reach. In our minds this means that meaning making still has to be the focus of writing experiences in classrooms and that what one has to say still needs to be valued.

In the early days of process writing, we and other researchers argued that the key to a good writing program was to create an environment in which children feel free to say what is on their minds. While we may now want children to interrogate what they say as well as the stances that are assumed given what they say, there is no interrogation without articulation. Writing – whether traditional or digital – still begins and ends in meaning.

By opening up curriculum to digital media and the everyday practices around which students create texts, students learn to interrogate and design a range of multimodal messages. In essence, students learn languages (written, digital, musical, art, and so on), learn through language (content, technique, concepts, etc.), and learn about languages and how they operate in a range of media texts (critical literacy, discourses). To engage in such work is to create a critical literacy classroom where students are able to reclaim writing as a thoughtful, social, agentive act.

## References

Albers, P. (2007). Visual discourse analysis: An introduction to the analysis of school-generated visual texts. In D. W. Rowe, R. T. Jimenez, D. L. Compton, D. K. Dickinson, Y. Kim, K. M. Leander, & V. J. Risko (Eds.), *56th Yearbook of the National Reading Conference* (pp. 81–95). Oak Creek, WI: National Reading Conference.

Doering, A., Beach, R., & O'Brien, D. (2007). Infusing multimodal tools and digital literacies into an English education program. *English Education, 40*(1), 41–60.

Emig, J. (1971). *The composing processes of twelfth graders.* Urbana, IL: National Council of Teachers of English.

Graves, D. (1983). *Writing: Teachers and children at work.* Portsmouth, NH: Heinemann.

Gray, L., Thomas, N., & Lewis, L. (2010). *Teachers' use of educational technology in US public schools: 2009 (NCES 2010-040).* Washington, DC: National Center for Education Statistics, Institute of Education Sciences, US Department of Education. Retrieved from http://nces.ed.gov/pubs2010/2010040.pdf

Harste, J. C., & Carey, R. F. (1999). *Curriculum, multiple literacies, and democracy: What if English/language arts teachers really cared?* (Monograph). Urbana, IL: National Council of Teachers of English.

Janks, H. (2010). *Literacy and power*. New York: Routledge.

Janks, H. & Vasquez, V. (2011). Critical literacy revisited: Writing as critique. *English Teaching: Practice and Critique, 10*(1), 1–6.

Lankshear, C. & Knobel, M. (2006). *New literacies: Everyday practices and classroom learning*. Maidenhead, UK: Open University Press.

Merchant, G. (2005). Electric involvement: Identity performance in children's informal digital writing. *Discourse: Studies in the Cultural Politics of Education, 26*(3), 301–314.

Vasquez, V. (1998). Building equitable communities: Taking social action in a kindergarten classroom. *Talking Points, 9*(2), 3–7.

Vasquez, V. (2000). Getting beyond *I like the book*: Putting a critical edge on kids' purposes for reading. *School Talk, 5*(2), 2–3.

Vasquez, V., Albers, P., & Harste, J. C. (2010). From the personal to the worldwide web: Moving teachers into positions of critical interrogation. In Baker, B. (Ed.), *The new literacies: Multiple perspectives on research and practice* (pp. 265–284). New York: Guildford.

Vasquez, V. & Felderman, C. (2012). *Technology and critical literacy in early childhood*. New York: Routledge.

Vasquez, V., Tate, S., & Harste, J. C. (2013). *Negotiating critical literacies with teachers: Theoretical foundations and pedagogical resources for pre-service and in-service contexts*. New York: Routledge.

VoiceThread, LLC. (2012). *Introduction*. Retrieved from https://voicethread.com/support/howto/Basics/Introduction/

# 15 Extension

## WRITING AS DESIGNING

### Reclaiming the Social and Multimodal Aspects of Writing

*Candace R. Kuby*

The chapter by Vasquez, Albers, and Harste helps us consider how identities "shape and are shaped" by writing practices. The numerous examples shared highlight not only the sociocultural aspects of writing but also the criticalness that happens when students inquire and display agency to make changes in the everyday. Vasquez, Albers, and Harste also demonstrate that digital technologies *are* writing, not an *add-on* to writing curriculum. The following vignette of second graders who created 3D puppets and scenery on a smart board shows how children effortlessly move between various modes and materials to communicate. These children (all student names are pseudonyms) actively reclaimed writing in school as a meaningful, digitally enhanced social act (see Jurich & Meyer, Chapter 16).

One August day, second graders scurry around Room 203 to find materials to design with in Writers' Studio. Gigi walks to her desk, grabs a hand puppet made from folded paper and goes to the round table where three girls are playing with animal hand puppets. While testing out the movements of their puppets, the girls discuss creating a play about the different animals' homes. A fifth girl, Ella, approaches inquiring about what they are doing and asks if they want her help. Only if she has a puppet, they reply. Ella asks Riley to help her make one.

Penny declares, "We need to make a scenery, let's talk about the scenery … it should be a little town where the puppets live." After a few seconds Gigi declares, "We can ask Miss Gutshall to draw the scenery on the smart board." Penny replies, "What in the world, are you crazy?" Gigi, walking to the smart board, uses her arms to explain how they can draw on the smart board with the four colored pens. Penny and Gigi approach Miss Gutshall with the idea.

MISS GUTSHALL: Talk to your group about what your plan is. If you're going to do it (scenery) on the smart board, what will you need for that? If you're going to do it on butcher paper, what you'll need for that? What's going to be your purpose for this [play]?

PENNY: I was thinking the story is of how they (animal puppets) all become friends. Like this show [I watched] it's about these six ponies and on the very first show they meet up and they become friends by having an adventure together.

MISS GUTSHALL: Can you meet with your group and make sure they all agree with your purpose?

Returning to the group, Gigi asks them about using the smart board or butcher paper. Penny and Gigi use their arms to sketch-out their ideas in front of the smart board. They ask the group members for their thoughts. They all agree to use the smart board and butcher paper. After a flurry of brainstorming, the girls begin working on different things: making puppets, collecting crates to stack up like a wall to hide behind with the puppets, and asking Miss Gutshall to get large green butcher paper. "This is going to be the best play ever!" Penny exclaims as she frolics around the room.

Neil approaches the girls and asks to help. Penny discusses with him the role of being the announcer. Neil responds, "I am going to make a puppet too." The girls agree Neil can make an announcer puppet that looks like a man.

As Gigi draws on the smart board, Riley asks to help out. Gigi tells her to draw flowers. In the following days, large green paper drapes over the crates and students create 3D houses on top for their puppets.

On the day of the play, the scenery is projected on the smart board and students crouch behind the crates. The play on friendships begins with much excitement. As the play concludes, the puppets move out into the crowd of second graders and ask, "Who will be my friend?"

The second grade children seamlessly integrated digital (smart board), alphabetic (play script), artistic (both drawing on the smart board and 3D creations of puppets and homes), media and pop culture (Penny's idea for the storyline from a TV show), oral language (negotiations as they designed and performed), and embodied literacies (movement of puppets and bodies to "draft" the scenery in front of the smart board). They used these materials, tools, and modes to communicate a message about friendship to their peers.

The girls had a pretty strong hunch that Miss Gutshall would allow them to use the smart board when they approached her. While Miss Gutshall wasn't always sure where folded paper puppets might lead students as writers, she learned to trust them (and herself). Students, when given time, space and access to materials, use what is "at hand" (Kress, 1997) to not only communicate, but to also change their world.

For these second graders, writers' studio was a time to design. It was not a time to simply use papers and pencils to write books, but to use a range of materials to create games, puzzles, maps, murals, plays, puppets, and 3D creations (such as train stations, skateboard parks, baseball stadiums, etc.) for others to use. In writing workshop, *audience* involves children reading their writing aloud to peers, but in a writers' studio, where children are designing with materials and digital technologies, students identify as producers. While producing, these students had a vision of someone not only listening to them share writing, but *using* what they designed. This initial exploration with paper-folded puppets turned into a play. Later these girls taught peers how to create paper-folded frogs. These new puppet designers used the original animal puppets as a mentor text to create frogs. The frogs functioned as game board pieces in a game they designed. Writing moved beyond writing for a *listening* audience to writing for others *to use*, take up, adapt, and redesign.

## Is This Critical Literacy?

Sahni (2001) uses the term "creative literacy" to describe the ways children demonstrate agency with those closest to them – teachers, peers, and family members. In the puppet vignette, the children used a play to begin conversations to interrogate friendship. By moving into the crowd of peers at the conclusion, the students reconstructed ways of being in relationships with each other and demonstrated how literacy is a vehicle for friendship. The play was about animals negotiating relationships and, in the process of designing, the students also negotiated their own relationships. For example, when Neil and Ella asked to enter the group, students thought about how additional designers would change the collaboration. Later in a conversation with Penny about designing artistic signs to name each hallway in the school (which she was proposing to the principal), she articulated to me the larger purpose was to make a "creative difference." The children saw social change in the creative differences they made in relationships with schoolmates.

At the core of writers' studio in Room 203 is collaboration. While early literacy scholars like Dyson (1993) describe social aspects of writing, examples given are typically of students sitting next to each other and conversing while working on individual texts. In Room 203, students fluidly and organically formed partnerships to co-design as writers. Students negotiated their roles as visionary, author, illustrator, researcher, and/or designer. These second graders were often part of numerous projects at once, yet managed their time and relationships with sophistication. Students took risks as writers and their agency with materials and partnerships fostered strong, sometimes unexpected, literacy identities.

## Reclaiming Writing: Perhaps it is About Designing?

As Vasquez, Albers, and Harste articulate, digital technologies are an integral part of writing, not an add-on. Their chapter encourages readers to consider the uses and purposes of writing. Students can produce and use writing to reclaim their learning, identities, communities, and relationships. The students in Vasquez, Albers, and Harste's chapter as well as the children in Room 203 designed as a way to express agency and have an effect on their world. Educators (and policy makers) should embrace expanded definitions of writing to include multiple modes and materials for designing. As educators, let us trust students and provide space, time, and materials for children to engage in such important work, where they (and we) can reclaim writing as purposeful, social, and transformative.

## Author's Note

I am grateful for the collaborative teaching/researching partnership with Tara Gutshall.

## References

Dyson, A. H. (1993). *Social worlds of children learning to write in an urban primary school*. New York: Teachers College Press.

Kress, G. (1997). *Before writing: Rethinking the paths to literacy*. New York: Routledge.

Sahni, U. (2001). Children appropriating literacy: Empowerment pedagogy from young children's perspective. In B. Comber & A. Simpson (Eds.), *Negotiating critical literacies in classrooms* (pp. 21–40). Mahwah, NJ: Erlbaum.

# 16

# DEMOCRATIC WRITING IN VIDEO PRODUCTION

## Reclaiming the Social Nature of Writing Practices

*Chuck Jurich and Richard J. Meyer*

In this chapter, we examine the complex social writing involved in children's video making as an example of one way to reclaim the social nature of all writing. We discuss the sociocultural contexts and processes that shaped the interactions of the authors including protocols and products, roles, and tools. We argue that video making is an opportunity for *democratic* writing, where multiple voices and contributions are included to shape the writing process. We observed how group writing in video making challenged the *"authoritative"* stance of traditional writing where a single author controls the entire content and process. Democratic writing moves away from many typical school literacy practices and mirrors the collaborative, experimental, and multimodal literacies that occur in many out of school contexts such as broadcast media, video game development, and web page design (Sheridan & Rowsell, 2010).

## The "Social-ness" in Reading and Writing

Literacy practices, including video making, may be considered from a sociocultural perspective that acknowledges the social origins of individual development and the significance of tools (both technologies and sign systems) to mediate social interaction (Vygotsky, 1978). This perspective of literacy explains reading and writing practices as transactional and social activities (Bloome, 1985; Goodman, 1982; Heath, 1983; Rosenblatt, 1978). Chuck's work with fourth and fifth grade video makers in an after-school club focused on the social processes and interactions of the students as they read and wrote together. While we center more on writing in this chapter, there were many readings/viewings of texts that included the social processes of composing, critiquing, and revising.

New Literacy Studies scholars recognize the importance of sociocultural contexts in literacies by studying the social practices that vary from one situation to another (Street, 2005). They acknowledge multiple contexts and multiple literacies composed in a variety of communicative modes such as linguistic, visual, aural, spatial, and gestural (New London Group, 1996). We examined student collective reading and writing as "literacy events," which were any occasion in which a text was integral to the nature of the participants' interactions and processes (Heath, 1983). The events in the video club, such as writing/revising a script or shooting a shot, were video recorded for analysis.

With its multimodal properties (scriptwriting, editing video, working with sound and music) and technological orientation, video making is generally considered a "new literacies" practice that is both physically and conceptually different from conventional print texts (Lankshear & Knobel, 2006). Explaining the new mindsets inherent in new literacies, Lankshear and Knobel (2006) discuss participation, distributed expertise, collaboration, and experimentation, and these are precisely what the students in the club exhibited during video production.

## The After-School Video Club

The site of our research was the Midway Elementary (all names are pseudonyms) After-School Video Club. Open to fourth and fifth grade students, the club met directly after school twice a week for approximately 90 minutes. Owing to space and supervision requirements, the club was limited to twenty students and there was an application to join that inquired about students' interests, motivation to make videos, commitment, and ability to work well with others. In addition to Chuck, the club had two other adult volunteers (one was a classroom teacher at the school and the other a graduate student) available to supervise students. The video club was based out of the school's computer lab. On the plus side of the lab, students had numerous technological writing tools at their disposal including computers (with their own exclusive login account), access to multiple video cameras, tripods, still cameras, LCD projectors, portable digital sound recorders, and printers. On the negative side, the layout of the lab was designed for individual activities and had no tables for students to gather and socially write together.

## Multiple Authorship in Video Production

In this section we share an example of group authorship: a crew shooting a scene for the video *The Attacks*. Next we examine the literacy events in the example and focus on the interactions of the multiple authors. We pay special attention to the sociocultural contexts and processes in video making including the protocols they followed, roles that they took on, the tools and objects they used, and the actual products (scripts, shots, completed videos) that resulted from their engagement.

## *Shooting* **The Attacks**

*The Attacks* is a four-minute "psychological thriller" about a girl who escapes from an insane asylum and, out of convenience, attacks the two unsuspecting protagonists. In a twist, they are saved by a second girl who, it turns out, is seeking her *own* revenge for the hurtful taunting the protagonists did to her many years earlier. In the end, the protagonists survive but learn that they shouldn't have been cruel, and the "insane attacker" is taken off to prison; however, the "revenge attacker," perhaps out of justice, manages to slip by unpunished. In the many months it took to collectively complete *The Attacks*, thirteen different authors in a variety of roles contributed to the making of the video. The two scriptwriters handed off the script to a director who, with the help of the producer, decided on a cast and crew. After filming, the cameraperson gave the camera to a team of editors who turned the shot footage into a final video. Each person's input was sizable and the final product was the end result of thoughtful and intensive deliberation, negotiation, and compromise.

Below, we join the filming after the crew's first two attempts to get a useable take had not been successful, mainly due to the word "emergency" which was extremely difficult for the actor (an English language learner) to pronounce. He was playfully teased by the cameraperson, his friend, and the humor kept the atmosphere light and fun. The director and markerboard operator were more serious and tried to support the actor in other ways. (Note: Video-recorded data are presented in screenplay format that provides a transcript of all speech as well as descriptive actions of the participants. Instead of using names, we used the roles of the participants as they are more informative to the discussion.)

INT. COMPUTER LAB – AFTERNOON – 2/7/2012
The lone Actor, Hispanic and learning English, is sitting in a chair with a telephone next to him. The Director surveys her copy of the script, which is covered with handwritten notes. There is an audience of kids around the perimeter of the camera chatting, watching, and waiting.
The Markerboard operator holds the clapperboard in front of the Actor's face and talks to him.
MARKERBOARD
(coaching)
Just say "Hi, this is Police Officer Joe. What's your emergency?"
ACTOR
(practicing)
E-mer-gen-cy… emer-gen-cy…
CAMERAPERSON
Just say "problem,"
(to the Director)
How 'bout we say "problem"?

MARKERBOARD
(thinking)
Yeah! Just say "problem"!
CAMERAPERSON
(playfully)
What's your problem, fool!
(Lots and lots of laughter by everyone in the room.)
DIRECTOR
No! No!
(to the Actor)
Say "What's your problem?" but not "What's your problem, fool!" Don't listen
   to this fool right here.
(She points to the Cameraperson and everyone laughs.)

In this segment, two competing suggestions were made to the actor; neither
came from the director. The markerboard operator's proximity to the actor gave
her access for a quick individual coaching session. She repeated the line to him,
offering a model for how to say the words. While practicing, the cameraperson
suggested he replace the word with "problem." The idea was appraised by the
crew, but the decision to use it was for the director to make. "Problem" may not
have been the ideal word but they were willing to experiment in order to make
progress. They continued:

DIRECTOR
Action.
ACTOR
(slowly, calmly)
Hello, this is Police Officer Joe. How can I help you?
(Several students in the audience look around at each other surprised and a
   little confused.)
DIRECTOR
Cut.
(There is still silence. Then, after a moment, a few people clap which builds up
   to everyone in the room.)
MARKERBOARD
That was pretty good.

Unannounced, the actor took the initiative to revise the dialogue further by
substituting the common phrase "How can I help you?" for "What's your problem?" While the crew was surprised, they didn't reject the take outright and
slowly warmed to it. The actor delivered the line cleanly but was the meaning
appropriate?

(The Actor stands and hams it up by bowing repeatedly. He starts to walk off.)
ACTOR
Thank you, thank you, thank you.
DIRECTOR
Sit down, Juan. One more.
(The Markerboard quickly erases and re-writes. The Actor sits back down
  smiling.)
ACTOR
One more?
MARKERBOARD
Quiet on the set!
DIRECTOR
Quiet on the set, please. Camera... Markerboard.
MARKERBOARD
Shot 48, take 4.
DIRECTOR
Action.
ACTOR
Hello, this is Police Officer Joe. What's your... e-mergency?
DIRECTOR
Cut. Good.
(The Markerboard looks over at the Cameraperson and nods approvingly.)
MARKERBOARD
(to the Director)
So what is this now? Shot 49?
DIRECTOR
No-no-no-no-no...
(And she flips through pages of her script searching.)

One of the protocols that developed in the video club was to capture a take that was "good enough" and then, if time allowed, do one more to see if they could get an even better one. We can see this protocol in effect when the director said "one more" and it was implied that the actor would try the original dialogue. If it didn't pan out, the crew already had an acceptable take tucked away in the camera. After the take was over, the markerboard operator knew it was time to move on. ("So what is this now? Shot 49?") For this shot, the production crew's job was done and it would be up to the video editor to figure out which take to use.

## Literacy Events in Video Making

In video making, a variety of social literacy events took place as two or more students interacted with each other while writing – or, perhaps more accurately, *composing*. Each literacy event in video making focuses on a different kind of text. Some texts are fairly concrete and conventional (e.g. scripts, props, costumes) but others, such as a "take" are more abstract. A take exists in two forms: as a fleeting but real-life performance right in front of the participants and also in a more durable but virtual form digitally recorded in the camera as a clip. Each participant in the literacy event above had a unique understanding of what happened. For example, the cameraperson saw the performance through the camera lens. If, during the improvised "How can I help you?" take, he had accidentally chopped off the head of the actor by misframing the shot, the performance would have been rejected by the cameraperson even if the line had been said cleanly. While lots of people on the set thought the improvised take was fine, the director's leadership perspective influenced her to request that the actor perform it one more time using the original line. In post-production, the take was viewed again by the editors. Figure 16.1 presents the stages of video making and also shows the activities that occurred and the types of texts produced and examined during each stage.

## Sociocultural Contexts in Video Making

In order to better understand social writing and multiple authorship, we looked at specific literacy events in video making and examined three important sociocultural contexts and processes: protocols and products (including stages of production), roles, and tools. We found these contexts to significantly influence how the different authors interacted. We summarize the relationship between these sociocultural contexts and processes across the various video-making production stages in Figure 16.1.

### *Protocols and Products*

The students produced videos in a three-stage process similar to the one used in major motion pictures, moving from pre-production, to production, and then post-production (see Figure 16.1). During the three stages, many products were created: a script, "takes" (an attempt), video clips in the computer, "sequences" (a collection of clips), "cuts" (complete drafts of the video), and lastly, the "final cut" of the video. Each product led to the next and they were substantially transformed, revised, and re-authored by many people before becoming the final cut. Not entirely linear, video club productions could temporarily jump back into a previous stage in order to improve their videos.

Protocols – contextually agreed upon procedures of operation – were established and followed in the video club. One such production stage protocol, enforced by the director, was that students would get one "good enough" take and then shoot only one more to see if they could improve it. Rather than risk erasing a take, another protocol was that students never re-viewed what they just shot on the camera, but waited until the footage was imported safely into a computer.

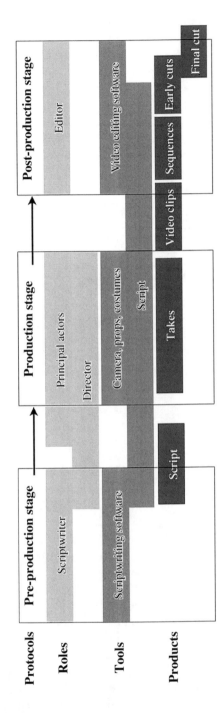

**FIGURE 16.1** Literacy events in video making.

It was much easier for a crew to capture additional takes and let the video editors in post-production watch all the shot video clips over and over to decide which to use. This process became an official working protocol of the production stage.

## Roles

Students working on video productions volunteered to take on specific roles, some of which had extensive responsibility and authorial power. These "major roles" – scriptwriters, directors, main actors, and editors – positioned the students as the principal author at any given stage of production. In pre-production, the scriptwriters were the principal authors with the most responsibility and power. In the production stage, the director and main actors assumed the power, while in post-production it was the editors (see Figure 16.1). "Minor roles," such as the markerboard operator, supporting actors and extras, and costume handlers didn't have the same control over content. Camera operators were positioned as a function of their skill level. Those with command over the camera were active contributors; others did little more than press the start and stop button.

Major roles such as director and video editor were usually offered to students by the scriptwriter(s) and producer(s) based on prior experience and expertise, but other roles were distributed without regard to student ability. On the set, *The Attacks'* director spoke very little but made the decisions, sometimes merely repeating what someone else said to show she both agreed and decided that a particular line of action was the right one.

An adult or teacher nearly always performed the role of the producer. Producers provided materials, organized groups of people, authorized projects, and controlled resources including the biggest one: time. Adults were usually the only ones in the club who had the access, power, and experience to perform these functions well, but producers were also creative contributors giving feedback and sharing ideas. This aspect of their role was often difficult for the adults/teachers because they traditionally viewed themselves as outside the creative work that children do. It was a significant realization that producers were real members of the crew and part of the creative process.

## Tools

Taking on a role implied learning how to use the specific tools that accompanied that role: scriptwriters used scriptwriting software; camera operators employed video cameras; actors engaged with props and sets; directors worked with scripts and people; and film editors used computers and video editing software. While roles helped divide up the labor and responsibilities involved in video making, the connection between tools and roles was so specific that some kids who specialized never handled other video making tools at all. Video editing, for example, is one of the more complex tasks one can do on a computer. Some students who specialized

| Stage | Activity | Text |
|---|---|---|
| Pre-production | Creating, writing, and/or revising a script<br>Deliberating on the merit of a script (reading)<br>Designing props or costumes; locating or deciding on a setting or location | Script<br>Script<br>Prop/costume/set |
| Production | Setting up a shot<br>Shooting a take<br>Evaluating the merit and quality of a take | Script/set/actors<br>Performance/take<br>Take |
| Post-production | Viewing/reading video clips for the first time<br>Evaluating and selecting a take of a shot while editing<br>Evaluating a video sequence (multiple clips together)<br>Evaluating a cut of a video (completed sequences) | Clips<br>Clips<br>Sequence<br>Cut |

**FIGURE 16.2**  Sociocultural contexts and processes in video making.

in video editing invested their time in mastering the tools of editing at the expense of not knowing how to write scripts. Figure 16.2 shows the tools, their relationships to each other, the stage in which they were used, and the texts produced.

The script was interesting because it was a product created by scriptwriters using screenwriting software; however, at the end of the pre-production stage, it transformed into a tool central to production and post-production. For the director, the script was a plan that guided her on what to shoot and where. For actors, the script provided words and direction. Editors used the script to make sense of video clips that were brought to them out of sequence. After the final cut was done, the script was discarded; its worth was gone.

Tools also mediated the social interactions between the various roles. In filming, the camera functioned as the center point of the interactions between the director, cameraperson, actors, and onlookers. The actor performed, not for the real audience in the room, but for the camera in front of him and, perhaps, an imagined audience when the movie was viewed. The cameraperson focused on what he was able to see through the viewfinder and nonactors were required to stay out of the "scene" or behind the camera at all times. The script mediated the interaction between the director and actor by both guiding and limiting their options. In the "Police Officer Joe" scene, the actor improvised a bit but did not stray far from the original idea. In post-production, the tools of the computer and video-editing software empowered the video editor because there was only one set of controllers, one keyboard and mouse. While others involved in the video making got to watch sequences and cuts and even make suggestions, the editors generally made the final decision mainly because of their firm control of the tools.

## Democratic Writing

As demonstrated by *The Attacks*, video making involved the collaboration of multiple people in different roles using specialized tools, providing an opportunity for democratic multiple authorship. During literacy events, participants engaged with each other closely as they read, wrote, and challenged ideas. In democratic writing, everyone was able to contribute in the process. Contributions came from random individuals of a large group (such as the cameraperson suggesting the word "problem" for "emergency") but also predictably by authors in assigned roles such as an editor, actor, or director. Authoritative single authorship, the conventional notion of one author controlling every aspect of composing, was exceedingly rare in video making. Still, the desire to control all aspects of the video making process, especially by focused directors or overbearing producers, was still present. Thus in video making, there wasn't a binary of democratic versus authoritarian group writing but a continuum, a question of *how* democratic, or authoritarian the process was.

Democratic social writing happened in real time (synchronous) when *The Attacks* crew shot in the computer lab where there were predefined roles: the director, the cameraperson, and the actor, each contributing to process and product. At times, authors broke their official protocols and stepped into other roles. Recall that after the crew decided to change some of the dialogue, the actor ended up changing it even more. Democratic social writing also happened over a length of time (asynchronous), when principal authors wrote and revised the text at various production stages and passed it on to the next group of authors. Asynchronous democratic writing occurred when directors were responsible for shooting scripts they didn't write and editors edited video footage they didn't shoot. At any given stage of production, principal authors handed over the authorial power to another group of people effectively collaborating asynchronously. Democratic writing was ultimately achieved through the checks and balances of major roles, established video-making processes and protocols, and the varying individual abilities of everyone involved in using the writing tools of video making.

## The Tenor of Interactions

As the students collectively, socially, and democratically read and wrote, we noticed that their interactions didn't always "feel" the same. We use the term "tenor" to describe the social and pragmatic relationships between participants in literacy events (Goodman, 1994). Tenor refers to the interpersonal functions of situational contexts: who is taking part, the nature of the participants, and their statuses and roles (Halliday & Hasan, 1985). Some groups argued a lot, while others were more inclined towards co-operative work. Some groups couldn't find their focus while others, like *The Attacks'* crew, tinkered and experimented their way to innovative results.

We consistently observed four writing tenors: *co-operative, collaborative, conflictive,* and *listless*. Each tenor was influenced by how democratic (or authoritarian) the participants were while engaging with the writing and how individuals socially interacted with each other, typically as a function of the context of their roles, tools used, and processes in place. A model of this relationship is depicted in Figure 16.3. The vertical axis is the dividing line between primarily authoritarian vs. democratic writing environments; the horizontal axis is the dividing line between contextually acceptable vs. unacceptable interactions and behaviors in any given sociocultural situation. The tenors fit in each of the four quadrants created by the intersecting axes.

The model helped us describe how students socially write by paying attention to how open the literacy event participants are to democratic writing. The model can't predict what will happen next but may help explain why some groups, such as *The Attacks'* crew, seemed to work well together and why others faltered. Examining the student interactions during the shooting of the "Police Officer Joe" scene, we found that the crew fluctuated between co-operative and collaborative tenors but was mainly collaborative. The word "emergency" was an obstacle for not only the actor but for the whole crew and the problem caused the tenor to switch from co-operative to collaborative as the group collectively searched for a solution. Multiple people contributed suggestions and everyone was open to the ideas. When the director decided on the course of action, the crew appeared to return to a co-operative tenor, however, the actor changed the line yet again and the crew's reaction showed that the mood was still collaborative.

The dynamic nature of group writing meant tenors could switch rapidly. With strong direction from a director, collaborative groups could transition to co-operative (single author with support) or, with the presentation of a perplexing problem, switch to a conflictive tenor (multiple contributors but no compromise or negotiation). While the collaborative tenor appears ideal, each tenor had its place. Sometimes being co-operative was the most efficient way to operate,

| | Authoritarian | Democratic |
|---|---|---|
| **Contextually acceptable**<br>Protocols and roles followed; tools used appropriately | **Co-operative**<br>*"Whatever to assist you..."*<br>One central author contributes and others co-operate and comply | **Collaborative**<br>*"I like that idea and..."*<br>Multiple authors contribute; everyone compromises and negotiates |
| **Contextually unacceptable**<br>Protocols and roles ignored; tools misused | **Listless**<br>*"Whatever...."*<br>One central author (or no one) contributes and others do not co-operate or comply | **Conflictive**<br>*"I like that idea but..."*<br>Multiple authors contribute but ideas conflict; no compromise or negotiation |

**FIGURE 16.3** The tenor of interactions.

especially when time was tight, and conflict could be an effective route towards innovation. In general, listlessness never was positive but there were times when the collective listlessness was an indication that the ideas and projects on the table were just not worth pursuing.

In this chapter, we examined the sociocultural contexts and processes of video making – protocols and products, roles, and tools – and demonstrated how they greatly influenced the interaction of multiple authors writing together. We discussed how these different video-making contexts promoted or discouraged democratic processes of writing and concluded that a variety of "tenors" – interactive moods – can unveil how democratic or authoritarian the group writing environment is. Video making is only one of many new textual forms that are challenging our conventional notions of how people write. In this sense, video making serves as a signifier of one of the many ways in which we may actively support teachers and students in reclaiming writing and continuing on the trajectory discussed in Chapter 1.

## References

Bloome, D. (1985). Reading as a social practice. *Language Arts, 62*(2), 134–142.

Goodman, K. (1982). *Language and literacy: The selected writings of Kenneth S. Goodman, Volume I.* London: Routledge & Kegan Paul.

Goodman, K. (1994). Reading, writing, and written texts: A transactional sociopsycholinguistic view. In R. Ruddell, M. R. Ruddell, & H. Singer (Eds.), *Theoretical models and processes of reading* (4th ed.) (pp. 1093–1130). Newark, DE: IRA Publications.

Halliday, M. A. K., & Hasan, R. (1985). *Language, context, and text: Aspects of language in a social-semiotic perspective.* Victoria, Australia: Deakin University Press.

Heath, S. B. (1983). *Ways with words.* Cambridge: Cambridge University Press.

Lankshear, C. & Knobel, M. (2006). *New literacies: Everyday practices and classroom learning* (2nd ed.). Maidenhead, UK: Open University Press.

New London Group. (1996). A pedagogy of multiliteracies: Designing social futures. *Harvard Educational Review, 66*(1), 60–92.

Rosenblatt, L. M. (1978). *The reader, the text, the poem: The transactional theory of the literary work.* Carbondale, IL: Southern Illinois University Press.

Sheridan, M. P., & Rowsell, J. (2010). *Design literacies: Learning and innovation in the digital age.* New York: Routledge.

Street, B. (2005). New literacies, new times: How do we describe and teach the forms of literacy knowledge, skills, and values people need for new times? In J. V. Hoffman, D. L. Schallert, C. M. Fairbanks, J. Worthy, & B. Maloch (Eds.), *55th Yearbook of the National Reading Conference* (pp. 21–42). Oak Creek, WI: National Reading Conference.

Vygotsky, L. (1978). *Mind in society: The development of higher psychological processes.* Boston, MA: Harvard University Press.

# 16 Extension

## DEMOCRATIC WRITING AND MULTILITERACIES WORK IN SCHOOLS AND COMMUNITY CENTERS

*Linda Skidmore Coggin and Carmen Liliana Medina*

Jurich and Meyer remind us of the significance of reclaiming the kinds of writing that are influenced by new literacies practices, and foreground democratic writing features like multiple authorship and collaborative engagement. Democratic writing, as a way of conceptualizing the relationship between new literacies and the writing process, is powerful for us. In our work we notice how new tools for writing (like digital apps and flip cameras) open up collaborative spaces because social interaction and improvisation support emerging co-constructed meanings. Our work in a rural second grade classroom and an urban community center kids' club serving Latino/a immigrant children considers the sociocultural contexts that influence social writing. New composing tools create an immediacy that pushes authors to improvise.

### In Second Grade

Our first example comes from a rural second grade classroom where children collaboratively authored stories about an animal they were researching. The students used an iPad app to digitally produce their stories and exhibited new literacies strategies as the stories emerged "in the moment" of composing. The students worked in groups of two or three to weave together content knowledge, imagined experiences, and multimedia tools. Students simultaneously wrote, published, and performed the story as they used an app to combine images, text, and voiceover to create a digital story for the classroom's big screen.

The literacy practices the second graders used to compose collaborative stories mirrored many of the strategies students use to individually author texts, as well as the multiple modalities and technological orientation that Jurich and Meyer describe. The tools and processes were malleable and responsive to improvisation as decisions made by individuals and in collaboration blurred the distinction between drafting, revising, and publishing that is typical in traditional authoring. Using multiple modalities to compose (written text, images, voiceover, design layout) offered multiple entry points for students to join the composing process and contribute their expertise.

In one instance, two collaborators looked at images of an arctic fox. Mike was reminded of places in previous writing that "went with" a proposed image and Cade focused on changing search terms to match his own imagined "predator" scene that he wanted to include in the story. These negotiations led to using specific word choices from Mike's previous writing with Cade's choice of image to create the first page of their story. On subsequent pages, they took turns typing sentences that merged previously written work and alternated choosing images for the page.

In the second graders work, the written, visual, and performed text was recursively created by:

- re-reading research notes and drawings made from web quests and other informational sources;
- re-reading their own writing "all-about" the animals;
- using "search" features to locate images, deciding on specific search wording to find the appropriate image;
- negotiating picture choices with a partner and as sole author of a "page";
- selecting what each would write or writing the sentences together collaboratively;
- making decisions about images and previously written text;
- working to merge what they identified as "interesting" or "good" from their individually authored writing with the work of co-authors;
- choosing collaboratively the pictures that would accompany singly authored print texts;
- making design choices such as layout of pictures or choice of multiple pictures and text (size and location) dependent on group makeup; and
- making voiceover decisions, such as who would read which page and what they would read together.

The students had immediate access to images via the Internet. They collaboratively shaped meaning as interactive authors when recording. Modal choices provided multiple avenues for students to insert their own expertise into the collective authoring. The authors quickly learned to change font size and location on the page by watching each other work and continually negotiated the placement of text in relation to images on the page. They experimented with design, viewed their piece, and made decisions together about the completion of their digital project.

## At the Community Center

Our second example highlights how the "story" children told shifted in response to multiple modal tools and audiences available to the author(s). Children from Latino/a immigrant backgrounds, ages 4–12, participated in multiple genres of individually and collaboratively authored writing about a family artifact in a community center kids' club located in a church. The idea behind the project was to engage children in inquiries about their lives in transnational, transcultural, and multilingual spaces. The church serves as a gathering space for the children's Latino/a community. The pastor, who is a Latino from Honduras, is invested in making the church a place that physically, spiritually, and socially invites the Latino/a community to develop close ties. Spanish is the dominant language in the building, including in the kitchen, where members of the church cook Latino food, the coffee room where members gather, and the library, which is filled with bilingual children's literature.

We initiated this project by asking children to bring an everyday artifact from home. The range of artifacts was quite wide and included "mundane" artifacts such as a key holder and more sacred artifacts such as a glass bell with a nativity scene that was given to a boy in memory of his infant brother's death. We explored the artifacts using multiple modalities; photography, visual arts, video and drama. These tools created new relationships and a rich space for recontextualizing the children's histories and relationships with the artifacts and the meanings they constructed.

Mario, who brought the nativity glass bell in memory of his brother, explored his artifact in several ways. His initial writing was three statements written on three separate sheets of paper and displayed with the artifact. The sentences in the order he wrote them were (original spelling):

> It is important to my family because it was for my brother that died.
> It's important also because of me.
> It's also important because theres god.

Working in a small group, Mario next took different photographs of the bell and statements in varied locations around the church and made a poster of the images of his family artifact. Finally, in another engagement, Mario created a video tour of his poster.

Mario might be considered the primary "author" of his work, but at this point the meanings he foregrounded shifted. As the camera recorded, he playfully said, "This is a far out thing with, you know that, that uh, comic thing," as he pointed to the words he wrote on the poster. At the end of the video, he looked into the camera and said, "So that's the end. On channel 6." This playful improvised talk aimed at the camera and his friend who was helping him with the video as both audience and collaborator distanced Mario from the seriousness of the meaning of the artifact and evoked a "TV news reporting" genre to imagine an established role for himself in this video making. In this instance, filmmaking included the audience and the mode of composing as participants in the writing, and influenced the how and what of the message.

Mario's improvisational video is an example of "in the moment" composing. It shifted between playful acting for an audience of peers and the gravity of his message. The flip camera served as his writing tool to make the story durable.

Similar to the second graders' digital text making, Mario's writing from previous events informed the filmmaking but not as a "script" for the new text. Looking closely at Mario's words, embodied actions, and design choices revealed how decisions made in the moment of filming with another student influenced his choice to re-center earlier meanings that were more serious and create new perspectives in response to the modal choices available and a new audience for the performance.

The idea of democratic writing, as presented by Jurich and Meyer, helped us make sense of the work we have been doing with diverse children. As we move forward in reclaiming more complex writing processes in classrooms and community centers, we are empowered by the idea that social writing could become a space for democratic practices that include collaboration, improvisation, and multiple authorships. Perhaps in this way we can also begin to reclaim agency and the creation of new ways of doing literacy that will help us transform other spaces into democratic ones.

# 17

# LISTENING TO COMPOSE SPACES FOR IDENTITIES, RELATIONSHIPS, AND ACTIONS

*Richard J. Meyer and Kathryn F. Whitmore*

The stories of children, teachers, researchers, and families that fill the pages of this book are evidence that reclaiming writing has already begun. Indeed, the thirst and hunger of the human spirit to put thoughts to paper, screen, art, or other media begins at a very young age and cannot be erased by a law, policy, or mandate. We think the essence of our humanity is the stories that we carry with us: stories of hope, activism, reaction, love, surprise, desire, hatred, and more. Stories originate from our relationships and experiences, and we compose stories and stories compose us throughout our lifetimes. O'Brien (1990) writes about the reasons for stories:

> Stories are for joining the past to the future. Stories are for those late hours in the night when you can't remember how you got from where you were to where you are. Stories are for eternity, when memory is erased, when there is nothing to remember except the story. (p. 36)

As we worked with the talented authors in this book, we found that every one of them deeply respects the stories that teachers and students bring to school. They lead us to an intensified appreciation for the ways in which teachers honor stories. In this final chapter, we focus on stories, defined quite broadly to include many genres (including nonfiction). We hone in on an overarching theme that we see underscores and expands the stories in *Reclaiming Writing*: the ways in which we listen influence the nature, breadth, content, and depth of the story. As we consider the importance, tentativeness, fragility, strength, clarity, and muddledness of stories, we argue that it becomes increasingly important to focus on the ways in which we "listen close" to children to learn about their identities, build relationships, and determine how to act as professional educators while supporting our students in actions they may take.

## Listening to Stories

The quote above from O'Brien (1990) comes from his book, *The Things They Carried*, which is a moving story about a man making sense of his experiences during the war in Vietnam. The idea of "carrying" is central to the book, as soldiers carried letters, photos, and other mementos of their lives as a way of staying connected to their homes. Some picked up other items during their time in Vietnam as a way of adding to what they carried. These portable objects represented moments within soldiers' lives and served as signifiers of important stories; indeed, these were the stories that composed their essences, their identities. O'Brien's book often causes his readers to think about what they carry (both real items and ideas within their minds) and these real or internal story signifiers wait within them, almost as a seed waiting to germinate. Germination occurs when someone listens. Tom Romano's daughter, Mariana, read O'Brien's book as she traveled through Europe, far from her father yet thinking about the ways in which O'Brien writes about his daughter and juxtaposing it with Tom and Mariana's relationship. Mariana wrote to her dad:

> O'Brien is so hip to so many things. I saw so many lessons in this book, not only about Vietnam, but how important it is to *write* and tell your stories and to *listen* to other people's stories ... And here's where one lesson lies ... about your story [referring to Tom's story about his own father] ... some people just don't want to *listen* to other people's stories ... sometimes [stories] have to be told to be dealt with ... Stories have to be told to keep people *alive* in a sense – even the person who is living has to be kept alive through stories ... (Romano, 1995, pp. 197–198, emphasis in original)

We are "kept alive" through our stories because someone listens; as Mariana's writing suggests, we answer each other's stories with more stories, and stories nurture the evolution of our lives. Stories, in this sense, may seem deeply personal and narrative in nature, but we suggest that the stories in this book help broaden and deepen what that word means. A story is the systematic recollection of a granddaughter coming into her writing life (Goodman & Goodman, Chapter 2), the retelling of the adventures of moving a classroom of fourth graders into using wikis (Blady & Henkin, Chapter 6), the compelling explanation of ways to teach children to argue for better water quality (Norton-Meier & Hand, Chapter 5), or vivid descriptions of the use of art (Martens, Martens, Doyle, & Loomis, Chapter 9) or song (Baskwill, Chapter 10) to enhance the ways in which meanings are composed.

In stark contrast stand too many contemporary stories about children, learning, and teaching in spaces void of meaning, such as those told by Gallagher (2009). Presenting many energy-draining and sad stories of book abuse in schools, he defines "Readicide" as "the systematic killing of the love of reading, often exacerbated by the inane, mind-numbing practices found in schools" (p. 2). The invention of a new word as part of a treatise that indicts school practices is humbling, especially for those of us that feel complicit in the practices, either because we weren't aware of the impact of what we were doing or because we complied with policies and laws rather than face being terminated from our jobs. Recent policies and laws led many of us to teach and research writing "in the cracks" with children, meaning we engaged in practices we knew to be consistent with our knowledge about writing and our intentions for children as writers, but we did so in secrecy in order to not commit *writicide*, the killing of the love of writing. Others, indeed many of the authors of this book, found that being informed by the literatures (stories) like those in their reference lists made it possible to challenge, ignore, or in some other ways craft lives and stories in opposition. Whether in the cracks or in open opposition, these stories were composed in spaces where identities and relationships grew and where voices moved to actions. They are the spaces where educators listened – to themselves, to each other, to children, to families, and to communities.

It is our conscious decision to receive and hear stories that allows us to listen and then enter them into the complex mix of who we are. We think deep and penetrating listening is the essence of what Rosenblatt (1978) meant when she presented the idea of a transaction as a unique relationship that one has with a text, whether it is received by listening, reading, or viewing. Even as we read or hear a scientific story, such as a report about water quality in Norton-Meier and Hand's chapter, its content dissolves into the already existing understandings and experiences we have of water. For some readers, Ms Margaret's students' stories will give rise to images of polluted water tables and contaminated streams and rivers. For others, images of possible actions, including legislation and litigation will come up. And for others, new questions about scientific concepts in their everyday worlds will be generated. Every story, then, is received in a way unique to individuals, open to further influence by experiences and relationships. The following sections focus on facets of listening that we uncovered as we read and considered the work in this book.

## Listening to Children

Listening to children with integrity, honesty, and intensity carries with it a responsibility to honor what we hear. Children's stories are at the center of this book because they – the children and their stories – are too often marginalized or dismissed by *the test* or *the standards* that must be addressed. When a louder and more powerful voice brackets what children say, the voice of the professional educator-as-decision maker is also dismissed. Reclaiming writing for children and their teachers means looking for spaces, in the cracks or in the open, to support writers in uncovering all that they can do. Bomer (2010) describes listening to writers well:

> I yearn for everyone in the world to *listen* to the music in kids' writing and focus our eyes on its originality, its vibrant and playful use of new words

and multiple languages, the way it collides with and borrows from multiple literacies: art, music, TV, movies, and games. I wish everyone could slow down and take the time to *regard* children's writing as art, especially the work of the many, many kids who don't fit into the square boxes that education values, the kids who produce the sparest pieces, the most obviously unreadable, or the most unappealing and uninteresting to us. (pp. 94–95, emphasis added)

When we *regard* children by listening to them intensely and offering the time, tools, and responses they need, they assume ownership of their writing. They invest in their work with passion, rigor, and intensity, and they are willing to revise and revisit in order to make their voices heard and their intentions clearly known. As we listen to children's questions, we search for what Bomer calls the "gems" in their works-in-progress. She suggests that we receive their work as something produced from passion, respect the work because of its sources and origins, and celebrate the power (Elbow, 1981) and potentials that rest within it.

Children's writing often implies questions and listening teachers recognize the questions as guides for practice. When a child writes "GNYS" (Bissex, 1980) for "genius," for example, implied questions are raised for the teacher: What do I know about spelling? Can I read this? What might I teach next? Why did the child write this? What's the point, intention, function, or purpose of the entire piece? Listening demands attention to implied questions that suggest something as immediate as teaching a spelling strategy (Manning & Ransom, Chapter 7) or as open-ended as holding a relationship-building conversation (Koshewa, Chapter 4).

It falls to us as teachers to listen (Johnston, 2004), to understand who our students are and what they value, and to rely on that information as the starting point for our teaching. We know these ideas are not new, as we've demonstrated from the late 1800s (Meyer & Whitmore, Chapter 1), but they may have fallen to the wayside as teachers, willingly or through coercion, moved the child to the side and made a predetermined curriculum the center of writing activity in classrooms or didn't teach writing at all. Reclaiming is the work of using what we hear and know, trusting children as learners and teachers as professionals, and looking to each other as sources of power, strength, and inspiration for making classrooms exciting places in which children write.

## Listening and Identities

Deep listening means we pay attention to children's languages, cultures, academic status, socioeconomic status, bodies, and more. Valdés (1996) writes about the distances between homes and schools for immigrant children. She explains that some children's teachers "viewed them as having communication problems or social development problems or as simply coming from homes where parents didn't really care a great deal about education" (p. 141). The deficit view of children that she describes makes clear that there are seemingly insurmountable borders between some children's home and school lives, yet throughout this book we demonstrate that by listening and responding, we can reclaim writing and concomitantly reclaim and support the identities from which that writing grows. When a teacher respects a child's need for song (Baskwill, Chapter 10), the joy of growing things where there used to be just dirt (Paugh, Moran, & Rose, Chapter 13), and the wealth of languages and cultures in the classroom (Van Sluys, Chapter 11; Flint & Rodriguez, Chapter 12), we honor, rather than dismiss, the substance of our own and our students' identities and our shared relationships in school. Malaguzzi (in Edwards, 1993) urges us to consider the *hundred languages of children* and he includes culture, movement, oral language, play, paint, song, and many more as the ways in which children can make meaning. He poignantly explains the confiscation of these languages, suggesting that schools "steal ninety-nine" of the one hundred creative ways in which children might compose.

Reclaiming writing is an active search for the ninety-nine and ninety-nine more. We want students to learn that words, songs, poems, and all of their languages and ways of making meaning can be crafted for impact, expression, manipulation, power, celebration, interrogation, and control. We want learners to know that their uniqueness (identities) drives their lives and that they can rely upon that in their writing lives. We want them to understand that their composing lives can lead to uncovering things that even they didn't know about themselves, their neighbors, their colleagues and friends, and the larger communities in which they live and function now and in the future. When writers add "designer" to their existing personal identities, they assume agency (Whitmore & Gernes, Chapter 3) over content and mode of expression.

Multimodal *tools* such as movie making, blogs, wikis, and art-infused books (to name only a few) are just that; they are tools. When they are employed in a community, their use is a function of the languages that are used, the nature of the community, the identities at hand and those that are anticipated as audiences. When children write about important issues and publish those on the web (Vasquez, Albers & Harste, Chapter 15), they are engaging in authentic and purposeful uses of writing. When they make movies and present them to others in the local area (Jurich & Meyer, Chapter 16) or beyond, they are doing important reclaiming work. Listening and responding to identities and relationships and using every (multimodal) tool at our disposal are central to reclaiming writing and to continuing the work of uncovering and discovering what writers might do next to express their identities. But this can only occur if we dedicate ourselves to listening to the children that stand before us and honor all that they represent.

## Listening and Relationships

Teaching is, above all else, about relationships. The uniqueness of each child is complemented by the uniqueness of each teacher, and it is within their relationships that teaching occurs. Rick (Meyer, 1996) wrote that "you teach who you are," meaning that we are who we are before, during, and after each pedagogical act, moment, and activity. If we are fundamentally curious and kind, we teach that; if we are mean-spirited and vengeful, we teach that; who we are with others radiates from us as we teach. The relational nature of teaching demands that we constantly interrogate who we are as writers, thinkers, and human beings and that we ask ourselves: "Are we serving this child well?" The brave educators that address this question are teaching in spaces where content is uncovered, language conventions are studied, and the full spectrum of possibilities for the uses of composing are actively explored.

Johnston (2012) explains that some of us may have what he refers to as a "dynamic view" of children as writers; from this perspective, we want to understand the processes in which writers engage and the decisions that they make in order to go about composing a piece of writing. On the other hand, from a "fixed view," the product is the most important part of writing. Johnston suggests that being *fixed* upon a product often undermines much potential that lies within the processes and, we would add, upon the relationships that are possible. As perhaps the penultimate example of a fixed view, he suggests that standardized tests, with that "eye on the prize" view of learning, have negatively affected relationships within classrooms. As pressure mounts to complete items rather than learn from processes or each other, relationships suffer and spaces for composing collapse.

Teachers forced into delivering prescribed curriculum likely feel angst, stress, and anxiety because they've let another voice appropriate their teaching. This sense of distance from one's self sometimes leads teachers to perfunctorily listen to children, but only as a vehicle for continuing with what is prescribed. Many children become disconnected because writing becomes work, reduced to a job that must be completed, rather than an idea, thought, feeling, or insight that demands exploration. When this happens, the relationships have shifted, the listening is light and superficial, and the classroom space is dominated by the standardized voice of invisible, distant curriculum writers. Reclaiming writing means understanding ourselves and honoring our relationships with our students by listening and making decisions about how to create spaces for the dynamic lives of writers.

## Listening to Empower for Action

In genuine spaces, where relationships and identities flourish, teachers can listen to the voices of children as the point of origin for action. Kathy refers to this as "looking small," meaning that the intense study of one child, one classroom, or one moment serves as a window into deeper understanding of every child, deeper consideration of the possibilities of what each writer can do, and an enriched view of the diversity of writers we face. Many "looking small" moments are included in this book. It was one girl, Reanna, and her determined songwriting, who enabled her teacher to reclaim writing curriculum (Baskwill, Chapter 10). And it was one boy, Antonio, whose story about a goat sparked Sanjuana, his teacher, to reclaim her bilingual students' oral languages and cultures as part of her teaching of writing (Flint & Rodriquez, Chapter 12).

By looking small, and listening carefully, we realize the uniqueness of each individual child and open ourselves to the possibilities for actions. This position stands in stark contrast to less child-centered perspectives, such as those articulated by Van Manen (2002).

> The theoretical language of child "science" so easily makes us look past each child's uniqueness toward common characteristics that allow us to group, sort, sift, measure, manage, and respond to children in preconceived ways. (p. 25)

We argue that "preconceived ways" were at full throttle during the dark ages of education for over a decade and that taking action to reclaim writing must begin with listening to children.

Quite often, voices of inspiration, sanity, and hope about teaching writing are nearby and it is from groups of teachers listening to each other that actions may arise. Teacher study groups and social forums that emerge naturally out of teachers' genuine curiosity and desire to engage in professional conversations are wonderful places to be heard. These are powerful places from which actions can emerge, as evidenced by the many Teachers Applying Whole Language (TAWL) groups that emerged in the late 1980s. These groups were such a significant threat to the louder voices of publishers and policy makers that a campaign was initiated to silence progressive practices, eventually leading to the (thankfully failed) *Reading Excellence Act* but followed by the even more damaging 2002 iteration of the Elementary and Secondary Education Act ("No Child Left Behind," in quotes because of how euphemistic that term turned out to be). Like almost all grassroots movements, fighting the larger machine proved too difficult for many TAWL groups and they disbanded. But, in the current climate, new groups have emerged (discussed below) to champion classrooms as places in which voices are honored.

Listening for action includes learning about what other outstanding writing educators are doing, thereby enhancing our repertoire for responding to our students' writing. Even during times when writing was marginalized, a few forums continued to support the teaching of writing, such as sites of the National Writing Project, the National Council of Teachers of English, the Center for Expansion of Language and Thinking, and other professional groups. These are places where some of us continue to listen and are heard, either live at conferences and webinars or through various publications.

We have assembled some of the most respected researchers and teachers of writing and invited them to present their most current thinking in this book.

Many of the authors rely upon critical literacy as the theoretical frame from which classroom activity is built. Some authors specifically cite critical literacists, while others demonstrate a critical literacy frame as they bring issues of power and equity to consciousness, honor the issues on students' minds, deepen understanding of issues through research and inquiry, and act upon the world. When we listen to our students with the kind of intense and respectful listening that we are advocating, actions necessarily follow, including inviting students to engage in the world. Christensen (2000) captures the tensions that teachers often feel about this kind of listening and explains how she faced and dealt with them.

> I couldn't ignore the toll the outside world was taking on my students. Rather than pretending that I could close my door in the face of their mounting fears, I needed to use that information to reach them. (p. 5)

Christensen was responding to the realities of the community in which she taught and knew that her curriculum must grow from there. For all teachers, there are joys, curiosities, interests, causes, and events to which our students may respond if we support them by listening intensely and participating in actions and possible solutions that are collectively composed.

Reclaiming writing for action means rewriting worlds so that the weak feel stronger, the vulnerable are supported, the fragile become more sturdy, the silenced gain voice, the oppressed gain power, and the strong understand that their strength must be accompanied by a sense of responsibility to help others become strong. Reclaiming writing involves cultivating senses of agency, responsiveness, presence, and voice within writers in order to act in, with, and upon the contexts in which we live. We know this work, although challenging, is joyful (Meyer & Whitmore, 2011).

As we imagine teachers engaging in such work with students in classrooms, we are well aware of the need for teachers to engage with other adults. For some educators, the desire to act upon our worlds means working with initiatives like Save Our Schools (http://saveourschoolsmarch.org) and United Opt Out National (http://unitedoptout.com/) or listening to others' compositions about resistance via avenues such as atthechalkface (http://atthechalkface.com/). Teachers are blogging and families are actively contributing to the movement (http://parentsacrossamerica.org). Students are responding nationally to tests by walking out or not attending at all (http://students4ourschools.org).

Empowered writers know that, "Words have been the source of the pain and the way to heal" (hooks, 1997, p. 208) and that hooks means *worlds* as much as she means words as we teach writers to write words and worlds (Freire & Macedo, 1987). Exerting one's right to write contributes to empowerment. Yet, no one can empower anyone else. It is up to us to create spaces within which we exert power, our students can exert it, and we collectively consider what such actions mean. This brings us back to the five pillars that are the foundation of this work.

## Five Pillars for Reclaiming Writing

Learning, teaching, curriculum, language, and sociocultural contexts are places to listen for unrealized potentials for reclaiming writing. When teachers open spaces to listen, we encourage writers to collaborate, listen to and view each other's work, and consider ways to invent, revise, design, use multiple modes, and reach real audiences.

Given the current standards-driven environment, reclaiming writing involves challenging, interrogating, undermining, ignoring, and working in other ways to keep relationships at the heart of writing activity. Honoring and actively receiving (listening to) children's identities is the essence of the political act of reclaiming writing because it means that we work to include in our classrooms and our research their: languages, cultures, living conditions, friendships, neighborhood events, TV shows, movies, eras and epochs that interest them, emotional states, tools, spirituality, and all else that we hear as we listen intently and intensely. The pillars help us consider ways in which writers can feel safe to be who they are and explore who they might choose to become by taking actions and by supporting and challenging each other, the school, the community, and beyond. When the true, deep, and authentic potential of each writer is on a journey to be realized, we will know that we have reclaimed writing.

## References

Bissex, G. (1980). *GNYS AT WRK: A child learns to read and write.* Cambridge, MA: Harvard University Press.

Bomer, K. (2010). *Hidden gems: Naming and teaching from the brilliance in every student's writing.* Portsmouth, NH: Heinemann.

Christensen, L. (2000). *Reading, writing, and rising up: Teaching about social justice and the power of the written word.* Milwaukee, WI: Rethinking Schools.

Edwards, C. (1993). *The hundred languages of children: The Reggio Emilia approach to early childhood education.* New York: Ablex Publishing Corporation.

Elbow, P. (1981). *Writing with power: Techniques for mastering the writing process.* New York: Oxford University Press.

Freire, P. & Macedo, D. (1987). *Literacy: Reading the word and the world.* South Hadley, MA: Bergen & Garvey.

Gallagher, K. (2009). *Readicide: How schools are killing reading and what you can do about it.* Portland, ME: Stenhouse.

hooks, b. (1997). *Wounds of passion: A writing life.* New York: Holt Henry and Company.

Johnston, P. (2004). *Choice words: How our language affects children's learning.* Portland, ME: Stenhouse.

Johnston, P. (2012). *Opening minds: Using language to change lives.* Portsmouth, ME: Stenhouse.

Meyer, R. J. (1996). *Stories from the heart: Teachers and students researching their literacy lives.* Mahwah, NJ: Erlbaum.

Meyer, R. J. & Whitmore, K. F. (2011). *Reclaiming reading: Teachers, students, and researchers regaining spaces for thinking and action.* New York: Routledge.

O'Brien, T. (1990). *The things they carried*. Boston: Mariner Books.

Romano, T. (1995). *Writing with passion: Life stories, multiple genres*. Portsmouth, NH: Heinemann.

Rosenblatt, L. (1978). *The reader, the text, the poem*. Carbondale, IL: Southern Illinois University.

Valdés, G. (1996). *Con respeto: Bridging the distances between culturally diverse families and schools*. New York: Teachers College Press.

Van Manen, M. (2002). *The tone of teaching*. Ontario, Canada: Althouse Press.

# CONTRIBUTORS

Peggy Albers
Professor
Georgia State University
Atlanta, GA

Jane Baskwill
Faculty of Education
Mount St Vincent University
Halifax, Nova Scotia, Canada

Shannon Blady
Teacher
Alamo Heights Junior School
San Antonio, TX

Linda Skidmore Coggin
Doctoral Candidate
Indiana University
Bloomington, IN

Michelle Hassay Doyle
Teacher
Pot Spring Elementary
Baltimore, MD

Charlene Klassen Endrizzi
Professor
Westminster College
New Wilmington, PA

Amy Seely Flint
Associate Professor
Georgia State University
Atlanta, GA

Marie E. Gernes
Doctoral Candidate
The University of Iowa
Iowa City, IA

Kenneth S. Goodman
Professor Emeritus
University of Arizona
Tucson, AZ

Yetta M. Goodman
Regents' Professor Emerita
University of Arizona
Tucson, AZ

Brian Hand
Professor
University of Iowa
Iowa City, IA

Jerome C. Harste
Martha Lea and Bill Armstrong Chair
    Emeritus of Teacher Education
Indiana University
Bloomington, IN

Roxanne Henkin
Professor
University of Texas at San Antonio
San Antonio, TX

Susana Ibarra Johnson
Doctoral Candidate
University of New Mexico
Albuquerque, NM

Chuck Jurich
Doctoral Candidate
University of New Mexico
Albuquerque, NM

Bobbie Kabuto
Assistant Professor
Queens College
New York, NY

Dick Koblitz
Adjunct Professor
Webster University in
St Louis, MO
University of Missouri in
Columbia, MO

Allen Koshewa
Elementary Teacher
Shanghai American School
Shanghai, China

Candace R. Kuby
Assistant Professor
University of Missouri
Columbia, MO

Lindsay Laurich
Assistant Professor
Augustana College
Sioux Falls, SD

S. Rebecca Leigh
Assistant Professor
Oakland University
Rochester, MI

Jenna Loomis
Teacher
Seventh District Elementary School
Baltimore, MD

Maryann Manning
Distinguished Professor Emerita
University of Alabama at Birmingham
Birmingham, AL

Prisca Martens
Professor and Assistant Chair
Towson University Baltimore, MD

Ray Martens
Associate Professor
Towson University Baltimore, MD

Carmen Liliana Medina
Assistant Professor
Indiana University
Bloomington, IN

Richard J. Meyer
Regents' Professor
University of New Mexico
Albuquerque, NM

Mary Moran
Teacher
Boston Public Schools
Boston, MA

Lori Norton-Meier
Associate Professor
University of Louisville
Louisville, KY

Patricia Paugh
Associate Professor of Curriculum and
    Instruction
University of Massachusetts Boston
Boston, MA

Kathryn Mitchell Pierce
Writing Specialist
Wydown Middle School
Clayton, MO

Marilee Ransom
Independent Consultant
Austin, TX

Sanjuana C. Rodriguez
Doctoral Candidate
Georgia State University
Atlanta, GA

Geoff Rose
Teacher
Boston Public Schools
Boston, MA

Lenny Sanchez
Assistant Professor
University of Missouri
Columbia, MO

Renita Schmidt
Associate Professor
The University of Iowa
Iowa City, IA

Michael L. Shaw
Professor
St Thomas Aquinas College
Sparkill, NY

Katie Van Sluys
Associate Professor
DePaul University
Chicago, IL

Vivian Maria Vasquez
Professor
American University
Washington, DC

Elisa Waingort
ESL Teacher
Academia Cotopaxi
Quito, Ecuador

Kathryn F. Whitmore
Ashland/Nystrand Chair
University of Louisville
Louisville, KY

Sandra Wilde
Professor
Hunter College
New York, NY

Karen Wohlwend
Assistant Professor
Indiana University
Bloomington, IN

# INDEX

academic language 187–90
action verbs 189, 191
after-school spaces: family night 178-181; student-led 84–5; technology think tank 83–6; video clubs 210–12, 229
agency 22, 147, 169
argument-based inquiry 58–66, 70; summary writing experience 65–6
art: art and meaning 125-129; art and writing 28, 39–40, 121-122, 132, 134
assignment, writing as 108–10
audience 226; digital media 50, 74
authoring cycle 106
Autism Spectrum Disorder 71–2

bilingual students see multilingual students
blogs 75, 76, 215, 248; peer response via 49
bookmaking 28, 38–39
Brown, Margaret Wise: The Important Book 36

care, ethic of 172–6
case study 12-22, 24-27, 39-40
CELT xiii
characterization 158–9
class magazines 55–6
code switching 164
collaborative writing 5; democratic writing 228, 236–9, 240–3; digital media 75, 85, 214, 216; learning spelling 93, 95; music 141–2;

playshop 198–208; tenor of interactions 237–9; texting 214; video projects 229–39; VoiceThread 219–21; wikis 73–81, 85; writing workshop 108
communication: capacity for 13; classroom strategies 42; digital media 75; science writing 63
community, building: after-school spaces 83–6; cultural differences 168–76; dialogic classroom 169, 170–1; ethic of care 172–6; expressing feelings 174–5; family literacy gatherings 178–80; family–teacher interactions 178–81; peer response groups 51; sharing concerns 173–4; storytelling 170–2; writing conferences 171–2
community learning: collective zone of proximal development 66–7; cultural imaginaries 198–208, 210; digital media 75; group presentations 186; language exploration 186; shared inquiries 107; shared reading 106; video projects 146–9; writing workshops 106–8
computers: educational use 215; multimodal tools 1–2, 3, 248; preschoolers 219; video projects 229; see also blogs; digital media; wikis
constructivist approach: to grammar 98–101; to spelling 88–91
creativity 4, 135–6: and democracy 4; use of technology 75
critical incidents 135–45

critical literacy: Critical Literacy in
Practice (CLIP) 217; digital
technologies 216–19, 226–7;
Global Conversations in Literacy
Research (GCLR) 217;
meaning 226; peer response
*see* peer response
cultural differences and
community-building 168–76
cultural imaginaries: idealized 198;
media 198, 203–8; playshop 198–208,
210–11; transnational 198–208; video
projects 210–12
curriculum 6, 7–8, 252; assignment-
driven 108–10; digital technologies
216; exploration-driven 108–10;
importance of vision 152–3; inquiry-
based 43, 88; NCLB Act 2, 9, 68, 70,
74; rigidity 43, 75, 83, 135–6, 249,
252; scheduling writing time 169–70;
science 58; subject integration 183;
verbocentric 30, 39; writing
workshops 104–13

democracy and creativity 4
democratic writing 228, 236–9; digital
media 228–39, 240–3; multilingual
students 240–3; in video production
228–39
design: aesthetic choices 32–3, 37;
learning by 28–41; transmediation
30–1, 37; as writing 224–7
dialogic classroom, multilingual students
169, 170–1
digital media: after-school spaces 83–6;
audience 50, 74; blogs *see* blogs;
collaborative engagement 75, 214, 216;
communication 75; critical literacy
216–19, 226–7; curricular framework
216; democratic writing 228–39,
240–3; global conversations 217–18;
history of educational technology
214–15; integration with other media
224–7; peer response via 49–50;
photo-sharing tools 219; preschoolers
219; public sharing 219–21; San
Antonio Writing Project 74; social
networking 76, 85, 218; students'
familiarity with 76; texting 214;
theorizing digital practices 216;
video *see* video projects; VoiceThread
219–21; wikis *see* wikis

drama: cultural imaginaries 198;
telenovelas 199, 203–8; video projects
229–32

editing 29, 44
Ellis, D.: *The Breadwinner* 131–3
empowerment: importance of listening
249–51; individual voices 34–6, 37
environmental texts 180
exploration, writing as 108–10
exploratory written language 21
expository texts 180

family: parent letters 14
family literacy gatherings 178–80
family–teacher interactions 178–81
feelings, expression 174–5
field (Systemic Functional Linguistics)
184, 190–1
first- and third-person storytelling 105
fishbowl strategy: peer response sessions
46, 47; songwriting 141–2
Foreman, M.: *A Child's Garden: A Story of
Hope* 122

gardening projects 182–91
gender stereotypes, investigating 221–2
genres: announcement 17; class magazines
55–6; essay 20–21; information genre
183; letter writing 15–17, 53–4;
narrative 17–18; personal 19–20;
persuasive 50, 53, 54–5, 183; story
genre 183; Systemic Functional
Linguistics 183–4, 188–9
global conversations: digital media
217–18; Global Conversations in
Literacy Research (GCLR) 217
glogs 73, 75
grading/evaluating work 110, 111–13
grammar, constructivist approach
98–101
graphic system 120
graphophonic system 119, 123, 131
Graves, D. 5–6
group presentations 186

Halliday, Michael: Systemic Functional
Linguistics 183
Herrera, Sara Poot: *Lluvia de plata* 164–6
history as writing subject 104
Holdaway, Don 114–15, 118
Houghton Mifflin reading materials 121

idea bank 43
idealized cultural imaginaries 198
ideating, writing as tool for 59, 63, 195
identity: identity texts 121; individual
 voices 34–6, 37; listening and identities
 244, 247–8; writing practices shaping
 25–7, 224–7
illustrations 18
illustrated journals 93; speech bubbles
 119, 124–5; symbolic representation
 125–8; transmediation 30–1, 37;
 writing workshop 107; *see also*
 multimodal composing
imaginaries, cultural 198–208
individual learning 106–8
information genres 183
informational texts 180
inquiry-based teaching 43, 58–59,
 70-71, 88
Internet *see* digital media
invention and convention 17–21, 24
 and spelling 89-91

journal writing and drawing 93
joy 2-3, 248, 251

Kidwatching 12
King, Coretta Scott 53–4

language 6, 8, 252; context of situation
 15; exploratory written 21; importance
 in science 59–60, 71; integrated
 language arts 183; social exploration
 186; Systemic Functional Linguistics
 183; *see also* multilingual students
learning cycle 195
learning writing 3–4, 6, 7, 252; marketed
 programs 3–4; personal nature 13;
 through play 3, 20
letter writing 53–4
Lin, G.: *The Ugly Vegetables* 184
listening: and identities 244, 247–8;
 influence of 244; integrated language
 arts 183; to build relationships 244,
 249; to empower for action 249–51
literacy: functions 180; social nature
 228–9; video projects 232–3
literature discussion 131-134

mathematics, argument-based inquiry
 70–2

meaning: connecting with academic success
 182–91; potential in language 182
mentor, teacher as 111–13
mini-lessons 95
miscues: culture of 50–1
mode: digital technologies 216; Systemic
 Functional Linguistics 184, 185, 190–1
multiage/multiyear classrooms 114–15
multilingual students 43, 152–67: building
 community 168–76; code switching
 164; connecting with 154–6;
 democratic writing 240–3; dialogic
 classroom 169, 170–1; English and
 Chinese 200-203; English and Japanese
 24-27; family literacy gatherings
 178–80; family–teacher interactions
 178–81; language of particular
 experience 156–7; peer response
 sessions 47; playing with languages
 159–61; poetry 34-35, 160–1;
 storytelling 170–2; translanguaging
 164–7; transnational imaginaries
 198–208; vision for writing 152–3,
 161, 164; writers new to English 153;
 writer's notebooks 154–5, 157; written
 language scripts 24–7
multimodal composing 228–9; analyzing
 picturebooks 123; artistic meanings
 124–8; color 121, 122; fifth grade
 131–4; first grade 119–30; graphic cues
 120; graphophonic system 119, 123,
 131; identity text set 121; New
 Literacy Studies 229; peritextual
 elements 128–9; picturebooks 120;
 semantic system 119, 123, 131;
 symbolic representation 125–8;
 syntactic cues 120; taking action text
 set 121–3; theorizing digital practices
 216; as tool for understanding 134;
 transmediation 30–1, 37; *see also* digital
 media; illustrations
multimodal tools 1–2, 3, 248
music 138–9; collaborative communities
 141–2; songwriting notebook 137–8;
 songwriting workshop 135–45

National Writing Project (NWP) 74
New Literacy Studies (NLS) 229
Nia, Isoke 146
*No Child Left Behind* (NCLB) Act 2, 9,
 68, 70, 74
nonfiction, organizational formats 105

notebooks 137–8; drawings and writing 93; multilingual students 154–5, 157; personalizing 154–5

O'Brien, T.: *The Things They Carried* 245
occupational texts 180
oral language 169, 170–1
orthographic features 16

peer response: blog responses 49; culture of critique 48–9, 50–1; Facebook 50; fishbowl sessions 46, 47; guidelines for 44–8; improving 42; influence of digital media 49–50; journal reflections 47; monitoring 47–9; multilingual students 47; role 42–51; social realities and 49; songwriting 141–2; videotaping sessions 47–8; writing workshops 105, 113
perception 195
persuasive genres 50, 53, 54–5, 183
phonological features 16
picturebooks: analyzing 123; artistic meanings 124–8; multimodal composing 119–30; peritextual elements 128–9; reading 107, 121
pillars: of reclaiming writing 3–6, 252
Pinterest critical literacy site 217
play: cultural imaginaries 198–208, 210–11; learning through 3, 20; play ethos 201; playing with language 159–61; playshop 199, 210–11; reclaiming writing through 3
poetry: multilingual students 34–35, 160–1; reading 115; writing 115–17; writing workshops 104, 115–17
political aspects of reclaiming writing 3, 6–7
popular culture 196, 208, 212
power: power and trust relationships 67–8, 85–6; student-led after-school clubs 84–5
PowerPoint presentations 85, 186, 219
presentations 85, 195; group 186; multimedia 186, 215, 218–19, 224–6; public sharing 219–21; VoiceThread 219–21
Prezis 75
process writing: importance 114–15, 117–18; writing workshops 104
punctuation 17-18, 25; constructivist approach 98–101; learning 16, 18

quick-writes 105

*Race to the Top* restructuring 182
reading: aloud to students 107, 115, 165; Houghton Mifflin materials 121; individual 106; integrated language arts 183; picturebooks 107, 121; poetry 115; shared 106, 115; social nature 228–9; teaching spelling 93, 95; writing workshops 104–5, 106
recounts 189
recreational texts 180
register (Systemic Functional Linguistics) 183, 184–5, 189
revising 3, 29, 44
roots of reclaiming 4
rural contexts 193–196

San Antonio Writing Project (SAWP) 73, 74
Say, Alan: *Drawing From Memory* 129–30
science: argument-based inquiry 58–66, 70; gardening projects 182–91; group argumentation 63; role of language 59–60, 71; subject integration 183; summary writing experience 65–6; weather experiments 193–6; writing about 58–68, 105
semantic system 119, 123, 131
Shakur, Tupac: *The Rose that Grew from Concrete* 183
sharing/publishing 29, 44; class magazines 55–6; as motivator 55
signal words 189
Silverstein, Shel 117
Six Trait plus one rubric 189
small, writing 139
social nature of writing 2, 24, 42, 228–9
social networking sites 76, 85, 218; peer response via 50
social participation: capacity for 13; Web 2.0 tools 75
sociocultural contexts 6, 8–9, 228–9, 252; and peer response 49; protocols 233–5; video projects 233–6
songwriting workshop 135–45; writer's notebook 137–8
speaking as integrated language art 183
spelling, learning 15–17, 18, 25, 87–96, 98–101; behaviorist approach 87–8; classroom practices 92–5; constructivist approach 88–91; developmental approach 88; family education 96; interactive writing 93, 95; invented spellings 88, 92, 94, 96; journal writing and drawing 93; mini-lessons 95;

syllabication 90; word walls 53; writing workshop 94–5
state/national standards: curriculum rigidity 43, 75, 83, 135–6, 249, 252; NCLB Act 2, 9, 68, 70, 74; writing workshops 110
sticky notes in preparation work 132
story genre/storytelling 183, 244, 245; cultural imaginaries 198; importance of listening 244–52; multilingual students 170–2
summary writing experience 65–6
syllabication 90
syntactic system 119, 123, 131
Systemic Functional Linguistics (SFL) 183, 187–91; genre 183–4, 188–9; register 183, 184–5, 189

taking action text 121–3
teaching 5, 6, 7, 22, 252; collective zone of proximal development 66–7; demonstrating writing 92–3; power and trust relationships 67–8; teacher as decision maker 68; verbocentric 30, 39
technical vocabulary 190
technology and schools 214–215
telenovelas 199, 203–8
tenor (Systemic Functional Linguistics) 184, 185
thinking, writing as tool for 59, 63
T.I. & Ritz, D.: *Power and Beauty: A Love Story of Life in the Streets* 207
topic choice 43–4
translanguaging 164–7
transmediation 30–1, 37
transnational imaginaries 198–9
trust: classroom strategies 42; teacher/ student relationship 67–8
Twitter 217

video projects 146–9, 210–12; after-school clubs 210–12, 229; collaborative 229–39; democratic writing 228–39, 240–3; investigating gender stereotypes 221–2; literacy events 232–3; New Literacy Studies 229; sociocultural contexts 228–9, 233–6
vision: importance 152–3; multilingual students 152–3, 161, 164; writing as an avenue for change 169
voice I, 21, 34–6, 37, 169, 182, 190, 246

weather experiments, writing centering around 193–6
wikis 73–81, 85, 215, 248; audience 74; class wikis 76–81; constructivism 79
Woodson, Jacqueline: *The Other Side* 107
word wall 53
writing: components of writing process 29–30, 44; creativity 4; democratic 228, 236–9, 240–3; as designing 224–7; integrated language arts 183; orthographic features 16; phonological features 16; reclaiming: current 5-6; history 4–5; political nature 6-7; shaping identity with 25–7, 224–7; social nature 2, 24, 228–9; time scheduled for 169–70
writing conferences 171–2
writing programs, marketed 3–4
writing workshop: ; assignments 108–10; audience 226; building community 168–76; celebrating products 106; collective writing 108; curricular framework 104–13; elements of writing craft 105; grading/evaluating work 110, 111–13; history reports 104; individual and communal learning 106–8; individual explorations 108–10; informal and formal sharing 105; mentoring 111–13; mini-lessons 95; multiage/multiyear classrooms 114–15; nonfiction 105; oral language 169, 170–1; peer response sessions 42–51, 105, 113; picturebooks 107; poetry 104, 115–17; process writing 104, 117–18; quick-writes 105; reading 104–5, 106; scheduling 169–70; shared inquiries 107; spelling development 94–5; state/national standards 110; structures 105; topics 105